UNLEASHING
OUR UNKNOWN SELVES

UNLEASHING OUR UNKNOWN SELVES

———————— • ————————

AN INQUIRY INTO THE FUTURE OF FEMININITY AND MASCULINITY

France Morrow

Foreword by Dee L. Aker

PRAEGER

New York
Westport, Connecticut
London

Library of Congress Cataloging-in-Publication Data

Morrow, France.
  Unleashing our unknown selves: an inquiry into the future of
femininity and masculinity / by France Morrow ; foreword by Dee L. Aker.
    p.   cm.
  Includes bibliographical references and index.
  ISBN 0–275–93587–6 (alk. paper). — ISBN 0–275–93837–9 (pbk. : alk. paper)
  1. Sex role—United States.   2. Femininity (Psychology)
3. Masculinity (Psychology)   4. Sex (Psychology)   5. Patriarchy—
United States.   I. Title.
HQ1075.5.U6M67   1991
305.3—dc20   90–39262

British Library Cataloguing in Publication Data is available.

Library of Congress Catalog Card Number: 90–39262
ISBN: 0–275–93587–6 (hb.)
       0–275–93837–9 (pbk.)

First published in 1991

Praeger Publishers, One Madison Avenue, New York, NY 10010
An imprint of Greenwood Publishing Group, Inc.

Printed in the United States of America

The paper used in this book complies with the
Permanent Paper Standard issued by the National
Information Standards Organization (Z39.48-1984).

10 9 8 7 6 5 4 3 2 1

For my family:
my husband, Charles, and our son, Ken,
my mother, Louise, and my father, Forrest,
my sisters, S. Morrow Paulson and Suzie Lee.

————with love and accomplicity

Contents

Foreword

Unleashing Our Unknown Selves: An Inquiry into the Future of Femininity and Masculinity is essential to our understanding of gender in human development. In an eloquent and masterful style, France Morrow exposes the obscurity and confusion inside and outside of academia about women's realities and men's priorities. Dr. Morrow leads the reader, regardless of her or his starting point, out of the fog of self-fulfilling prophecies of diminished capacities to plateaus where many, from various disciplines and with genuine concerns, can explore alternative futures.

Beginning with gender divisiveness to demonstrate and achieve gender inclusiveness and plenitude (and the profound healing that implies on a personal, relational, and global level) is a daring aspiration. It requires going beyond the conventional boundaries of patriarchal histories, cultures, and psychotherapies. It requires discipline of a multidimensional order and self-trust. Breaking taboos or new ground is born of integrity and vulnerability, of which the last is a most rare commodity in academic glass towers.

France Morrow not only aspired to unveil our acumen, she succeeded. Remaining vulnerable (open), disciplined, and true to her intuition as she searched through time and master thinkers' works, she articulates the sources of tragedy and hope that many of us sense and see in personal and public lives.

As I go from peasants to presidents and continent to continent, recording the oral histories of individuals amid societal challenges, I observe the cultural and historical and psychological web of gender expectations and proscribed psychosexual development. On occasion, in communities crippled as much as the individual women and men within them who are caught in justification of domination and abuse, I have found women who have tapped what has been always locked away or hidden by custom and belief. Somehow a potent self emerges, one seemingly made from the many selves and gender natures within which France Morrow identities our "majority" and "minority" selves. In an ostensibly compassionless world, this potent self is reconciliatory, without revenge, and tremendously capable, creative, and stable. The women come from Central America, East Africa, Texas, Vietnam; the explanation of how this is possible comes from Dr. Morrow's work.

The extrapolations made via her "subjective discipline" (and I would accent discipline) in classical, feminist, and interdisciplinary examinations of the essential nature of bisexuality confront us with our individual and societal self-diminished realities. Enlightened that we have become the embodiment of our myths, metaphors, theories, and axioms that were developed in a patriarchal glass house on the hill with the fog below and the clouds above, we are called to action. Faced with the fact it is a participatory universe, we may as well choose to make it a more conscious, positive, partnership venture that is not destructive of society or self.

Overcoming the feminist perspectives still limited by patriarchal assumptions, which in themselves tend to fall into negative, monolithic, objective ruts, we can begin to use the power of maternal "accomplicity" that France Morrow manifests for us. In this realm where body and mind are no longer split and our uniquenesses and similarities are equally cherished, we create a healthy world. This is the realm of *Unleashing Our Unknown Selves*.

France Morrow has given phenomenological and vitalistic illumination to the simple yet profound words of Carl Rogers, another teaching, exploring colleague concerned with dispelling what impedes and clarifying what enhances personal and societal evolution: "What I am is good enough, if I can only be it." France Morrow tells us how to be it.

                    Dee L. Aker
                    Director, United States International University

Preface

Studs Terkel has recently used the image of the "Great (Continental) Divide" to symbolize the deepening chasms in American life. Terkel enumerates a multitude of splits — economic, religious, and racial — that separate us from each other and from our roots. Even more, Terkel insists, this Great Divide cuts us off from "our very selves" (Terkel 1989, Foreword).

In this study I suggest that the tragic estrangement from our very selves has everything to do with an unexamined divisiveness of gender. I further suggest that among the foundations that have crumbled are centuries-old ideas about femininity and masculinity and about their interrelationships. *Unleashing Our Unknown Selves* is a hopeful book because it presents a new theory of psychosexual development that is also a theory of psychosocial evolution. Sometimes foundations can actually be walls blocking the light.

In the twentieth century, theorists have come to realize that it is impossible, and perhaps not even desirable, to attain a totally objective perspective. It is essential, however, to let readers know "where one is coming from." My own perspective is interdisciplinary, the only perspective possible when treating gender problematics, and it is therefore a critical and normative perspective. In order to compare across cultures, genders, and generations, and across disciplines, one must self-consciously choose categories of comparison and be prepared to make explicit the valuations underlying those choices. My perspective is that of qualitative social psychology. Finally, my perspective is that of the disciplined subjectivity endorsed by Sigmund Freud, and to which Freud's disciple Erik Erikson referred as both an essential element of the therapeutic encounter and an inescapable element in the advancement of all the social sciences. The psychoanalyst, the anthropologist, and the sociologist each must recognize, Erikson said, that "his [*sic*] studies will demand ... that he develop the ability to include in his observational field his human obligations, his methodological responsibilities, and his own motivations" (Nelson 1957, 99). By including within my observational fields my obligations as a woman as well as my responsibilities and motivations, I believe that I will contribute to closing that practical and theoretical hiatus signaled by Freud when he queried years ago, "What do women want?"

Every book is a collaborative effort. Often colleagues are unaware of just how much their advice, suggestions, and example have assisted and inspired. Throughout many years of thought and research, I have accumulated numerous intellectual debts. At critical moments in the early development of my theories, I was supported by three unusually perceptive persons. Prof. Stanley Aronowitz, now at The Graduate Center, City University of New York, provided indispensable guidance and encouragement. Norma Chinchilla, Professor of Sociology and Women's Studies, California State University, Long Beach, helped me learn about her disciplines. And Jay Martin, Leo S. Bing Professor, University of Southern California, and a member of the faculty, Southern California Psychoanalytic Institute, provided much needed criticism and encouragement.

I am deeply grateful to Dr. Joseph L. White, clinical psychologist and Fellow of the Menninger Foundation, for his enlightened guidance. Equally enthusiastic and steadfast in support have been the accomplished writers, historians, and social critics Profs. Peter Clecak and Mark Poster of the University of California, Irvine. Without their unflagging interest in and support of my ideas, this book could never have been completed. I also heartily thank Dr. Ashley Montagu for his attention to an early draft, as well as for his sympathy, helpful suggestions, and encouragement.

Notable among many others who have lent me a friendly ear and provided advice and moral support are Viviane Wayne, Prof. Leslie Rabine, Dr. Robert Newcomb, Geneva Lopez, and Edna Meija, all of the University of California, Irvine. Vivian Lennertz, a professional in the health sciences, and Prof. Doris DeHardt, a clinical psychologist, provided valuable suggestions throughout multiple revisions.

Finally, I could not neglect thanking my colleagues at the United States International University's Graduate School of Behavioral Science, Irvine, California, for providing both moral support and inspiration. I especially want to thank the Graduate School's director, Dr. Dee Aker;

clinical psychologist Dr. Daryl Freeland; and my colleague, Dr. Max Lerner. My doctoral students at United States International University — most of them seasoned professionals in the fields of psychotherapy and medicine — have been a continuing source of inspiration.

I greatly appreciate the financial support I received from the Josephine de Karman Fellowship Trust during the early stages of manuscript research. Paul Macirowski, Alda Trabucchi, and Krystyna Budd, my editors at Praeger, have been most helpful and supportive. In addition, I am grateful to Kimiko Miller for her assistance. The indispensable part played by my family during the writing of this book is also warmly acknowledged.

UNLEASHING
OUR UNKNOWN SELVES

1

Introduction: The Peaceful Kingdom

*Only technology advances, while the story
of humanity has come to a complete stop.*
Takeo Doi

THE WASTELAND

We are living in the midst of an emergency. Telephones are ringing;
letters, magazines, newspapers, and journals are piling up on every side;
errands demand running; meetings require attending; machines and
relationships are breaking down; our children are clamoring; and our
parents and our planet are sick or dying. Each day the pace quickens:
Another coup or election surprise in Central America; another crisis in
the Middle East; another liberation movement crushed or rising; while
financial deficits are growing in Washington, Sacramento, New York, and
in our own bank accounts. Einstein, it appears, forgot one law of
relativity: As the planet shrinks and human populations and communications burgeon, time also contracts. The faster we run and the harder we
work, the fewer hours remain in which to still the ever-accelerating blur,
the too-muchness of our waning, weeping century.

We have reached, we are told, a "turning point"; a new age is aborning,
a new paradigm appearing. In sum, we are in the midst of a revolution in
consciousness. The worlds of family and work, of female and male, are
converging just as global competition increasingly pressures both men
and women in America to work harder than ever before. Yet amidst the

futurists' talk of third waves, genetic programming, parallel processing, and ever more efficient killing devices, our daily lives feel diminished.

We feel diminished in our daily lives, I suggest, because the "story of humanity" *has* come to a complete stop. In fact, it is difficult to imagine how anything can be experienced as moving and progressing when pictured against the rushing roar of all those engines of progress. Technology advances inexorably while evolution in human relationships has stalled. Every year thousands of new chemicals are introduced into the biosphere; annually thousands of new products burden and, occasionally, unburden us; knowledge grows exponentially, and the engines of death grow ever more clever—whether in the guise of nuclear or biochemical warfare, or in that of mutating viruses. Long ago the German philosopher Goethe understood how that which merely informs us, diminishes us. We require more of the future than an "information age." Information alone, technological progress by itself, cannot sustain our global household's growing hunger for meaning and for communities of caring. Along with these growing hungers also grows the awareness that nature is dying and that our human families are endangered species.

This study contributes to our growing awareness of humanity's stampede toward perdition, but, above all, it contributes a possible antidote by means of an analysis of the chasm growing within our species. I am referring, of course, to that great fatal divide which is our present sex/gender system. Underlying all the other schisms of class, race, and ethnicity is that schism most repressed and least considered: the schism between men and women, between masculinity and femininity. *Unleashing Our Unknown Selves* explains why an understanding of the cultural gender divisions within our Western patriarchal civilization and within our Western selves holds the key to our survival, as well as to our material and spiritual evolution. I believe that viewing the world's cultural life "steadily and whole" will affirm at least one nearly universal truth: Neither man's story, nor the story of humanity, can continue until woman's story is told.

In her prescient book *Toward a New Psychology of Women* (1986), Jean Baker Miller acknowledges the last two decades' rich outpouring of writings about women, authored by women. She also acknowledges that although women are finding their own authentic voices and beginning to tell their own stories, much work remains to be done by women to bring to bear upon the problems of humanity theories that incorporate women's experiences and women's points of view. Miller's two major concerns are also my concerns: First, there indeed remains a theoretical hiatus in the human sciences that can be bridged only by bringing forth the whole and steady visions of women. Second, these unborn theories—

of society, family, individual, and their interrelationships — must take into central consideration what Miller calls "the pervasive threat of violence" in the lives of women (Miller 1986, xxiii). I propose to demonstrate that for both girls and boys growing up in patriarchal cultures, Miller's "pervasive threat of violence" manifests itself not only as actual physical violence, but as the symbolic violence that comes from growing up in a society where femininity is denigrated and its genuine powers are denied. This present violence, symbolic and real, represses our warring inner selves.

Everyone agrees that the battle of the sexes continues to rage. I will show that men as much as women are the casualties of this warfare. I will lead to where the bodies are buried, and I will point to those half-selves of the opposite sex that each sex represses — unknowingly mutilated — deep within. But if men monopolize power — cultural, military, economic, and institutional power — how can women ever aspire to complete equality? Just as there exists no satisfactory analysis of the early psychosexual development of girls and boys within families rent by the power conflicts of mothers and fathers, so also there exists no satisfactory analysis of why men should relinquish some of their cultural, military, economic, and institutional power to women and, in turn, share in women's genuine powers, especially the power to build and nurture relationships.

In this study of "our unknown selves," I present a theory of the origins of our divided selves that is also a theory of the relationship between femininity and masculinity. It is a theory of psychosexual development that is simultaneously a theory of psychosocial evolution.

Fortunately, we are beginning to understand on a global scale that nurturance and strength and the strength of nurturance are neither feminine nor masculine qualities but, rather, human qualities. We must further recognize that *sexuality as culturally elaborated has been the primordial organizing principle of all human societies.* Human qualities have been assigned, not by nature, but by culture to women and to men. Real biological differences have been incorporated, absorbed, and at times superseded by infinitely more powerful cultural differences. These cultural differences have been elaborated over millennia and have been incorporated — literally embodied — in our nervous systems. Over the course of generations, social body becomes individual body.

The chasm between those qualities culturally assigned to men and those assigned to women has also dangerously widened because patriarchal cultures and their symbolic language structures have grown exponentially over the last two centuries. In the dizzying flux of fashion and event, we have failed to understand that the most momentous change of all, a change that will revolutionize human consciousness more than any technological advance, is, simply stated, the breaching of the barriers erected by socially constructed gender categories. It is not that a new femininity is emerging from the womb of masculine culture—although there is some truth in this view. Our best hope for the rapid spiritual evolution of both women and men is the release in each sex of the repressed qualities of the other sex, so that both sexes may be what they have never yet become: whole. Our survival as a species demands no less.

My own activism has taught me about some of the links between personal concern and public conscience. It has demonstrated to me that one person joined by many other "ones" *can* make a difference. Like many others, I have begun to trace the links between the limits of our planet's ability to absorb the waste products from human activities and the resulting inevitable limits our species must put upon its burgeoning populations. From my studies I have learned that where women gain education and economic power, birth rates drop. I have also begun to learn about the grinding poverty, about the ceaseless productive and reproductive work that is the lot of the majority of the world's women. In a world where women contribute two-thirds of all hours worked, women are rewarded with only one-tenth the wages of men and they own only 1 percent of world property (Eisler 1981, 41:9). If, as has been said, the state of a civilization can be discovered by investigating the status of its women, then I have learned that the level of civilization attained by the world as a whole is dismally low indeed.

In the twentieth century there have been volumes written about the estrangement of man from himself and from nature; next to nothing has been written about the estrangement of man from woman, from his mother, and from his feminine self. Nothing has been written about the estrangement of woman from her masculine self. Carl Jung mentioned the need for balance between *anima* and *animus* within each self, yet he spoke scornfully of women attending the "animus factories" that U.S. universities represented to him. And Jung's concepts, like the Eastern concepts of *yin* and *yang*, represent universal, ahistorical, abstract ideas that function as pristine objects of worship, untouched by the grim, prosaic sexual warfare of everyday life.

Fortunately, it is once again becoming acceptable to speak of national and personal malaise because the signs of social and personal disintegration are closing in around us. We humans are poisoning Mother Earth— and ourselves—on a global scale unimaginable a few decades ago. Worldwide our air is becoming an unbreathable chemical soup that blackens our lungs and burns holes in the earth's protective ozone layer; our drinking water is being poisoned, and our forests and farmlands are rapidly diminishing while our vast mysterious oceans heave the dead and dying onto the world's littered shorelines. Every year over 86 million more human beings are born and must be fed (Brown et al. 1989, 22), while every year the earth's topsoil dwindles by 25 billion tons (ibid., 49). We are consuming our natural resources faster than nature can replenish them, and we have exceeded nature's ability to absorb our wastes. In the United States, for example, nearly one-third of solid waste landfills are scheduled to close within five years, yet 85 percent of U.S. baby diapers, to give but one concrete example, are disposable — 18 billion dirty diapers per year are contributing close to 5 percent of household waste and exposing sanitation workers to disease (*Science News* 1989,135: 141).

Mankind's rape of Mother Nature is beginning to put a price-tag on those "best things in life" that were supposed to be free — fresh, clean air, pure water, sunshine, and spring showers. On a national level, the signs of social decay are every bit as discouraging as those we have noted in the world of nature. Within the last ten years the United States has gone from being the largest creditor to being the largest debtor the world has ever seen. Among industrialized countries we are by far the most violent: During the last two decades the rate of U.S. homicides has doubled to ten times the average rate found in the other nineteen most industrialized nations (Weiss 1987,132: 59). Every six minutes a woman is raped; domestic violence has become epidemic; the teenage suicide rate has risen 300 percent over the last two decades (Edwards 1988,70: 297); between 1981 and 1986 child-abuse cases in the United States increased 90 percent (*New Perspectives Quarterly* 1990,7: 23). With only 5 percent of the world's population, we manage to consume over 60 percent of the illegal drugs produced annually in the entire world (Washton & Boundy 1989, 12). The violence of poverty afflicts over 20 percent of American children (nearly 50 percent of black children); women make up two-thirds of the poor adults in the United States (Tavris & Wade 1984, 27). If the United States represents the future of developing countries, then the future appears grim.

We are living in the midst of multiple crises, multiple emergencies. Naturally, given the complexity of our world today, each crisis has multiple causes — it is not possible to single out definitively one reason underlying all pollution, poverty, violence, addiction, and despair. Yet considering the importance of sexuality and gender to all levels of social production and reproduction, I cannot help but wonder why so few theorists have tried to trace the ramifications of the massive cultural power inequalities of men and women. The causal linking of women's inferior social position with such well-researched and universal modern problems as the poisoning of the planet, the arms race, the population explosion, drug and other addictions, violence and poverty — these causal linkages may seem exaggerated to many, but that only testifies to the low level of importance given the social subordination of the female half of the species.

We do know that the dominant culture that has produced the degrada-tion of both the natural environment and the social environment is masculine and patriarchal. White males occupy 97 percent of senior management jobs in American industry (Schachter 1988, IV:1); white males hold the most important positions in science and technology (Bleier 1986, 21); in higher education about 90 percent of tenured full professors are male (Andersen 1983, 85); over 75 percent of the writing jobs in American movies and television go to white men, the majority of whom are younger than forty (Bielby & Bielby 1989, Foreword); and 95 percent of the seats in the U.S. Congress are held by men. Although women now make up 45 percent of the U.S. labor force (*New Perspectives Quarterly* 1990, 23), they earn scarcely more now in relation to men than they did in 1939. The Bible (Leviticus 27: 3–4) states that a woman is worth 30 shekels whereas a man is worth 50, and, indeed, a woman in 1990 earns little more than 60 cents for every dollar earned by a man (Boris & Honey 1988, 111:34). Yet there are many indications that, despite their economic power and cultural dominance, many men — even some powerful "Anglos" — are deeply distressed by the violence, addictions, and ugliness in their lives. A recent survey reported by *Time* magazine found that 56 percent of the men polled were willing to give up 25 percent of their income if they could then spend more time in personal or family activities (Wallis 1989, 134:89). In *America's Quest for the Ideal Self* (1983), Prof. Peter Clecak summarizes the most hopeful trends in our socity today when he notes that the twentieth century's "democratization of personhood" is giving birth in the latter part of the century to a search for small communities of caring in which individuation may proceed.

Paradoxically, one most hopeful sign is the growing awareness that, as psychologist Rollo May has stated, something is "radically wrong in man's relation to himself" (May 1986, 66). May believes that man has "become fundamentally problematic to himself" (ibid.). In this study I will elaborate upon and extend the work of Sigmund Freud and that of many women theorists who understand that modern man's fundamental problematic is the cultural splitting of the human species into feminine and masculine genders and the arrangement of these genders into a hierarchical order wherein feminine qualities are viewed as both subor-dinate and inferior to masculine qualities. If this hierarchical order prevails over the forces now working toward its dissolution, femininity and masculinity have no future. They will disappear along with the earth itself in the self-destructive fury of powerful men alienated, not from themselves, as one reads in the existential literature, but alienated — split off — from their *feminine* selves.

In *Unleashing Our Unknown Selves,* I focus on the neglected explanatory power of what I believe to be our last, best hope, namely, the explanatory power of a theory that systematically explores the crippling of *both* men and women by the cultural subordination and invisibility of the latter. In this study I present a theory of how our present-day definitions of femininity and masculinity cripple and limit children of both sexes, beginning in the cradle. I ask a question too long ignored by the dominant culture: What are the effects upon developing infants and children — both female and male — of the bloody battle of the sexes raging overtly in physical blows between mother and father and more covertly in the psychic blows children sustain from their mother's vulnerability in patriarchal cultures?

In examining this question, I am contributing to what Betty Friedan has called "the second stage" (1986) of the women's movement. My model of psychosexual development does affirm the difference between women and men while explaining why men will benefit by women's attaining equality in political and economic power. Presently, men are not only being corrupted by their growing cultural powers; they are also succumbing in growing numbers to death and addiction under the weight of patriarchal responsibilities. In the nineteenth century, John Stuart Mill had already recognized the crippling of men by their power. Mill declared that "even a really superior man almost always begins to deteriorate" as he exercises absolute power within families (quoted in Bassein 1984, 26). Given the epidemic of wife and child battering by husbands and fathers, given the pervasive threat and reality within American society of rape and murder of women, given the economic realities of impoverishment with divorce, and the marginal existence of most single women, and given glass ceilings, fatigue, and resurrected discrimination, can one blame women if vulnerability also corrupts?

Human beings, Sigmund Freud justly claimed, need both love and work in order to hope for a measure of happiness. The importance of the work of men and of work to men has been widely recognized. Work develops men and men develop their work: the dialectic is well known. Less well understood is the evolution of our concept of love. As human societies have developed, human beings have come to expect more from love, but without understanding that love has been relegated to the supposedly unchanging spheres presided over by women. Love has been seen by the dominant society as the work of women, but not as a quality that evolves with the evolution of human potential. Love is seen as a gift of grace, gracefully given by women to men and to children. Love, seen as the sphere of women, has been split from work, seen as the sphere of men. Since women and their spheres are by definition inferior, a deadly contradiction has been growing within the heart of men's reason. Love itself has become split between the transcendent and the tainted; work has become split off from love.

Today human survival depends upon the integration of our feminine selves with our masculine selves, upon the integration of our work with our loves. Split apart, neither gives satisfaction; split apart, humanity's story has not only stopped, it may be ending.

STRAW MAN

Human beings seek validation from their social group, often unconsciously, by living in accordance with the values of that social group. If men seek self-esteem and recognition — manhood — through work, through the heroic deed, it is not because men have inherited a "good works" gene. Similarly, if women seek self-esteem and recognition — womanhood — through nurturing relationships, neither is it because they alone have inherited the gene for nurturance. The most recent research on gender differences demonstrates nurturing capacities in young boys and reveals a rapid disappearance of those qualities used in the past to distinguish between the sexes. No longer can one assume that girls will, on the average, out-perform boys on tests of verbal ability and boys will out-shine girls on tests measuring spatial and mathematical abilities. The gaps between the genders have all but narrowed down to invisibility (Feingold 1988, 43:95; Jacklin 1989, 44:128). As the cultural context has changed, so have the abilities that were previously used to make gender distinctions.

Unfortunately, although objective tests of ability and interest do show that old gender distinctions are breaking down under the weight of changing educational opportunities and a relaxing of gender stereotypes, many sensitive critics of American life see that the chasm between the sexes is once again beginning to widen. Our feelings regarding acceptable feminine and masculine behavior have not, on the whole, kept pace with our possibilities; our lack of imagination is impoverishing our potential for change. Researchers find that gender is still the most important predictor of the activities of grammar school children and that women and men inhabit "different planets" in terms of sensibility and attitudes (Medrich et al. 1982). Politically, the gender gap is now a recognized phenomenon. Women's new self-consciousness regarding their gender's lower social status is a healthy first step toward an identification with other women who may belong to different racial, ethnic, national, class, or religious groups. Indeed, as the twentieth century draws to a close, sisterhood is becoming global (Morgan 1984). The rapid evolution of political consciousness and power of Japanese women during the late 1980s is but one striking example of a worldwide rise in women's self-awareness. Worldwide, women are seizing power on behalf of the issues that will define the twenty-first century, issues centered in planetary housekeeping and global householding.

These issues require new analyses of our culturally constructed gender distinctions. Inextricably interwoven with our ideas regarding biological sexuality, our ideas of femininity and masculinity constitute the bedrock of both our selves and our societies. The great anthropologist Margaret Mead has commented that it is difficult to imagine any society that does not found itself upon the sexual split within our species. Yet, Mead's life work was devoted to breaking apart the rigid identity that patriarchal culture has developed between female and certain kinds of femininity, between male and certain kinds of masculinity. She demonstrated that although all societies may found themselves upon gender distinctions, there is nothing immutably decreed by nature concerning the qualities each gender is assigned.

That gender constitutes a caste more important and fundamental than any other group category can be dramatically illustrated by the findings of one researcher who asked young boys what they would do if they turned into girls. "Kill myself" was a typical response. By contrast, when girls were asked how their lives would change if they were to become boys, they replied that their lives would change for the better, that they might be given a chance to go to college (Tavris & Baumgartner 1983, 160: 92–95). Numberless studies demonstrate that parents still prefer to have boy babies. Unfortunately, missing are the studies that would show us how this preference deforms boy babies, girl babies, and the men and women they become.

Western culture, or American culture, is still essentially a culture of hero-worship, and by definition heroes can only be male. Modern man is still Faustian man, not just selling his soul in order to attain power, youth, and riches, but selling off—killing off—the very earth that nourishes him. In the feverish and brutally competitive race to prove themselves through individual heroics, modern men not only are sacrificing themselves, their feminine potentials, but they are also jeopardizing the very survival of humankind. Although the hour is already late, a new way of understanding the models of masculine heroism, the hidden heroism of women, and the ways in which both heroisms become incorporated into the selves of men and women as developing children will give us the insight necessary for the radical changes our survival as a species requires.

I have already enumerated some of the daunting crises facing humanity and have suggested that our best hope for solving these crises lies in a new understanding of the origins of cultural gender distinction, of the feminine and masculine selves at the core of each human self. I have suggested that each woman harbors within herself a repressed masculine self, and that each man harbors a repressed feminine self. I have further suggested that the social and spiritual evolution of each human soul requires the liberation and integration of these unknown and undeveloped selves. This is the revolution in consciousness that is required.

My assertions echo those of the founder of depth psychology, Dr. Sigmund Freud. Indeed, the theories presented here are deeply rooted in Freudian psychoanalysis because the specter of Freud is still haunting Western cultures, even as the twentieth century draws to a close. The very mention of Freud's name never fails to evoke passionate response. In fact, the amount of emotional energy Freud's ideas continue to elicit astounds me and confirms me in my own understanding that the secret potentials of Freudian psychoanalysis for further development remain as yet untapped.

Unfortunately, as argued by Russell Jacoby in *The Repression of Psychoanalysis* (1983), the revolutionary potential of Freudian psychoanalysis was lost when Freud's followers fled the Nazis. Transplanted to the United States, psychoanalysis melted into the medical model of the American psychiatric establishment. Whatever potential remained for a progressive social psychology was negated by the distorted image of Freud as an antiwoman apologist for neurotic Victorian upper-class men. Today, however, a growing minority of theorists—women and men—are busy exhuming the original Freud, scrubbing away the thick patina of object relations theory, and pointing to the substantial Freud behind the straw man. Women theorists in particular are beginning to understand that a Freudianism transformed by the factoring in of women's experiences promises to provide a social agenda capable of healing many of the splits within American society and within American selves.

While the dominant culture's ideal well-adjusted individual—identical with its ideal of masculinity—exhibits rational objectivity, Freud argued for the importance of a disciplined subjectivity; while this same dominant and patriarchal culture argues for the desirability of separating thought and emotion, Freud's system presents such separation as pathological; while the dominant culture models maturity as separation from others, Freud developed a theory of the individual as generated both by the social group and by family relationships. Unfortunately, *this* Freud is not as well known as the straw man some of us love to hate. This study presents another view of Freud, a view well understood by Freud's closest students, by Peter Gay, by Russell Jacoby, by Juliet Mitchell, and by Abraham Kaplan — and this study takes Jacoby's "revolutionary" Freud one step further.

From before Freud's time until the present, the dominant patriarchal culture has founded itself upon sets of polarities, or dualisms. The poles of these dualisms are, in fact, mutually exclusive because their arrangement is hierarchical as in man/woman, reason/emotion, work/play, soul/body, activity/passivity, independent/dependent, and so on. Many theorists of both sexes have pointed out the identification of the first term of each pair with masculinity and the second term with femininity. Because the feminine terms are seen as inferior, as nonessential qualities to be mastered, if not eliminated altogether, I submit that the dominant culture is not, in fact, dualistic but monistic. The importance of this observation lies in the inability of the dominant culture to account for or to cherish difference. Patriarchal culture cherishes only those qualities it espouses as self-descriptive and self-identical. Alone among prominent masculine systems of thought, Freudian psychoanalysis is founded upon dualistic modes of analysis that recognize how important sexual differences are to the social structure, while emphasizing the bisexuality warring within each human individual.

Today no one denies that rational civilization, the Western patriarchal civilization of Enlightenment reason, is in crisis. The deepest cause of this crisis, and a central problematic of modern life, is the equating of women with sexuality/pleasure, the low esteem in which the feminine gender and its attributes are held, and women's lack of economic power. It is quite simply impossible for women to attain sexual freedom and promote their own vital interests as long as they do not possess economic freedom equal to men. It is not possible for men to experience the joys and warmth of close human relationships as long as they are strangers in their homes.

The importance of sexuality has often been emphasized by modern philosophers, most recently by the respected French philosopher Michel Foucault, who commented in his *History of Sexuality* that

[sexuality is expected to supply us with] our intelligibility ... the plenitude of our body ... our identity. ... Hence the fact that over the centuries it has become more important than our soul, more important almost than our life; and so it is that all the world's enigmas appear frivolous to us compared to this secret, minuscule in each of us, but of a density that makes it more serious than any other.

The Faustian pact, whose temptation has been instilled in us by the deployment of sexuality, is now as follows: to exchange life in its entirety for sex itself, for the truth and the sovereignty of sex. Sex is worth dying for. It is in this (strictly historical) sense that sex is indeed imbued with the death instinct. (Foucault 1980, 156)

In all of his emphasis upon the importance of sexuality, Foucault remains but a pale echo of Freud. Yet neither man succeeded, finally, in cracking the hidden sexual codes. The importance of sexuality lies quite simply in the hidden importance to human evolution of women, of woman as repressed sex, and of woman as unknown self, repressed within the psyche of modern man.

To all our modern problems of frantic fragmentation, time sickness, and nicely formated "narcissism," the original Freud offers two antidotes: One is his *shibboleth* of (bi)sexuality, the other his insistence upon the reality and the pertinacity of the unconscious. On both of these Freudian offerings, modern neo-Freudianism, especially in the United States, has turned its back. The problems of sexuality have been trivialized or reduced to problems resolvable by the sexual mechanics of Masters and Johnson. The problems of the unconscious have been rationalized, codified, and institutionalized, their mysteries drained and falsified. In the dominant neo-Freudianisms of object relations theory and "cultural" Freudianism, the splits between subject and object, and between subjectivities and objectivities have widened and been set in concrete.

In all of the above, there is no place for a fresh look at gender in its widest cultural ramifications. Quite simply forgotten is the truth that in patriarchal cultures subject is always male, and object, female. This study of the future of femininity and masculinity reasserts the primacy of the Freudian emphasis upon sexuality, but here it is sexuality taken in its broadest cultural manifestations as gender — and, most important, as *woman*. I will show why Freud remains essential to the development of modern psychological understanding as I critically transform Freudian categories. Freud is a worthy foundation for a "womanist" psychoanalysis because Freud remains the only twentieth-century thinker to initiate a theory of human being/becoming based upon the sexual nonidentity of "bisexuality," that is, of overlapping gender categories. In this way Freudian psychoanalysis has set a central place at the patriarchal table — at least potentially — for women.

THE FUTURE OF DIFFERENCE

Feminist theorists have commented that all members of a repressed group look alike to the members of the dominant group. Tragically, members of repressed groups themselves often share the prejudices of the dominant group. However, with the most recent women's movement there has fortunately come a growing awareness by women of the great differences among themselves. This awareness of difference is most welcome and healthy—as long as it does not stifle their continuing growth in awareness of conditions they still share with other women in male-dominated societies. To argue for difference *or* for similarity is a fruitless task and prevents women theorists from escaping the circularity of the dominant culture's either/or logic. Individual *or* society, reason *or* emotion, spirit *or* body, work *or* pleasure, reality *or* fantasy, fact *or* value, masculinity *or* femininity—such are the unproductive dichotomies of much masculine discourse. Indeed, the hidden agenda of such circularity often is maintenance of the cultural status quo.

Much theoretical energy has been expended by women in arguing for or against women's likenesses to men. Valuable insights have accrued from these debates, not least among them the limitations and paradoxes inherent in rigidly emphasizing *either* women's similarities *or* women's differences. Women are aware that any of their differences from men have and will be used against them by the dominant male culture, which still holds most of the power to define and label these differences as inferior. To avoid labels of inferiority, women from George Sand to Simone de Beauvoir have emphasized women's similarities to men.

Today, some important women theorists such as Jean Baker Miller, Carol Gilligan, Betty Friedan, and Nancy Chodorow have reaffirmed women's differences as special and valuable. This significant theoretical advance also contributes to women's self-esteem, but it is not without its drawbacks. One danger, recognized by the above theorists, resides in viewing women as essentially superior to men. Viewing women as naturally superior ignores the influence of the cultural context, which most women theorists do believe is more important to the development of feminine and masculine qualities than genetic endowments. But if one emphasizes culture over nature, then logical consistency demands that women remain in the subordinate positions that produced these socially superior and valuable characteristics. Feminist theorists must find ways to move beyond these paradoxes. (For further discussion of these issues, see Eisenstein & Jardine 1987 and Hare-Mustin & Marecek 1988, 43: 455–64.)

In *Unleashing Our Unknown Selves* I move beyond the essentially masculine parameters of these debates to a consideration of the relationship between femininity and masculinity as it develops within the persons of individual women and men in early childhood. I consider how natural similarities and differences are always mediated by cultural contexts and masculine power structures. I demonstrate the advantages to men, as well as to women, of changing these contexts and power structures. The contradictions within the dominant culture are now becoming visible even to those affluent Anglo-Saxon men who are this culture's staunchest defenders; even they are beginning to realize that radical change in both the workplace and the homeplace is unavoidable.

Even within what Anne Wilson Schaef (1985) has called the "White Male System" there exists a profound uneasiness and a dissatisfaction with Faustian individualism. This uneasiness was perhaps first expressed by Albert Camus in 1957 in his acceptance speech for the Nobel Prize: "And the man who, as often happens, chose the path of art because he was aware of his difference soon learns that he can nourish his art, and his difference, solely by admitting his resemblance to all" (O'Brien 1958, 201: 31). Camus was underlining the falsity of the then popular notion of an opposition between individual creative genius and the social context. Earlier, philosopher William James had declared in much the same spirit that "the community stagnates without the impulse of the individual. The impulse dies away without the sympathy of the community" (James 1953, 242). Both these men understood the reciprocity inherent in individual and social evolution. Not only is individual difference impossible outside a cultural matrix, but so is individual progress impossible without cultural standards by which progress can be measured. In fact, I submit that one of the unconscious motives of men in their historical assimilation of the feminine to the eternal unchanging forces of nature was to produce the constancy against which men could then chart their own progress and development.

It is important today that women recognize their similarities to other women *and* their unique differences. "Nothing human is foreign to me" should be a motto for both women and men; "nothing women do is foreign to me" is at this time an even more important motto for all women if women are to grow in the identifications with other women necessary for them to become a force for change in the world. Writer Adrienne Rich echoes Camus's sentiments quoted earlier when she urges women to understand the "paradox contained in 'my' experience of motherhood." Rich states that "although different from many other women's experiences, [my experience of motherhood] was not unique" and "only in shedding the illusion of my uniqueness could I hope, as a woman, to have any authentic life at all" (Rich 1981, 22). As they strive for authentic life within and without the spheres traditionally reserved for them by men, women need to affirm and respect both their similarities to and their differences from other women, as well as their similarities to and their differences from men.

Kaplan has claimed that an epistemology, a theory of how we know, worthy of Freud's system has not yet been developed. This study draws out from Freudian metapsychology the seeds of an epistemology that allows for transformations across levels of consciousness and that explains the origins of our bisexuality; it further explains how a recognition of this overlapping of gender categories — this bisexuality — within each human self will help bring about genuine change. For Freudian psychoanalysis represents a radical transformation and expansion of the concept of science itself. Knowledge comes, Freud recognized, from nonidentity, from differences culturally grounded in the unconscious. A reversal of the patriarchal suppression of differences, beginning with the most fundamental — those of the female sex — will effect a cultural revolution more profound than any resulting from the dissolution of distinctions based on class or race. An understanding of human bisexuality as it develops within each female and male will lay the foundation for future femininities and masculinities far better than those that we may now imagine.

My aim is to develop a new model of psychosexual development. Our present crisis in life's meaning, our crises in love, work, and community, can be met only with a perceptual revolution leading to a revolution in how gender relations are structured within our Western civilization and within our Western selves. The wastelands within and without stem from the dominant culture's denigration of body, emotion, values, pleasure, relationship, and the feminine. The close identification of the feminine, of women, with all these so-called lesser qualities has brought about the repression of men's feminine selves and has prevented in most women the development of their masculine selves.

An important assumption of this study is that the sexual division of nature into two sexes, despite the ambiguities involved in this division, has served all cultures as a primordial organizing principle, even when cultural meanings of gender have differed. I suggest that the fundamental dualisms, the dichotomizing tendencies of the human mind, are founded in this sexual division and reinforced by this division's cultural elaboration as gender distinctions. These divisions represent the deepest cleavages in the human species, and over millennia they have become freighted with unconscious, symbolic, and traditional meanings. The feminist theorist Shulamith Firestone first expressed this idea when she enquired, "Why postulate a fundamental Hegelian concept of otherness as the final explanation — and then carefully document the biological and historical circumstances that have pushed the class 'women' into such a category — when one has never seriously considered the much simpler and more likely possibility that this fundamental dualism sprang from the sexual division itself?" (Firestone 1979, 7). My new model of human development will take seriously this fundamental sexual schism in our species, and that means taking women seriously. Certainly, being taken seriously must be one thing that all women want.

This study calls for an end to the war between the sexes; it contains a call for detente and for *glasnost* between men and women. Sexual warfare constitutes one of the primary sources of intrapsychic conflict in both women and men; sexual warfare is also a primary source of the increasing violence in our society. This study seriously considers the needs of women, but it equally considers the needs of men. Human potential has been culturally divided between culturally constructed paradigms of femininity and masculinity. By tracing this division to its origins in early childhood development, I show how each woman harbors an under-developed masculine self, and each man, a repressed feminine self. Finally, I affirm the importance of the differences that do exist between women and men, and that these differences are as important as the equally undeniable similarities men and women also share. Unfortunately for feminism, it is often misconstrued as denying all differences between men and women. For example, in December 1988 Benazir Bhutto became the first woman leader of a modern Islamic nation. When she was interviewed by the American press, she declared, "I am not a feminist [because I have always thought that] men and women were different" (Fineman 1988, I:8).

The necessary model of human development presented here is founded upon differences, but differences grounded in the samenesses of cultural bodies. In this way psychosexual development becomes psychosocial evolution. I am hopeful that men, too, will be curious about a model of human development that promises to grant them greater freedom to be themselves, to escape the gender prison of a narrowly conceived masculinity.

In Chapter 2 of my study I analyze the dominant paradigms of patriarchal culture, especially as illustrated by the important work of Thomas S. Kuhn. In Chapter 3, I show how Freud's system holds the dialectical keys that open doors out of the logical impasses in which patriarchal thought finds itself. I also indicate how Freud's system incorporates Kuhn's paradigm and also partially transcends it. My critique and transformation of essential Freudian categories is designed to pass beyond the spurious dualisms of the dominant culture.

Chapters 4 and 5 present, analyze, and deconstruct the six myths of patriarchal culture that prevent us from moving beyond sexual warfare. I also develop an alternative perspective upon the early development of girls and boys and explain why we are still prisoners of our present gender arrangements. Like Freud, and unlike Kuhn, I emphasize the coexistence of two selves (paradigms), overlapping and grounded in the patriarchal culture, yet relatively autonomous from each other. The theories of *accomplicity* and of the *paradigm change* (or stillbirth) of Oedipal selves I present here will help us resolve philosophical, as well as practical, problems of subject/object, mind/body, and male/female schisms, will help us overcome the stasis of masculine identity theories, and will help us find the paths to genuine change. The story of humanity, hung up on the peg of gender rigidity, will begin to unfold once more.

In Chapter 6, I further develop my new perspective on psychosexual development, revealing the insights that this womanist angle of vision provides on such phenomena as sadomasochism, homosexuality, and so-called normal sexuality. I demonstrate the power of this new vision by selecting a few salient problems at the intersection of psychoanalysis and culture, most notably the concepts of symbolic death and psychic rape. I explain why Norman O. Brown's significant study of Freudian psychoanalysis, *Life against Death* (1977), fails as a philosophy of history: Brown's "resurrection of the body" fails as a solution to repression and to the denial of death because Brown himself fails to acknowledge the dimension of the symbolic: the reality of symbolic death and of symbolic immortality. Brown fails to understand the symbol as metaphor, and sexuality and the body as symbolizing woman for patriarchal men. Finally, Brown fails to recognize that woman, body, sex — all three terms — also equal symbolic death in the masculine lexicon. A transformed psychoanalysis, I conclude, will recognize that instead of a resurrection of the body, Western culture must facilitate a resurrection of women and of the repressed feminine self within each man.

In Chapter 7, I outline a few principles of a womanist psychotherapy and summarize the major concepts presented in this study. (The term "womanist" has been suggested by writer Alice Walker in order to extend feminist concerns to minority and working-class women.) I conclude that, as the twentieth century draws to a close, the existential truths of women's lived experience are beginning to confront the truths of masculine culture, just as the worlds of family and work are converging. By bringing the light generated by this clash to bear upon Freudian psychoanalysis, I have begun a transformation of Freudian categories of analysis — principally those of the Oedipus complex, of 'bisexuality,' and of the unconscious. I believe that this transformation constitutes a major advance in both psychoanalysis and feminist theory. I fervently hope that this new theory will unleash the unused capacities of both women and men and will aid us in our long struggle to transform our lives.

2

The Structure of Gender Revolution

It is striking to realize that in the psycho-analytic writings on the psychology of women, the greatest amount of material is on their sexuality. This finding is a comment in itself.

Jean Baker Miller

MAN THE MEASURE

Although we Americans proudly trace important roots to the civilization of the early Greeks, we are surprisingly silent on one important aspect of this heritage. The Greeks recognized many forms of love, all springing from the love of beauty, identified by the Greeks with the wise and virtuous soul. However, love for the Greeks was split between the earthly Aphrodite and the heavenly Aphrodite, between love of body and love of soul, and the latter — the highest form of love — was most likely to be portrayed by Greek philosophers as the love felt for a young man. The Greek scholar K. J. Dover notes that in the ambience of Socrates "intense eros was experienced more often in a homosexual than in a heterosexual relationship" (Dover 1978, 164). That Greek culture was patriarchal is well known; that Greek philosophy rose on the backs of slaves is also known, if not loudly trumpeted.

However, the homosexual aspects of Greek civilization often remain but a quiet whisper, an inconsequential footnote to our cultural understanding. The sexual threads in the fabric of Greek social relations have been unwoven: Nineteenth-century male scholarship portrayed Greek women as standing apart, hardly above the slaves, and that has remained the dominant view. The nineteenth-century Victorian writer Edward Carpenter thought that both the strength and the weakness of the Greeks could be understood by their reduction of love for women to "mere sensuality," while "the *romance* of love went to the account of [masculine] friendship," which was quite openly erotic (Bronski 1984, 25). Today, feminist scholarship, justifiably eager to restore balance, reminds us of the historical forces women have exerted; feminist scholars study the voiceless masses of women in history along with individual "great women," as, for example, the wise Aspasia, adviser of Pericles and teacher of Socrates.

In truth, Greek culture was neither the sanitized heterosexuality of most school texts nor the idealized homosexuality of specialized scholarship; rather, it exhibited a distinctive bisexuality. Dover informs us that "Greek culture differed from ours in its readiness to recognise the alternation of homosexual and heterosexual preferences in the same individual, [and in] its implicit denial that such alternation or coexistence created peculiar problems for the individual or for society" (Dover 1978, 1). While permitting the privilege of education to some women, the Greek patriarches still segregated the majority of upper-class women in private quarters remote from the rest of the household activities. While enjoying the company of their educated *hetaerae*, the producers of our Western traditions still preferred sexual and intellectual intercourse with young men whose companionship alone led, they thought, to mutual spiritual advance. Thus, the infamous Cartesian splitting of the human person into mind and body, the notorious seventeenth-century "dissociation of sensibility," already had a rich history dating back at the least to this Greek dissociation of most women from the ideal of reason, which remained masculine; the majority of women were identified with reproductive sexuality and with the body. Plato, of course, split the generic human into male and female, the former associated with advance into perfect knowledge of the eternal and ideal forms and the latter associated with mere animal reproduction. These became the fundamental human typologies of patriarchal culture.

In the sense that these male-defined divisions of a sex/gender system have remained the fundamental cultural organizing principle of Western civilization, we have yet to experience a culture that is thoroughly heterosexual. Only one sex, the male, has been responsible for the kinds of cultural production — history, science, technology, and art — that have been consciously transmitted and that have shaped our conscious historical awareness. Writer Adrienne Rich has noted that all women "are trained to identify with men, whether with the males in power to whom they may be attached, or — as emotional sympathizers — with the men of an oppressed group. Identification with women *as women*, not as persons similar in class or race or cultural behavior, is still profoundly problematic" (Rich 1979, 287). Until the cultural contributions of women are recognized as equal to those of men, until we no longer live in a one-sex cultural milieu, I submit that we will be living in a homosexual culture (here I use *homo* from the Greek *homos* meaning "the same"). Ironically, this homosexual culture is profoundly homophobic, or self-hating.

Yet, I argue that it is only through *difference* that material-spiritual evolution becomes possible. Material-spiritual evolution requires that we recognize and respect the value of those who differ from us sexually, ethnically, religiously, and racially.

Unfortunately, the measures of what is human have been defined over millennia by privileged men and remain today the yardsticks by which Western men and women determine their worthiness and progress. Until recently, women in the U.S. military had to sign codes of conduct in which they declared themselves "American fighting men." And although we are told that the words *man* and *mankind* are generic terms that include the females of the species, studies have demonstrated that young schoolgirls believe themselves excluded by such usage. Language shapes us in more ways than we know, and there are many cultural codes that shape us below the level of cognition, codes that determine how we use time, space, and our relationships with others to define and assert our femininity and masculinity. Important cross-cultural analyses of space and time structuring have been made by noted anthropologist Edward Hall, whose observations convinced him that "men and women often inhabit quite different visual worlds" (Hall 1969, 69). Later I will argue that the essential differences between the ways women and men use time and space have important consequences for the development of traditional femininity and masculinity in children.

Along with the growth of the women's movement, awareness has been growing that gender itself confers status: To be born male in an androcentric (male-centered) culture automatically renders one superior to those born female. Ann Oakley, a British feminist sociologist, has stressed the need to differentiate between the concepts of anatomical or biological sex and those of gender. "A 'gender role,' " Oakley states, "is a role assigned on the basis of biological sex, which defines specific personality traits and behavioral responses as appropriate to a person of that sex. Biologically, people are male or female; culturally, they are pressured to be masculine or feminine" (Oakley 1976, 82). Males and females are naturally differentiated by their possession of male or female genitals and secondary sex characteristics. Gender refers to masculinity and femininity, and these latter concepts are culturally determined.

The human race is divided into two biological sexes, female and male. Generally, cultures construct two genders, feminine and masculine, upon this biological, "natural" foundation. Modern biological science has found, however, that even biological sex is multidimensional. Sexual attribution is usually dependent upon external genital morphology at birth that can be ambiguous. Other determinants of biological maleness or femaleness are interior sexual anatomy (presence of ovaries/uterus or vas/prostate) and chromosomal characteristics (presence of XX, XY, XYY, XXY, or XO configurations; only the first two are considered normal female and male, respectively). Further biological determinants are hormonal levels. Considerable overlap between the sexes exists, however, because some normal males produce fewer male hormones (androgens) than some females and, vice versa, some females produce fewer female hormones (estrogens) than some males.

Although it is not common, some cultures construct more than the usual two gender categories. The Mohave Indians allow phenotypic females to adopt a masculine gender role and status called *hwame*, and phenotypic males to adopt a feminine gender role and status called *alyha*. The *hwame* and *alyha* adopt the dress, customs, and behavior of the gender opposite their phenotype and then are permitted to marry individuals of their own phenotype. The Navajo have a third gender category for intersexed individuals (those whose genitals at birth appear neither masculine nor feminine). Intersexed individuals may dress alternately in male and female clothing and carry out the tasks of either sex with the exception of war or hunting. Other cultures are more rigid and recognize only two gender categories; in these cultures newborns with ambiguous genitalia are killed (Martin and Voorhies 1975, 84–107).

Although modern anthropological and biological research has discovered the complexity of male and female sexual attribution and among some peoples the multiple gender statuses that correspond to deviations from the usual biological sexual dichotomies, the fact does remain that even supernumerary sexes are created in relation to masculine/feminine bipolarities. Furthermore, clinical studies have proven many times over that in the majority of cases (with the exception of hypogonadal males), cultural attribution overrides biological factors in what is called core gender identity. If the parents, or others in the parental role, do not doubt the gender of their child—even if they have made an incorrect assessment based on ambiguous or malformed genitals—the child's core gender identity will accord with this social attribution.

Biological theory, developed almost without exception by men, has insisted upon the superiority of the male, and, as psychoanalyst Clara Thompson has stated, only in recent years have men and women begun to realize that this masculine superiority is not biological fact (Miller 1978, 72). From Aristotle until the end of the seventeenth century, semen was considered the vital ingredient in human conception (Tannahill 1980, 344). Just as the male was assumed to provide the essential spark of life through his semen, he was also assumed to be the stronger sex, as well as to represent the prototype of humanness. The human male has been the ultimate measure of "man."

However, recent discoveries in the biological sciences have demonstrated that the fragile, "second" sex is indeed hardier than the male. More male embryos are aborted before term, and although more males are born than females (about 106 males for every 100 females), far fewer males reach young adulthood. Furthermore, brain physiologists have discovered that

the resting state for the central mechanisms of gender (i.e., masculine and feminine behavior as contrasted to "sex") *is female. Only if the fetal brain (hypothalamus) is organized by androgen does masculine behavior result.* And, if normally occurring androgens are blocked in the male, then, once again, femininity appears. Apparently the brain makes do with one type of anatomic system: if it is activated with androgens, it is the "bedrock" of masculinity; without activation, it will subserve femininity. (Stoller in Miller 1978, 278)

It would be foolish for feminists to launch a "Woman the Measure of All Things" campaign on the basis of these new biological findings. Given the importance of cultural interpretations and cultural valuations, recourse to the "factual" meaning of discoveries in human biological nature is always moot. It is important, however, to focus attention upon biological discoveries that counter masculine ideology's endless dichotomizing, which has so often constituted femininity as the weak and inferior afterthought of either God or nature.

Therefore, should it be surprising that in a society where men alone set the standards of normality and abnormality, feminine traits are by comparison with masculine traits seen to be abnormal, inferior, and even a little mad? Many recent researchers have noted what Oakley calls the "situation of 'structural ambivalence' " that exists for women in patriarchal cultures (Oakley 1976, 81). In short, the activities that patriarchal cultures define as primary female activities, above all, marriage and motherhood, along with the personality characteristics defined as feminine, namely, docility, nurturance, expressiveness, and openness to others, are dysfunctional in masculine domains and are, in fact, held in lower esteem than traits and activities culturally defined as masculine.

Ihsan Al-Issa, professor of psychology at the University of Calgary, has written an entire book, *The Psychopathology of Women* (1980), in support of the idea that mental illness in both women and men constitutes a deviation from gender roles. In the course of his research and clinical practice, Al-Issa has found that the least-powerful members of a culture are those most apt to stand accused of madness. Therefore, Al-Issa believes, the vulnerable social position of women, coupled with the intrinsically unhealthy sex-role characteristics prescribed for women, helps explain their continuing higher rates of depression and their higher treatment rates for psychiatric disorders. Al-Issa asserts that "society and its professionals have sanctioned typical male behaviors and considered them the ideals for mental health. Because of this, women are thrown into unresolvable conflict and are damned whatever they do. Whether they show masculine or feminine behavior, they are considered sick" (Al-Issa 1980, 29).

Women, then, are reduced to the choice between behaviors considered mature and adult, but unfeminine, or behaviors that although considered feminine are also not respected. As Elizabeth Janeway expresses women's dilemma: "The more feminine a woman is, the less can she be part of the major, ongoing trend of life in our society" (Janeway 1971, 100). Yet professors of psychiatry like Ihsan Al-Issa and Robert Stoller have demonstrated that there is no other quality more intimately linked to a sense of who we are than that of gender. Gender distinctions are the cornerstone of self and society.

Along with Shulamith Firestone, I assert that the origins of human dualistic thinking begin in sexual dimorphism. Unfortunately, however, Firestone espouses a Rousseauistic viewpoint that urges the destruction of that which she believes is suppressing humankind's natural sexuality and erotic potential (Firestone 1979). Firestone argues that the main inhibiting factor is the patriarchal family and that its abolition would permit "natural" polymorphous human sexuality to be resurrected.

My own viewpoint is more complex than a Rousseauistic opposition between the "good" sexuality of natural, uncivilized humans and the "bad" sexuality of moderns: There is, I submit, no natural sexuality, polymorphous or other, that can be resurrected when civilization is renounced. A humane sexuality cannot exist apart from cultural and historical processes. Firestone, along with Freud, does correctly understand that modern civilization has brought about a stultification and stunting of erotic potential on the part of both sexes. But this sexual malaise is due, not to the suppression of sexuality "itself" or "in-itself" — which does not exist — but to the suppression of the female person and her sexuality through patriarchal ideologies and economic structures and through pre-Oedipal parenting practices within patriarchal families.

Sexuality, along with femininity and masculinity, has over generations been defined and shaped by men through the medium of patriarchal culture. Moreover, since the beginning of the nineteenth century and the Industrial Revolution, an accelerating masculinization of culture has occurred due to the exponential increase in the production of knowledge by men and the multiplication of cultural codes and languages written in male script. Unfortunately, as patriarchal culture has expanded, women as outsiders to this culture have grown ever more distant and different from men. And this difference has been defined — by men — as constituting inferiority. Some men, psychoanalyst Robert Seidenberg among them, have noted and complained about the intolerance of men for differences of all sorts — religious, racial, sexual, and academic. This intolerance of those who differ (implied is "differ from the powerful white middle or upper-class male") is attributed by Seidenberg to men's deep-seated fears of women, fears that have been clinically uncovered during psychoanalysis (Seidenberg in Miller 1978, 326).

Patriarchal theories have constructed the female as absolute other and used this otherness as the basis for women's presumed inferiority. Yet as Freud's system emphasizes and as modern biology and anthropology now indicate, each individual, whether female or male, contains characteristics of both sexes. Flawed as Freud's model of human development may be, it still may serve as the basis for a theory that can include the female gender because, unlike the spurious dualisms of most masculine thought, Freud's model includes a *dialectics of difference within a cultural matrix.*

The psychoanalyst Erich Fromm, both follower and critic of Freud, has claimed that "the concentration on sex actually deflected from the criticism of society and hence had in fact partly a politically reactionary function" (Fromm 1981, 135). To the contrary, I agree with both Freud and philosopher Michel Foucault that sexuality — as culturally constructed gender differences — is the central problem of this postmodern age. Furthermore, the flight from problems of sexuality represents a fleeing from the problems of women, and from their sexuality as constructed by patriarchal culture and as it exists in potentiality. It is also a fleeing from the problems of the body — by attribution and default the queendom of the feminine — and, lastly, it is a fleeing from the problems of bodily decay and death. Left behind are potentials for emotional development. Above all, because affective and cognitive development must develop in reciprocity, I detect the crippling of cognitive growth in patriarchal cultures. Finally, there exists a flight on the part of men from an inalienable, even if repressed, part of themselves, that which I call their *majority selves*, a part honored in myth as representing a lost paradise.

Sexuality, then, in its broader ramifications as gender distinctions, represents the primordial schism, the prime organizing principle of patriarchal culture, and the source of ubiquitous dualisms and ineluctable intellectual dichotomizing. Every facet of culture is relegated to either the feminine or the masculine, and the essential difference between the two, from the viewpoint of our patriarchal culture, is that the latter evolves into the transcendental spheres of spirit and intellect, whereas the former is forever mired in matter, in immanence, in the body and its imperious needs. Woman as sexual, natural, emotional creature represents the unchanging and enduring eternal against which man measures his growth and progress; she is the secure port receding on the horizon as man's ship adventures into unknown seas. Thus defined as an unchanging sphere of natural pleasure, the private realm, queendom of woman, can have no problematic articulation with the kingdom of public enterprise. It is port, continuity, and backdrop to the public stage, to the officer's deck, where leading men take action.

I find, however, that despite the historical depth of contemporary misogyny, a new vision of women's lives is struggling to be born and that this new vision is aided by significant changes in the cultural ethos. These favorable cultural changes spring in part from the closely interrelated women's, ecological, peace, and holistic health movements. They can be briefly summarized as follows: First, new historical schools have found that the spheres assigned to women — the spheres of family and the affective life — are not stationary and unchanging; they are historically evolving. Family relationships are not static and transhistorical. Feminist writer Shelia Rowbotham's insight that sexual love and "the feelings generated by the particular sexual relationship come out of the totality of human social relations" is becoming more widely understood (Rowbotham 1976, xxx).

Second, and reinforcing the above discoveries, have been the many cross-cultural research findings of cultural anthropology that illustrate the enormous overlapping range of behaviors defined as feminine or masculine. Gender is now understood as culturally constituted. Third, Western cultural climates are more accepting of dual or multiple realities due to the powerful influence of the paradigm-shattering findings of modern particle physics and its principle of complementarity. This new vision affirms the importance of relationships in a "participatory universe" that centrally implicates the knower in the constitution of the known. Fourth, new research in biology, biochemistry, and medicine and the brain sciences is abolishing the old mind/body schisms and bringing forth a powerful model of mind-body interaction.

Fifth, studies of early childhood are radically changing our understanding of infants and young children, with an emphasis on the importance of early cognitive growth as opposed to studies of purely affective and sensorimotor growth in babies. Sixth, although there have been recent setbacks for women, reliable contraception is on the cultural horizon. Despite the protests of a vocal minority and the rulings of reactionary judicial bodies, control over a woman's own body — and therefore over her own destiny — is becoming a firmly embedded female entitlement. Seventh and last, the recent revival of interest in Freudian psychoanalysis, particularly the interest in the original Freudian texts, has also revived interest in the broader aspects of sexuality, in women's development, in the problems of early childhood development and child care, and in the unconscious aspects of personal and cultural reality.

Many abstract theoretical problems are intimately related to problems of sexuality and the sexes because masculine philosophy has been blinded by rationalistic monisms that cut us off from the potentials of our other selves. Yet, as European social theorist Alain Touraine has stated, the solutions to these abstract problems will arrive as we pass "from a monistic industrial culture in which man assumed the guise of Nature's master to a vision where man [*sic*] and nature are different, yet complementary" (Touraine 1989, 6:34). Central to this new vision will be the complementary differences of women and men.

In the sections that follow, I discuss in more detail the dominant patriarchal paradigms that are causing both men and women personal anguish and are promising cultural destruction. The remainder of this study is devoted to presenting a new model of psychosexual development, a model based upon the Freudian paradigm, but one that transforms it, moving beyond it as women's experiences are factored in. I demonstrate why monolithic conceptions of truth that neglect the cultural truths assigned to women and the truth of women's lived experience can comprehend neither the scope of the real nor of the ideal, nor of the fantasized, nor of their interrelationships. Philosopher William James has stated:

To no one type of mind is it given to discern the totality of truth. Something escapes the best of us—not accidentally, but systematically, and because we have a twist. The scientific-academic mind and the feminine-mystical mind shy from each other's facts, just as they fly from each other's temper and spirit. (James 1953, 198)

Until recently Freud's insistence upon maintaining a dualistic system was correct because female and male, the culturally constructed feminine and masculine, did "fly from each other." The unprecedented fact of late twentieth-century patriarchal cultures is that these truths — the truths of women's reality, the truths of men's reality — are beginning to confront each other. As they do, I believe with Rich that "sexuality, politics, intelligence, power, motherhood, work, community, intimacy will develop new meanings; thinking itself will be transformed" (Rich 1981, 292). I propose to present a model that will bring us all — women and men alike — a little closer to this global transformation.

GOOD-BYE TO THE MEN FROM EITHER/OR

The American branch of Western culture is not noted for its warm acceptance of either philosophy or social theory. Our archetypical contribution to both is pragmatism, or as one wit put it, "the theory of non-theory." Thinkers in the dominant culture pride themselves on their problem-solving capabilities in the here and now, on being hard-headed and hard-nosed; not half-baked, but hard-boiled. Within American universities, the greatest prestige goes to the "hard" sciences, and even among these there exists a hierarchy of "hardness," led by mathematical physics and engineering. It is no accident that the "harder" the discipline, meaning the more mathematical, the fewer women one will find studying that discipline.

One would think that women would at least be found successfully practicing in the top ranks of the arts and "softer" social sciences, since these are the university disciplines in which women students equal or outnumber men. With the exception of a few recent breakthroughs by women film producers and directors, however, women artists, journalists, script writers, composers, and television producers are scarcely visible in the higher echelons of their respective fields. Although women have made some advances within psychotherapeutics, they are clustered in the lower-paid and lower-prestige fields of social work and family counseling. Within education, women are scandalously under-represented among administrators and among tenured faculty at the college and university levels. The "two cultures" that British social critic C. P. Snow warned us about some years ago are more than a regrettable possibility; they are the realities that battle for ascendancy within the wider Western culture and, indeed, within each Western breast. However, I submit that more fundamental than the two cultures—that of science and that of art—Snow brought to our attention are the two cultures represented by Western women and Western men.

Contrary to views still prevailing, there was no return of women to the home after World War II. Women's participation in the workforce has continued to grow steadily from the postwar 1940s, through the family togetherness of the traditional 1950s, right up until the present (Ryan 1983, 253–54). The additional responsibilities women have assumed since the mid-twentieth century—their two full-time jobs, the continuing denigration of the feminine by the dominant patriarchal culture, and the escalating expectations that women must meet working both at home and "abroad"—all of these realities have fueled the women's movement. These realities have also created deepening anxiety, frustration, fatigue, guilt, and depression among the vast majority of women—as well as a growing vision among many as to what must be changed. With the acuity of perception that comes naturally to the outsider, women have begun to produce cogent critiques of the dominant cultural paradigms and have been highly represented in the civil rights, women's, ecological, peace, and holistic health movements, all of which seek to change our dominant reality.

This dominant patriarchal reality has been characterized by the spurious dualisms of the either/or, by a one-dimensional linear logic, and by the compartmentalization of human discourse and disciplines. In the universities the academic disciplines are busy following Voltaire's dictum to cultivate their own gardens—walled, of course; in business and government bureaucracies executives build mini-empires and secure them against invasion by neighboring departments; in medicine the human body is broken down into smaller and smaller subentities that supposedly have nothing to do with each other. Writer Robin Morgan cites the example of sociologists who study population growth and social reproduction while claiming that the study of women is not relevant to their inquiries. Architects solve the problems of the underclass by building high-rise pigeon-roosts that have rapidly become the twentieth-century version of medieval fortresses, blood-stained by the shoot-outs of competing juvenile gangs, and narcotics pushers. The dominant languages of all professions are masculine in their monotonous insistence upon metaphors of war and masculine sporting life, both of which have become big business.

Fortunately, the exhaustion of the Western intellectual tradition and the bankruptcy of the present patriarchal social system is beginning to be widely recognized. Early in the twentieth century, the philosopher Edmund Husserl realized that the "crisis of European sciences and European man" was a crisis in the conception of reason itself. Husserl decided that he must "save human reason," and thus he attempted to resurrect philosophy as a "rigorous science" (Husserl 1965, 7). Husserl's critique of Western reason's decay and his wish to "reground" reason in both history and invariant structures of subjectivity were soon echoed by critics belonging to the Frankfort school of sociology, many of whom came to America during the Nazi era. These thinkers claimed that the "substantive reason" of earlier eras, most particularly that of Greek thought, had become merely instrumental reason, the latter serving neither the whole man nor the whole nation, but degenerating to the slavish servicing of capitalistic greed. Fromm summarizes their concerns when he says: "Reason as the means for discovering the truth and penetrating the surface to the essence of phenomena has been relinquished for intellect as a mere instrument to manipulate things and men. Man has ceased to believe that the power of reason can establish the validity of norms and ideas for human conduct" (Fromm 1967, 5).

It is important to understand that the twentieth-century crisis in man's reason reflects a crisis in one of the most fundamental of the dominant culture's schisms, namely, that between reason and emotion, or objectivity and subjectivity. Of all the spurious dualisms of patriarchal thought, this is the duality most often used to differentiate the rational, objective male from the emotional, subjective female. Fromm went on to delineate the crisis of Western reason from the viewpoint of masculine thought when he stated, "The development of man's intellectual capacities has far outstripped the development of his emotions. Man's brain lives in the twentieth century; the heart of most men lives still in the Stone Age. The majority of men have not yet acquired the maturity to be independent, to be rational, to be objective" (Fromm 1969, xiv).

Substantive reason, Fromm declares, has been reduced to instrumental reason that manipulates and destroys nature and other men through ignorance and greed. Man is split between feeling and thinking, Fromm asserts, with reason worshiped as end all and be all by thinkers from the Enlightenment philosophers down to the present. The dominant culture ignores, Fromm continues, what "Spinoza had seen, that affects, like thought, can be both rational and irrational" (Fromm 1963, 13). Of course, Fromm here begs the question, which is, if men have lost their grip on substantive reason, how can they determine which affects are reasonable, let alone which reasons are reasonable? Furthermore, Fromm leaves unanalyzed, and unquestioned, the equating of maturity with independence, objectivity, and rationality (presumably rationality of the right kind).

Of all the either/ors of patriarchal thought, the split between reason and emotion is the most pervasive. Fromm's idea that the emotional or affective spheres can also be rational is unique because for most Western thought the affective and the emotional — those cultural attributes assigned predominantly to women — are seen as irrational and as more primitive than reason. Affect is without structure or logic and, therefore, usually seen as unintelligible and eternally the same. Writer Gordon Rattray Taylor has remarked in *The Natural History of Mind*: "The failure of science to provide even a sketchy but convincing account of emotion suggests to me, very strongly, that some major factor in the story [of mind] is still unidentified" (Taylor 1979, 291). I submit that the splitting of reason from emotion and the identification of emotion with women, with the feminine gender, and with this gender's presumed historical stasis has prevented science from understanding Taylor's missing factor and developing a "convincing account" of human emotional development.

There are many other varieties of the either/or dichotomizing tendency of patriarchal thought. Western philosophers since Plato have taken a stand for the precedence of *essence* (the ideal, formal structure, the immortal soul) over *existence* (the actual ephemeral contingency, the perishable body) or, as with Sartre, asserted exactly the reverse, namely, the precedence of existence over essence. Typically, in this variety of the either/or, the problem of the relationship of essence to existence, remains unexplained. No matter from which of these poles man derives himself and his cultural productions, still left unexplained are the processes of becoming and their relationship to being. Being is eternally opposed to becoming, and time's arrow either shoots straight into the infinitely unknown or chases its tail in futile unending cycles. Above all, the categories of analysis, the undergirding patriarchal system, are viewed as a priori, unchanging, transhistorical — no development or changes are allowed for in the categories of analysis themselves.

Yet another variety of the either/or involves patriarchal man's struggles with his own personal origins. This is the either/or of self or (m)other. Typically, patriarchal man proclaims himself self-created and visualizes himself as *either* a product of a male God-head that he fashions in his own image, *or* as a product of efforts he himself has made after having reached the age of reason and cut himself loose from his maternal environment. Having cut themselves off from their roots in their pre-Oedipal mother-complicated childhoods, men must also account for the social-solidarity of their self-made selves. Their solution, from philosopher John Locke to Freud's primal horde and parricide theories, has been to claim that individual men come together and agree to a social contract that spells out the laws and terms of their association. In this way men found families, clans, tribes, cities, and national governments. Some twentieth-century theorists, most notably the American sociologist Talcott Parsons, have called attention to the tautological nature of social-contract reasoning (see also Roazen 1968, 154). This reasoning is tautological because a contract is based upon an agreement that presupposes the common language and rules signaling an already thriving social life. Also, women are totally missing from this masculine origins equation.

All of patriarchal thought, then, is characterized by its dualistic conception of reality; but it is a peculiar dualism in which one reality of the pair — of the either/or — becomes more real than the other, becomes *the* fundamental reality that transcends, masters, or even annihilates the other. For patriarchal thought, then, truth ultimately is not dualistic but monistic. Univocal truth becomes grounded in reason that, as instrumental reason, makes use of the tools of mathematical measurement and a linear compartmentalizing Aristotelian logic. Language remains the key cultural level to which all others are coded, but the languages of mathematics and physics represent the rigorous ideal to which all other discourse aspires.

Clarity, brevity, simplicity, and efficiency are ultimate values in both language and life. Without language, thinking cannot exist, and man's self does not exist without thought and reason. Anything tainted with subjective values is suspect and inferior. For most Western patriarchal theories the affective, the emotional — the cultural attributes assigned to women — are seen as irrational and as more primitive than reason; affect is without structure and remains, therefore, unintelligible.

Another tendency of patriarchal thought is to affirm a reality *either* "out there" *or* "in here," a reality that man can approach asymptotically, step by step, but never quite reach or know "in-itself." Reality is considered extensively and intensively infinite; it is "an infinitely divisible profusion" (Giddens 1977a, 138). Man can approach the truth of these infinite realities only through the experience of appearances that reflect the structure of reality. These conceptions render reality, in effect, one-dimensional, and so the scientist's task becomes one of furthering mankind's asymptotic approach to truth. The very idea of an asymptote presupposes the linear and one-dimensional and represents an essentially positivistic formulation: Neither the natural nor the social sciences have anything to contribute to the world of values. As for philosophy, it remains an "underlaborer," capable only of pointing out logical inconsistencies that hinder the progress of the scientific march toward truth (Giddens 1977b, 29–89). Philosopher Jay Ogilvy calls this conception "the paradigm of the univocally determinate object towards which all descriptions converge like ever more accurate measurements" (Ogilvy 1979, 85). Even in contemporary intellectual models where several "modes of knowing" are allowed, reality is still reduced to "*a level of consciousness, and this level alone is Real*" (Walsh & Vaughan 1980, 238). Patriarchal reality is thus characterized by being monolithic (not dualistic) and intelligible, that is, reasonable; where it is comprised of levels, it is hierarchical; but, in essence, reality can be reduced to one level that "*alone is Real.*"

These prevailing one-dimensional conceptions of the dominant culture, especially the idea that reality can be continuously approached by a converging series of discrete steps, harbors the Faustian impulse that seeks validation of masculine individualism and masculine immortality. For if reality is not continuously approachable by discrete steps, as for example, critical realism claims, if reality is fundamentally discontinuous and fundamentally implicates the knower in the innermost structure of the known, then masculine genius and masculine immortality become impossible as traditionally defined. Reality would then have to be rethought in terms that would challenge the viability of the Faustian project, which is to see (prescience) and know (omniscience) all to the end of time or, should this prove impossible, at least be part of that immortal tower of giants upon whose shoulders Faust stands to grasp immortality itself.

As a result of these dominant values and ideals, patriarchal thought lacks a cultural model of becoming; it experiences grave problems when attempting to explain not only origins but also any transitions and change. Yet it is obvious to all in these closing years of the twentieth century that humanity as a whole is experiencing a paradigm change upon a vast scale. Desperately needed are models that can explain change and becoming on both the level of society and that of the social individual. I suggest that masculine models cannot account for change and becoming, social or individual, nor for evolution from origins, because for patriarchal thought it is essential to deny any rootedness or merging, whether in mother, country, or nature.

Rootedness equals impotence for the male, I suggest, because rootedness equals merging with those cultural attributes masculine thought has simultaneously defined as feminine and weak. They are weak, not because they are feminine, but because masculine individuation grew at the expense of the feminine defined as constant, unchanging, and incapable of evolution—and therefore incapable of immortality. Therefore, the themes of separation and independence, of individualism and immortality, find themselves supported by a world-view and a reason that divides and separates. The emphasis of dialectical thought upon fusion (synthesis), interdependence, and reciprocity translates for patriarchal thought as *contamination* with the feminine, with immanence, and with death.

The dominant traditions in Western thought have proclaimed that dualities have arisen because of *man's* self-consciousness. They have further proclaimed that these dualities are destructive and that they must and can be overcome. Various models have been brought forward, all of which tend to reduce the reality of duality, of genuine difference – which I assert is founded upon the sex/gender split in our species – to one more "fundamental" monistic level of reality via identity theories, metaphors of reflection, and theories of mimesis and correspondence or of isomorphism and homology. It is interesting to note how neatly the male/female dichotomy fits into the dualisms the dominant culture is at pains to describe, separate, and above all hierarchically order so that the female terms are mastered, controlled, and finally reasoned away as inferior to the male terms:

MALE	FEMALE
subject	object
mind	body
reason	emotion (or the irrational)
transcendence	immanence
social laws	everyday cultural mores

The distinguished scholar and sociologist Zygmunt Bauman, while commenting on the phenomenon of the marginal man, states our cultural reality as regards the sexes most dramatically:

The deeply rooted popular belief that trespassing in existentially separate realms testifies to a superhuman power in the trespasser; the act of striding over the borders, entering the territories one does not belong in—modelled perhaps in the commonsensical, but archetypal image on the sexual violation of the primordial opposition between male and female—is seen as the ultimate measure of the transgressor's acumen, dexterity and dynamic potency. (Bauman 1973, 131)

Here we have it loud and clear: "existentially separate realms," "male and female," "primordial opposition," "sexual violation." Such "deeply rooted popular beliefs" regarding absolutely separate "territories" are still organizing our understanding. Once again I submit that other, more abstract problems are rooted in this "primordial opposition between male and female," between culturally constructed masculinity and culturally constructed femininity. The revolution that must take place in these "primordial" gender structures can come about only through a new model that examines the *relationship* between femininity and masculinity at their origins in developing female and male infants and children. In fact, a new angle of vision on this critical relationship is becoming possible because of the many changes now occurring within patriarchal culture itself.

These present-day changes in the dominant scientific paradigm are best exemplified by the early twentieth-century view of the universe as essentially discontinuous, a view born with the new discoveries from within that stronghold and inner sanctum of Western reason, mathematical physics. Here the masculine monolith has cracked, and cracked mightily. Quantum theory tells us that we live in a statistical universe wherein phenomena at the subatomic level have only a tendency to fulfill our experimental expectations. Modern microphysics has dissolved matter into energetic moments and into that which has become known as the atomic zoo. At the level of the electron microscope and the collisions of subatomic particles, matter becomes completely mutable: Particles vanish into energetic moments that recoalesce into other particles, proving subatomic particles to be simultaneously indestructible and destructible. Nature appears as a complicated web of relations between the various parts of the whole. These relations always include the observer in an essential way (Capra 1977, 67–69). The universe is one which in a profound sense is "a participatory universe" (ibid., 128).

The new physics has introduced paradox into the very heart of matter, not only requiring new epistemological sophistication but also calling for a total abrogation of old subject/object, materialist/idealist oppositions. The masculine either/or has died with these discoveries and, I suggest, so has the old sex/gender system underpinning this vision of reality. Physicist Werner Heisenberg explains the new vision: "A clear distinction between matter and force can no longer be made in this part of physics [quantum mechanics], since each elementary particle not only is producing some forces and is acted upon by forces, but it is at the same time representing a certain field of force. The quantum-theoretical dualism of waves and particles makes the same entity appear both as matter and as force" (Heisenberg 1962, 160). Heisenberg explains that our scientific models do not reflect some isomorphic or indexical relationship between themselves and what is "really" out there. Rather, our natural science models describe "nature as exposed to our method of questioning. This was a possibility of which Descartes could not have thought, but it makes the sharp separation between the world and the I impossible" (ibid., 81). This vision of reality also makes impossible the sharp separation between the dominant culture's I and its definition of femininity as alien other and as nature.

The philosophical conclusions being drawn from the new quantum-mechanical vision of reality, being drawn by some male theorists as well as by feminist thinkers, are that our methods of questioning, our points of view, the forms of our questions, our experimental apparatuses — all these interact with nature in such a way as to help determine being itself. The I and the not-I interact; epistemology and ontology constitute reality in reciprocity. And, in a statistical universe, chance is ontologically real. In a profound sense the universe is the unit "social individuals–culture–universe" and can be understood as changing and as emerging into the future through a *dialectics of difference.* I suggest that these new understandings are revolutionizing our conceptions of our worlds of human interrelationships, especially those between the sexes.

For now, I must limit myself to suggesting that a new epistemology is required and that philosopher Abraham Kaplan is entirely correct in believing that Freud's system, more than any other, holds the keys to this new epistemology of the relationship between gendered humanity and natural evolution. One can no longer rely upon men's reason, the monolithic principle of the dominant culture. Although these ideas are still highly controversial, even within physics, Heisenberg thinks that the paradoxes introduced into our new vision of the universe are inescapable, that the universe is not simply a participatory web of interrelationships, but one in which subjectivity is inextricably woven.

The limitations upon total objectivity cannot be resolved by better measuring equipment or techniques. In addition, the limitations now understood as inherent in the nature of reason and formal systems of logical discourse, especially statistical methodologies, underline once again the need to develop that disciplined subjectivity so neglected within the thinking of the dominant culture — neglected because subjectivity has traditionally been equated with the irrational feminine.

Happily, the last thirty years have seen the beginnings of a post-positivistic philosophy of science within patriarchal culture. This new philosophy's significant tenets emphasize that "1) theories are underdetermined by facts" and "2) all observation statements are 'theory-impregnated' " (Giddens 1977b, 11–12). Moreover, some theorists are now expressing the essential understanding that the problem is not to decide "whether a proposition is a fact or a theory . . . [but] which theory [since from one point of view, a fact is also a theory] to consider as the interpretative one" (Dixon 1973, 17). This dialectical reciprocity of fact and theory, this understanding that facts themselves are constituted, is another opening onto an epistemology that will include the insights and realities of women.

These discoveries in modern particle physics and their philosophical implications represent a new vision of reality that feminist thought has espoused as closer to the existential realities of women. These discoveries point to a universe whose principal characteristics are those of "interconnectedness," of "dynamic and continuous motion or flux," of "foundationless" reality (i.e., no one fundamental level of reality). In such a universe an inextricable linkage is affirmed between knower and known; the nature of reality is viewed as statistical, probabilistic, and paradoxical. The either/ors of the dominant culture, namely, the ideas regarding essence/existence, matter/energy, ideal/real, fact/value, and objectivity/subjectivity—all these either/ors must be rethought, along with the deepest either/or of all, the one underlying all the rest, the primordial opposition between masculinity and femininity.

Some thinkers—Fritz Capra in his *Tao of Physics*, for example—and some feminist theorists such as Morgan are emphasizing the similarities between the view of the universe emanating from modern quantum physics and the world-view of Eastern mysticism. Unfortunately, those aspects of reality that have been repressed in our patriarchal Western cultural contexts—and that *are* related to women's realities—continue to be confused by some thinkers with an ultimate, mystical level of reality. But it is not a question of replacing the dominant culture's logic and reality with women's logic and realities. The problem this study addresses is, rather, one of lifting inner repressions of both women and men through a new outlook on the processes of early psychosexual development. The problem is to liberate real, existing contemporary women—and men—from patriarchal restraints built into their very nervous systems over the course of generations.

Therefore, I must emphasize that I am not promoting a mystical vision, nor insisting that all is an interconnected whole. I explicitly reject the notion of totality as it applies to human cultural theories, since, unfortunately, this notion tends to result in ideological totalitarianisms. The intuitive and mystical outlook must be liberated, not in order to defeat the logical and dichotomizing outlook, but in order to complement it. Both outlooks are needed by social individuals. The basic flaw in mystic philosophy is the same as that in masculine rational philosophy: Neither has a well-developed concept of culture, nor of the unconscious as mediating time, nature, and individual development. Mysticism believes that each individual can, by assuming the correct introspective or meditative attitude, leap into the center of the cosmic dance and, by dancing with the cosmos, achieve spiritual perfection. Masculine thought believes that salvation is open to the individual genius capable of reasoning his way to a bigger and more inclusive paradigm by means of which he will have heroically edged humanity closer to ultimate truth. I subscribe neither to cosmic dancing nor to heroic ultimate truths.

To further clarify my stance, I will contrast these two traditions, the mystical and the rational, by means of two quotations: In Zen Buddhism wisdom is expressed by the statement, "The instant you speak about a thing, you miss the mark" (Capra 1977, 21). And in the best example of rationalism, rationalism beginning to transcend itself, Heisenberg comments: "Insistence on the postulate of complete logical clarification would make science impossible. We are reminded here by modern physics of the old wisdom that the one who insists on never uttering an error must remain silent" (Heisenberg 1962, 86). One tradition insists that truth is found in contemplative silence; the other, that without speaking, truth cannot be found. Which tradition is correct? They both are, of course, for in human life there is a time to speak and a time to refrain from speaking. The relationship between these two attitudes adheres in the necessary ambiguity of speech and the fleeting eloquence of silence.

Most will agree that the whole of the twentieth century represents a period of rapid and mind-numbing transition — whether to a new golden age of postindustrial peace or to nuclear annihilation, only the passage of time will reveal. Writer Roger Walsh has stated that "we may be witnessing a paradigm transition in which one of our most fundamental paradigms, the bedrock of Western science, the classical Greek concept of the universe as essentially atomistic, divisible, isolatable, static, nonrelativistic, and comprehensible by reductionism, is in the process of replacement, not just for physics, where evidence for such a shift was first obtained, but for all sciences" (Walsh & Vaughan 1980, 222). I do affirm that this paradigm switch is now taking place. In this chapter's next section, I analyze the work of Thomas S. Kuhn in order to demonstrate how Kuhn's model of scientific change can help us to understand Freud's model of individual development. This comparison of Kuhn's paradigm switch with Freud's Oedipus crisis permits me to present new principles of early psychosexual development as well as a vision of potential *glasnost* and peaceful cooperation between the sexes.

PARADIGMS OF MASCULINE REVOLUTION

As the pace of sociocultural change accelerated during the nineteenth century — a time when both the historical and social sciences came of age — the dominant culture began to focus on theories of change and history: Theories of evolution and theories of stages of development proliferated. However, by the early years of the twentieth century, a reaction had set in and the diachronic (linear and temporal) analyses of the late nineteenth century were giving way to synchronic (structural and spatial) analyses. Whether the focus was on the immediate and apparent, as in functionalist theories, or on the transhistorical and hidden, as in the later structuralist movement, the search was on for the enduring configurations of social-institution (Durkheim, Radcliffe-Brown, and Talcott Parsons) or social-individual (Freud's later work, Piaget, and the gestalt psychologists).

The gestalt psychologists, particularly, perfected the idea of an ahistorical apprehending in terms of a priori mental configurations — a neo-Kantian modification of the prevailing positivistic view of reality/nature as extensively and intensively infinite. Philosopher of science Thomas S. Kuhn drew upon their work in an interesting fashion: He projected the selective and constituting power of the mind's gestalt onto the problem of scientific unity and development, attempting in the process to explain change, scientific progress, and the production of new scientific worldviews.

Kuhn's *Structure of Scientific Revolutions* (1970) caused a sensation when it was published in 1962, and it remains today the single most-quoted source within the social sciences. The great significance of Kuhn's model of revolution resides in his attempt to explain how one scientific tradition evolves into a new and superior scientific tradition. In so doing Kuhn hoped to abolish the schism between another one of the troublesome either/ors of masculine theory, namely, that between structural/spatial models and those predominantly historical/temporal. Kuhn embarked on the search for no less than the structure of evolutionary processes — the structure of development — within science. Since Kuhn's model will serve as a touchstone in my analysis and transformation of Freud's model of psychosexual development, it is important that we examine it in some detail.

Kuhn's modern classic, *The Structure of Scientific Revolutions* (1970), analyses the nature of scientific progress, tackling both the problem of change and that of development. For Kuhn, progress in science is cumulative only when certain values and goals are shared. He calls activities of the resulting scientific community "normal science," and he assimilates their shared values and goals to the idea of a gestalt. The scientific gestalt of normal science, Kuhn calls a "paradigm." When this shared set of values and goals, this paradigm, breaks down, normal science enters a revolutionary, or interparadigmatic, phase.

Of course, Kuhn's central problem is how to explain the change, the transition, from one paradigm to another. Keith Dixon comments in

Sociological Theory that "naive falsification makes the mistake of assuming that at the point of crisis science is divided into two areas—the problematic and the unproblematic, theory and brute data" (Dixon 1973, 17). Kuhn assumes that at the point of crisis science is divided between the paradigmatic (normal science) and the interparadigmatic ("pools" of discrete, unrelated facts).

In addition, Kuhn proposes that scientific revolutions lead to scientific progress. Yet Kuhn also introduces the idea of the incommensurability of scientific paradigms. In brief, Kuhn proposes that periods of scientific normalcy (paradigmatic periods) follow revolutionary (interparadigmatic) periods, and that these periods of normal science are not comparable. However, Kuhn also asserts that each ensuing period of normal science represents progress when compared to that which precedes it. Of course, noncommensurable paradigms can by definition have no basis upon which to be compared. Because Kuhn creates absolute categorical separations between science and society, between periods of normal science and periods of interparadigmatic breakdown of normal science wherein all that exists is a "pool of facts", Kuhn's model cracks apart under the weight of its logical inconsistencies.

Now, the crucial question is, how does change occur, how does one build bridges from the either to the or? This is the great second-level problem of relationship. I suggest it is a problem that the dominant culture with its insistence upon hermetically sealed categories, one-dimensional rationality, and absolute objectivity is ill-equipped to resolve. Specifically, as Kuhn tackles these interrelated problems of change and relationship, the question becomes, how does one get from one paradigmatic level to another, from one "normal" paradigm to the next *superior* "normal" paradigm? As Kuhn has postulated the idea of paradigmatic progress in science, a new paradigm must be a better paradigm. This idea of progress cannot, however, be logically derived from what Kuhn states are the characteristics of preparadigmatic and interparadigmatic periods wherein a "pool of facts" exists and fact gathering is a "nearly random" or "arbitrary" activity. These latter views seem to imply a theory-independent reality "really out there"—views explicitly denied by Kuhn elsewhere in his essay. As mentioned, Kuhn also posits the idea of the incommensurability of the various periods of normal science. This latter idea, however, he himself logically undermines in two ways: first, through the presentation of the idea of scientific progress, which presupposes that different competing paradigms must in some sense be comparable; and, second, by implicitly ascribing a monolithic character to normal science and scientific methodology.

Kuhn tries to extricate himself from the first difficulty by asserting that the scientific community of experts will somehow know (intuitively, perhaps?) when they have found a better paradigm-gestalt. As he goes along, however, Kuhn himself realizes that this formulation really is not cogent, so later on in the book he settles the question once and for all (he hopes) by proclaiming: "The transfer of allegiance from paradigm to paradigm is a conversion experience that cannot be forced" (Kuhn 1970, 151). Also, he declares that the decision to accept a new paradigm "can be made only on faith" (ibid., 158). So we travel the road to truth with Kuhn by first submitting to logic, then to the authority of experts, and finally, as in religion, we find scientific truth by fiat from above.

The second way in which Kuhn tries to bridge the gap between periods of paradigmatic normalcy (and thus deny the linear and monolithic character of scientific methodology implicit as well as explicit in his discussion) is by asserting that scientific progress comes about through the infusion of new blood, as when young scientists enter a field for the first time or when scientists come in from another discipline. He also briefly focuses on the swift gestalt switch, the sudden illumination in the middle of the night. However, Kuhn does not elaborate on these assertions, coming as they do toward the end of his arguments, and he never resolves the contradiction he falls into when he states, on the one hand, that paradigm switch (made analogous by Kuhn to gestalt switch) occurs all at once or not at all (those who would rather fight than switch will die out, he says); and, on the other hand, the assertion that scientific discovery "is a process and must take time" (Kuhn 1970, 55).

Moreover, when Kuhn posits the necessity of scientific revolutions, he is raising to an ontological principle the nature of scientific causality and it is not even that causality as understood by the Heisenbergian model of a statistical universe. Rather, it is that of the old empirical science, namely, that whenever a given cause is set in motion, one must necessarily and at all times come up with the same, predictable effect.

I contend that many of the confusions, ambiguities, and inconsistencies found in Kuhn's model are due to his valiant attempt to bridge the gap between the dominant masculine intellectual tradition and the opposing traditions of Hegelian dialectics and Heisenbergian quantum mechanics. Kuhn, in effect, is using the logical linear models of Euclidean and Newtonian science and attempting to factor in Hegelian ideas of dialectical progression. Normal science is presented as thesis, the growing number of anomalies as antithesis, and their resultant clash is presented as productive of a new synthetic normal science, but one on a higher level of development.

Many of Kuhn's problems arise, then, because of the difficulty he has in achieving both consistency and completeness while trying to apply the concept of dynamic whole processes to problems of scientific change by way of a linear, atomistic, and additive Aristotelian logic. Kuhn attempts to explain the structure of evolutionary change within science but fails; one cannot derive principles by which to judge one paradigm better than another when the paradigms are seen as categorically separate and noncommensurable.

Some critics have stated that Kuhn's difficulties stem in part from his having neglected to analyze the institution of science, that is, science as a bureaucracy, and the ways in which this institution interacts with other social, economic, and political institutions. However, I must agree with Kuhn when he asserts that recourse to these external factors will not modify the main theses he has developed. For no matter how large or inclusive the extension of referential frame, it cannot be an infinite regression, and the same logical dilemmas must recur, given the system of logic within which both Kuhn and his critics labor.

Kuhn's presentation is monolithic and monological in several ways: Most significantly, science is presented as the sole means by which truth is attained, and the contrast between the period of paradigmatic normal science and the period of interparadigmatic proliferation of "anomalies" and "arbitrary" facts is absolute. Kuhn is criticized for not allowing interaction between the two periods; but for Kuhn to have done so, he would have had to abandon his use of Aristotelian logic — he would, in fact, have had to transcend the paradoxes of this system of logic, paradoxes that demonstrate the impossibility of simultaneously achieving both consistency and completeness (Pagels 1988, 272–73 & 291–95; Dossey 1982, 192–94). Such a transcendence would have entailed the forging of (1) another system of logic or rationality, one "such as Hegel's where inconsistencies [contradictions and differences] function as principles of conceptual development" (Feyerabend 1978, 191), and (2) a concept of culture.

Transcendence of logical paradox means abandoning the monistic viewpoint of the either/or, an outlook that forever confronts theories (or paradigms) with facts (or "pools" of raw, unorganized data). Transcendence of this outlook means recognizing that science is rooted in a cultural world with preinterpreted meanings, with myths and mind sets, and that problems cannot be treated one by one but must be treated "as parts of a pattern" that extend far beyond immediate domains (Feyerabend 1978, 52). Again, as the theorist Imre Lakatos has stated, "whether a proposition is a fact or a theory depends on our methodological decision . . . [and] the problem is which theory to consider as the interpretative one" (Dixon 1973, 17). Indeed, the idea of interpretation cancels the certainty of preestablished indexical relationships; interpretation throws open doors into cultural contexts and cultural values. At this point, however, the thought of the dominant culture flounders: Once outside the mansion of logical discourse, masculine thought sinks into the quicksands of subjectivity and the irrational. So the either/or thinking of most masculine theory has delineated the problem for itself: *either* the rational *or* the irrational; *either* objectivity *or* subjectivity— *either* masculine *or* feminine.

One of the great values of Kuhn's *Structure of Scientific Revolutions* resides in its so clearly exposing the inability of scientific logic taken as monolithic to account for development and change. By introducing into his analysis the concept of discontinuity, of the incommensurability of paradigms, Kuhn has hammered another crack into the monolith of linear logic. The next steps necessary, those resulting in theories of the relationship between cultures and sciences, Kuhn could not take. For although he could initially admit that science has been contaminated by myth, he could not admit to what extent all knowledge—including that of science—depends upon the mythopoeic imagination. Kuhn could not recognize that scientific paradigms represent a culture's selective systems, organizing experience in precisely the same ways in which cultural myths and cultural metaphors select and organize experience (Pagels 1988, 150). Kuhn, along with the dominant culture, could not recognize that growth of knowledge requires a disciplined subjectivity whose methodology relies upon intuition, upon leaps of imagination, and upon courage and persistence in the face of uncertainty, loss, and ambiguity. In the final analysis, even the culture of scientific endeavor is a culture of tragedy.

BEYOND SEXUAL REVOLUTION

Kuhn's model of the structure of scientific revolutions presents us with some of the logical paradoxes endemic to patriarchal thought. Kuhn fails to see the logical inconsistencies in his essay because he is unable to analyze his own presuppositions. This should not be surprising, since they have been the presuppositions of much of Western civilization for centuries and are constitutive of the modern Western scientific world-view. Kuhn presupposes a monolithic scientific paradigm reflective of an equally monolithic natural reality. He presupposes a clear-cut boundary between normal science and the interparadigmatic periods between progressing "normal" periods of science. His model fails, in fact, to account for either paradigm change or paradigm progress because his model ignores the rootedness of scientific communities in their cultural communities, and it therefore ignores the overlapping of simultaneously existing and conflicting paradigms and world-views. Yet Kuhn's model of progress was eagerly accepted as an advance over previous models because it did attempt to resolve thorny problems of progressive change by means of the *metaphor* of the paradigm, namely, the idea that there exist interrelated selective principles that characterize and unify a given period and a given community.

As the twentieth century is ending, the multiple emergencies enumerated earlier, in conjunction with the accelerating pace of change, signal that humanity as a whole is experiencing a paradigm change — and this upon a vast scale. Desperately needed are models that can explain change, development, and becoming on the level of society and on that of social-individuals, female and male. Further, models are needed that can shed light upon the relationship between social structures and individual psychic structures and their reciprocal development.

What, then, are the elements required for a satisfactory theory of social change, of the psychosexual development of women and men, and of their interrelationships? Why, once again, does patriarchal thought find itself trapped at every turn in the stasis of logical paradox? I have already suggested that the dominant culture is weighted down with a number of paradoxical schisms, the deepest of which is that between culturally defined femininity and masculinity. In fact, I have asserted that this cultural dichotomy operates as the primordial organizing principle of Western culture and that the sex/gender system is generative of other cultural schisms. Over the course of millennia, but especially over the course of the last two hundred years, men have slowly obtained the greatest powers of cultural definition through their increasing control of cultural symbols (metaphors) and communication codes. Men, therefore, have obtained the power to define women and their spheres and activities as inferior.

I have further suggested that men have not done this at a blow — as in the "world historical defeat of the female sex"; neither has the subordination of women occurred as a result of a conspiracy by men. Rather, slowly over many generations, men have gained greater and greater control over cultural evolution. While gaining these cultural powers of production and definition, men have assimilated women to nature, to the unchanging natural, so that women as nature have fulfilled the need for a constant and unchanging point of reference for individuating and individualistic men. Also, as the spheres culturally assigned to women grew ever more rapidly apart from the spheres of men, the desexualized edifices of patriarchal culture were cordoned off from contamination by that which is feminine because the feminine defined as nonevolving soon came to be perceived as weak, dependent, and inferior. In this way developed over centuries the fundamental model for all oppression: that of sexism.

Many characteristics of patriarchal culture's values and theories can be explained by this need to avoid contamination by the unevolved feminine. In particular, the rigidity of linear logic and the compartmentalization of patriarchal thought derive directly from these perceived dangers of contamination. The inability of patriarchal thought to develop models of change and development that satisfactorily avoid the paradoxes of transition from one state to another also find their source in the desire not to trespass in "existentially separate realms." The unpopularity of dialectical thought, as well, finds its source in the same avoidance strategies because dialectical interaction breaks across categorical imperatives; it mingles the pure and the impure; it sullies clarity with ambiguity and taints certainty with indeterminacy; it proclaims the necessity of loss and tragedy in order that progress and evolution might occur. Needless to say, dialectical thought is not beloved by the dominant culture.

The spheres belonging to women and to men have been separating mightily since the nineteenth century with the growth of masculine scientific, technological, and cultural power, and with the growth of the masculine philosophical systems and theoretical models characterized here as essentially monistic. Even the ways in which time and space are experienced and structured have become ever more different for the two sexes. This, indeed, has been testified to in the work, already quoted, of anthropologist Edward Hall. The consequences of these differences between mothers and fathers for the psychosexual development of children are of monumental — and neglected — importance. Is it possible, I ask, that the resolution of logical paradox and problems of human change and psychosexual development depend upon systems of thought that, like Freud's, refuse to abandon duality, refuse to abandon subjectivity, psychic reality, and the symbolic constitution of truth; refuse, in short, to suppress bisexuality and the reality of the female other?

I submit that problems of change and development can never be solved within a one-dimensional monological system — not even one like that, for example, of British social theorist Anthony Giddens, whose system does begin to comprehend the need for structural, or cultural, mediations. A system that explains change and development, whether on the level of society or on that of the individual, requires at least two models that are complementary — that is, nonhierarchical. These models, however, cannot be monolithic and totally continuous. They must be visualized as having temporal and spatial gaps between them, gaps that are mediated and bridged by principles of interaction both isomorphic and nonisomorphic, that is, by principles that simultaneously embrace similarity and difference. As the next chapter demonstrates, Freud's metapsychology is rich with clues for just such a system.

Freud's model of psychosexual development resembles Kuhn's model of scientific evolution because Freud views the pre-Oedipal period as one paradigm of self dominated by mother, and the post-Oedipal period as another — superior, yet noncommensurable — paradigm dominated by father. The Oedipus crisis itself represents that critical interparadigmatic period in which the self is fractured and rehealed, or partially healed. Yet although Freud's model of psychosexual development harbors some of the dominant culture's schisms, particularly in his Oedipus complex model, Freud also transcended most masculine models because he described dialectical principles that bridge the gaps between parts of the self and between self and society, and because Freud discovered the importance of two types of rationality, namely, primary and secondary process thinking.

Like Freud's, and unlike Kuhn's, my own model of psychosexual development emphasizes the coexistence of (at least) two selves within each self, selves that overlap each other and are grounded in the patriarchal culture, yet are relatively autonomous from each other. The theory of the paradigm change (or stillbirth) of self at the time of the Oedipus crisis, which I elaborate in Chapters 4 and 5, helps to resolve the philosophical problems of the subject/object (male/female) split and of the stasis of masculine identity theory. My theory, therefore, does account for genuine change and development. In contrast, Kuhn's paradigm model, along with modern structuralist theory, illustrates the ways in which the dominant culture handles concepts of identity and of difference. Gaps between levels — between paradigms, between conscious and unconscious structures — are suppressed by means of theories of identity or of linear progress or of homological relationships and correspondences that, in effect, close off completely any opening to progressive change.

In the next chapter I lay the final plank in my theoretical foundation, leading up to my own paradigm change theory, with an analysis of Freud's metapsychology in its relationship to both masculine analytics and feminine dialectics. I suggest that Freud's theory of the founding of the masculine adult self in an identification with the father, resulting in the formation of the superego, represents the ultimate masculine monism and identity theory. Nevertheless, I also argue that Freud's system simultaneously transcends the dominant culture's limitations because Freud stubbornly clung to the dualistic elements in his system. Further, by rejecting Jung's and other monistic systems, Freud kept alive in psychoanalysis the problematic of the other, which is the problematic of the female gender — the dualistic battle of the sexes yet to be dialectically resolved.

The new vision of women's lives presented here through the medium of a transformed Freudian psychoanalysis reveals that neither women nor men can hope to attain their full stature as human beings while each sex's bisexual potential remains stunted and repressed. Furthermore, without the full powers of whole human beings, our century's multiple crises cannot be brought to peaceful resolution. In the second week of April, 1984, *Time* magazine's cover announced, "The [Sexual] Revolution Is Over," whereas in December of 1989, *Time's* cover trumpets that as "women face the '90s," they have "had it," and the issue goes on to question if there is a "future for feminism" (Leo 1984, 123; Wallis 1989, 134). In *Unleashing Our Unknown Selves*, I begin to lay theoretical foundations so that the real revolution — that of the female gender, that of women — may now begin again.

3

Sigmund Freud: Bridge to the Future

WHY IS FREUD ESSENTIAL?

Of all the seminal twentieth-century thinkers, Sigmund Freud provides the broadest bridge from the nineteenth century into the twenty-first century. Freud's capital importance for feminist philosophy, social theory, and psychology lies in his positing of sexuality as the crucial enigma of modern life. Freud tenaciously insisted upon the central importance of sexuality for both our cultural and self-understanding. Because the patriarchal culture equates sex and the female, and because sexual divisions permeate every fiber of our social-selves, to retain Freud and yet belittle his obsession with problems of sexuality is also to dismiss the problematic of the cultural feminine and of Western women. To dismiss Freud and retain problems of sexuality and gender is to dismiss the most powerful analysis of intrapsychic *and* interpersonal conflict yet devised, an analysis that places the genesis of femininity and masculinity at its core.

Freud's greatness lies in his refusal to abandon either his *shibboleth* of sexuality or the dualities he saw as related to sexuality. Most important is Freud's emphasis upon the original bisexuality of the human being, the bedrock upon which he founded his theories. That which to others was a natural given, namely, femininity and masculinity and (male) genital sexuality, was for Freud a riddle requiring solution. In brief, Freud is essential for feminist psychology because, when patriarchal sexuality is decoded, one discovers the synonyms woman, death, and body. Freud's analyses of the genesis of femininity and masculinity in early childhood brought to center stage concepts of body-ego, of castration's symbolic death, and of woman as mother — all subsumed under the libido's insistent sexual drives.

Empirical studies of child development in recent decades have proven Freud wrong on several counts. For example, young children develop a core gender identity before the age of Oedipus crisis; they are not necessarily aware of the female's lack of a penis; they do not suddenly acquire a superego, or conscience, at the age of four or five with Oedipus complex resolution. In addition, recent investigations into the nature of memory have cast doubt upon the reliability of childhood memories. Despite these findings, it has still proven impossible to banish the idea of an Oedipus complex in some form. Too much clinical material remains unexplained if the Oedipus complex is totally abandoned; too much passion and controversy still surround the theory for it to be considered dead (for the results of empirical investigations into Freudian theory, see Fisher & Greenberg 1977, *The Scientific Credibility of Freud's Theories and Therapy*; Lee & Herbert 1970, *Freud and Psychology*; Mullahy 1948, *Oedipus: Myth and Complex*).

One could best characterize the twentieth century by the prominence of concern with three M's: memory, metaphor, and madness. Freud's work is central to all three concerns, and, contrary to received doctrine, his system also harbors a concept of culture. Popular analyses of Freud typify him and psychoanalysis as the apotheosis of subjective and self-centered individualism. I do not share this opinion. On the one hand, Freud refused to posit an individual unconscious in addition to a cultural unconscious, as did Carl Jung, because Freud insisted that the unconscious *is* social. For Freud, psychosexual development regulates psychosocial evolution. On the other hand, Freud never saw himself as treating solitary individuals because for him other individuals — in particular parents — are always involved in the genesis of gender and of neurosis, and in the psychoanalytic cure. The self for Freud is social and bisexual in its origins and cannot develop without love from others.

Psychoanalysis was a militant social psychology before immigrating with Freud's followers to England and the United States during the Nazi era. Otto Fenichel summarized his, and Freud's, views as follows: "Neuroses do not occur out of biological necessity, like aging. . . .

Neuroses are social diseases . . . the outcome of unfavorable and socially determined educational measures, corresponding to a given and historically developed social milieu. . . . They cannot be changed without corresponding change in the milieu" (Jacoby 1983, 120). Freud was one of the first great students of humanity to argue powerfully for a relationship between the "dis-ease" of individuals and their cultural surround.

Freud explicitly argued for the reality of social representations, for the reality of the collective mind; as he put it, a *social* psychology would be impossible without conceptions that ensure continuity as individual consciousnesses are extinguished. Also, the impulses continuously flowing from the Freudian unconscious id provide a continuity and foundation for the ego's intermittent bouts and degrees of consciousness (Freud [1913] 1950, 158). For Freud, then, psychoanalysis is a social psychology. Moreover, Freud did not hesitate to draw general conclusions from one case study. This methodology makes sense only when one views the individual as a social-individual embedded in a cultural matrix. For Freud the individual unconscious was, from its inception, intimately related to the cultural unconscious because of the inheritance of acquired traits. I suggest that this scientifically suspect notion, if interpreted in the light of body-ego awareness and cultural repression, deserves another hearing.

Toward the end of his life Freud became ever more concerned with cultural neurosis and with the possibilities for curing these social ailments. He began to interpret the Lamarckian idea of the inheritance of acquired characteristics: The Lamarckian need, Freud said,

which creates and transforms organs is nothing other than the power of unconscious ideas over the body, of which we see relics in Hysteria: in short, the "omnipotence of thoughts." Purpose and usefulness would then be explained psychoanalytically; it would be the completion of psychoanalysis. Two great principles of change or progress would emerge: one through (autoplastic) adaptation of one's own body, and a later (heteroplastic) one through transmuting the outer world. (Jones 1961, 350)

Freud here envisions human beings as ultimately capable of evolving by harnessing mental forces that will be efficacious in changing both body and cultural surround. Freud's vision propels us toward the self-conscious social transformations necessary for the cure of cultural — and personal — neuroses.

The dim contours of new scientific paradigms are beginning to give substance to some of Freud's most suspect speculations. On the one hand, the work of geneticist Barbara McClintock demonstrates mechanisms of rapid evolution by means of DNA changes brought about by interaction with the total organism and, therefore, with the cultural environment (Keller 1985, 158–76). Besides McClintock's work, the work of John Cairns at Harvard's School of Public Health also appears to have reopened the question of rapid mutation in direct response to environmental constraints, a Lamarchian idea not taken seriously for over fifty years (Cairns et al. 1988, 335:142–45). On the other hand, the work of neuroscientist Jonathan Winson presents sophisticated and convincing arguments for the evolutionary development of the unconscious as located in interactions among the brain's hippocampus, limbic system, and prefrontal cortex, with repression accounted for by a half-second processing lag between sensations applied to the human organism and conscious awareness of these sensations (Winson 1986, 234–35). Finally, writer Norman Cousins's seminal work in the field of mind-body interaction, epitomized by his latest book, *Head First, The Biology of Hope* (1989), assembles impressive scientific evidence for the "autoplastic" power of ideas over the body.

All these recent scientific discoveries undermine patriarchal culture's monolithic conception of rationality, a rationality that identifies the masculine ego with reason and separates both from unconscious, cultural, bodily and emotional (or maternal) mediations. Yet as Freud so well understood, and as Dr. Ashley Montagu reminds us, "emotions are extraordinarily accurate sources of information . . . listening to them is often more revealing than the spoken word" (Montagu 1981, 165). Freudian psychoanalysis shows us how to "listen" to human emotional expression for its own particular kind of rationality.

From the evidence for interactive models of human/cultural evolution now developing in several disciplines, feminist psychology must synthesize a new vision of psychoanalysis. I propose that this new vision will represent the "completion" of Freudian psychoanalysis, the realization of "autoplastic" and "heteroplastic" potency for the change and progress that Freud himself envisioned. I submit that these latter powers for change depend upon the enlargement of each gender's competence within the domains now culturally reserved for the other gender. Only with such enlargements can the human imagination find release from the rigidity of gender repressions.

Russell Jacoby has noted in *The Repression of Psychoanalysis* that "the antipsychoanalytic wind has weakened, and a renewal of interest in psychoanalysis can be registered in diverse fields" (Jacoby 1983, 136). Jacoby further comments that "lessons drawn from pigeons and encounter groups, the romanticization of mental illness, and quick therapies are themselves vulnerable to grave criticism. Nor have these antipsychoanalytic psychologies generated social or political theories of any substance; here psychoanalysis remains alone" (ibid.). The insights and revolutionary impetus of the original *political* psychoanalysis, transformed by feminist vision, are indispensable for resolution of the multiple crises humanity faces entering the new millennium.

Especially significant are the reality and dignity Freud accords to memory, fantasy, and subjective experiences in their own right. Freud ends by radically transvaluing masculine values as he roots the ego's reason in the passions of the mind — a mind inextricably blended with body-ego. Freud's greatest contribution is the idea that the irrational — associated with women by the dominant culture — has a latent rationality that can be deciphered, that the unconscious exists as an analyzable force. Freud modified French philosopher Blaise Pascal's cryptic comment regarding the inability of reason to know the heart's reasons: Freud declared that he had discovered how to decode the "reasons of the heart."

While maintaining the preeminence of bisexuality as a cultural force constituting both female and male, Freud elaborated his theories of culture as memory; of culture as metaphor; of culture as madness. "Our patients fall ill from their reminiscences," Freud declared, and their symptoms, like their dreams, symbolize a primal crime that cannot be totally expiated. Freud's origin myth states that primitive man slew his father because he sexually desired his mother and sisters. With his brothers, primitive man founded the social order that by means of the incest taboo and exogamy prevents a recurrence in reality of this murderous act. Yet each child, according to Freud, is doomed to reenactment of this crime in fantasy. Furthermore, Freud asserts, *fantasy is real.*

Freud traced neurosis in adults to their sexual experiences as children. He discovered that in all childhood seduction, whether fantasized or real, the child (usually a girl) reacts with repressed excitation. Here Freud had unknowingly stumbled upon the masculine culture's structuring of sexual response for *both* sexes. Freud's theories suggest that the banal perversity of sexual power conflicts is hard-wired into the nervous systems of both male and female infants and is represented in each sex by warring masculine and feminine elements, Thanatos and Eros incarnate. Freud's theory of the constitutional bisexuality of both men and women serves as a long denied counter to the essential "homosexuality" of masculine culture.

Now enters another central legacy, Freud's logic of paradox. Culture becomes mad in the Freudian legend because humans are faced with untenable choice. The original objects of desire — the mother and father — are forever forbidden. Civilization demands sublimation of desire, while the superego rewards this effort with ever-increasing guilt.

At his most pessimistic, Freud saw no choice for the social-self, trapped between conflicting realities; no choice but destruction of the other, or destruction of the self. Here, indeed, is a definition of madness to ponder. In the following chapters, I present a feminist angle of vision capable of finally resolving these Freudian paradoxes: a womanist psychology that views Freudian psychoanalysis as a theory of cultural change driven by the contradictions of the patriarchal sex/gender system.

Unlike the masculine dualisms of essence/existence and of mind/body, which in the final analysis reduce one term to the other, Freud's split models of body-ego and superego, of unconscious, preconscious, and conscious mind, maintain a nonisomorphic, nonlinear and nonreducible interaction between the conscious and the unconscious, between the body and the mind. Freud stood alone in defending and asserting the validity of interactive dualisms. When confronted by a monistic consequence of his system's evolution, that is, when the ego-instincts were also found to be libidinous, Freud was quick to repair, by reconstructing a dualism of Eros and the death instinct, what he recognized as an unacceptable identity.

Of course, Freud's major contribution to social psychology, his Oedipus complex theory, is a theory of the founding of the adult male self in an identification. But Freud viewed this as a problematic founding over a fundamental split within the self, and I argue that Freud found the resolution of the Oedipus conflict through identification with the father more problematic as his system and thinking deepened and matured. Freud's present-day French follower O. Mannoni well distills this problem when he typifies the process of identification as "the socially accepted form of lost uniqueness" (Mannoni 1974, 185).

Other former students of Freud who have had significant contemporary impact in America, such as Erich Fromm, Erik Erikson, Karen Horney, Alfred Adler, and Carl Jung, have all neglected or denied the central importance of sexuality. The one notable exception to this retreat from sexuality, particularly that of early childhood, has been the French neo-Freudian Jacques Lacan, who has insisted, as I do, upon a return to Freud's major themes of childhood sexuality and the unconscious. Unfortunately, Lacan's reinterpretation of Freud's system destroys just those dialectical elements that feminist thought should expand: Lacan enforces an absolute demarcation for each developing child between the pre-Oedipal time of the mother and the post-Oedipal time of the father. Furthermore, Lacan declares the latter paradigm of self superior to the noncommensurable earlier paradigm of self.

Although Freud's system does lend itself to Lacan's reinterpretation, Lacan's neo-Freudianism falls into the same logical impasses as does

Thomas S. Kuhn's system of progressing, but noncommensurable, scientific paradigms. Lacan arrives at his reinterpretation of Freud, however, by neglecting and suppressing the dialectical elements and complex clues Freud gives us for overcoming the absolute separation between developmental periods. Lacan closes the openings left by Freud, openings that suggest both how individuals can change and how our socially defined gender categories can be changed.

In fact, most of the dominant culture's modern schools of Freudian psychoanalysis have been regressive because they have reduced the rich multidimensionality of Freud's thought to the one-dimensional. An example of this tendency among cultural neo-Freudians can be seen in Fromm's *Forgotten Language* (1980). Fromm reduces Freud's insistence upon the necessity of dream interpretation grounded in the specificity of each patient's life circumstances, to the transparency of immediate understanding, eliminating in this way any need for the tracing of associative links of signification. For Fromm, dreams represent a symbolic language that "is the one universal language the human race has ever developed, the same for all cultures and throughout history" (Fromm 1980, 7). This is a rather strange stance for someone who has insisted upon the crucial importance of Karl Marx's principles of historical and social specificity. Fromm's formula typifies masculine *temporal* one-dimensionality.

The one-dimensionality of Lacan and other structuralists consists in reducing the Freudian idea of the ego to an "image," or inner icon, that reflects the self-reality given to the child in what Lacan calls the "imaginary" period of the mother-child dual relation (Lemaire 1981). Although Freud did employ metaphors of mirrors and telescopes in describing the developing ego, the weight of Freud's metaphoric expression restores dimension to his concept of the ego. Lacan's neo-Freudianism trips and falls over its own errors of *spatial* one-dimensionality.

That Freud and Freudian psychoanalysis have been viewed as enemies of women is understandable, given the directions taken by psychoanalysis in modern Western cultures. But, as writer Paul Robinson comments, "nothing testifies more eloquently to the liberating effect of [Freud's] ideas than the extraordinary role assumed by women in the early years of the [psychoanalytic] movement" (Robinson 1984, 18:65). Nearly a third of the European psychoanalysts who immigrated to the United States during World War II were women. Freud was centrally concerned with blocking the medicalization of psychoanalysis, and his failure to do so in America has resulted in what Jacoby calls the "defeminization" of analysis in this country. While nearly a third of immigrating psychoanalysts during the 1930s were women, today less than half that number of practicing psychoanalysts in this country are women (Eiler & Pasko 1988, 619).

Freud was aware of the dominant society's crippling of women's sexuality and intellectual development, and he explicitly stated that we should not underestimate the coercive power of social mores that "force women into passive situations" (Freud [1916–33] 1966, 580). Freud championed the sexual as well as the social emancipation of women, condemning, as Lucy Freeman and Dr. Herbert S. Strean point out in *Freud and Women*, "the practice of *coitus interruptus* as causing anxiety in women" and arguing that sexual fulfillment was dependent upon better means of contraception (Freeman & Strean 1987, 200). Near the end of his life, Freud wrote to his son Ernst that because "women were forbidden to think about sex . . . they acquired a dislike for thinking altogether" (ibid. 203). Here Freud makes clear his beliefs regarding the impossibility of separating sexuality and sexual emotions from cognitive development.

Of course, Freud shared some of patriarchal culture's prejudices about the "weaker" sex; but to his credit, Freud failed to repress his own sexual ambivalences, his own feminine self, and his growing knowledge of the ways in which patriarchal culture cripples women. He was especially encouraging to his women followers and, in fact, chose his youngest daughter Anna as his intellectual heir. In all these ways, Freud was light years ahead of his contemporaries, and it is upon the pillars already erected by Freud that a more humane psychoanalysis can be built that will carry both women and men into the twenty-first century as whole human beings.

FREUDIAN DIALOGUES

First, let us examine the ways in which Freud's system represents a break with the dominant patriarchal culture of his — and our — day. As previously discussed, most masculine theories are implicitly or explicitly monistic and based upon linear Aristotelian logic and ahistorical Kantian rationalism. One level of reality is fundamental and key to all others, although this universal transcendental reality remains in important respects forever un-knowable — a "thing-in-itself." Nonetheless, this one fundamental reality can be approached asymptotically through a time that is essentially homogeneous in character. Truth is grounded in instrumental reason and logic, but reason itself cannot be logically grounded.

In addition, language represents for the dominant culture the key level of reality to which all other levels are coded, while the basic characteristics of the symbolic languages of mathematics and physics represent the ideal to which all other languages should aspire. The foundation for knowledge is empirical sense data, that is, the world of facts as given. Clarity, brevity, simplicity, efficiency, these are the central values in both language and life. Without language, thinking cannot exist. The ultimate value for patriarchal science and ideology is that of objectivity. Anything tainted with subjective values is suspect and inferior.

Objectivity, in turn, depends upon a logic of subsumption based upon clear definitions that separate and delimit concepts as they define them; in this way boundaries are rigidly maintained between categories. Patriarchal thought lacks the theories that can bridge across levels of abstraction; error cannot be accounted for where "facts" are "given" and "recorded" as sense data by percipients. No concept of progress can be justified, nor can one system of values be preferred to another; neither can change and/or development be seen as possible when all relationships are based upon correspondences, homologies, isomorphisms – in short, upon identity theories. The philosopher William James has noted that these masculine logics of identity leave change unaccounted for. James complained that "monism is inevitable only when you assume that in order for one thing to become another, or to be related to another, it must be the same as the other. Then there is no change, there are no relations; difference is mere appearance; there is only identity without difference, and that is all" (James 1953, 37).

And, indeed, "identity without difference," the hidden principle in the heart of men's reason, accounts for the dominant culture's inability to model change and development, as well as for the tautological nature of patriarchal origin myths. Social theorist Max Horkheimer provides us with an analogous insight when he states in the *Eclipse of Reason*, "The view that philosophical concepts must be pinned down, identified, and used only when they exactly follow the dictates of the logic of identity is a symptom of the quest for certainty. . . . It would make it impossible to convert one concept into another without impairing its identity" (Horkheimer 1974, 167). So it is that the dominant culture's Faustian quest for certainty, expressed in its fear of difference, supports the status quo and forecloses openings to change.

Patriarchal culture identifies itself with the conscious and masculine mind, with individual reason, with the factual, objective, exterior world of politics and power. These spheres are rigidly cordoned off from those identified with the feminine, namely, the irrational unconscious, emotions and intuition, the interior world of subjectivity, and the material vulnerability of the body and sexuality. Furthermore, as French philosopher Michel Foucault has noted, the equation female = sex was expanded because patriarchal culture also made sex "identical with its body" (Foucault 1980, 123–24). Paradoxically, the sexuality so alienated in the female body is quintessentially male genital sexuality.

How different was Freud's attack upon all these spurious dualisms! In particular, Freud attacked the idea that aside from reason, all was unintelligibly irrational. When arguing the case for lay analysis, Freud had an interesting answer for his protagonist who had protested the idea of interpretation by exclaiming: "Interpret! A nasty word! I dislike the sound of it; it robs me of all certainty. If everything depends on my interpretation who can guarantee that I interpret right? So after all everything *is* left to my caprice" (Freud [1927] 1969, 54). The assumption here is that facts must speak directly and univocally or one is faced with a multitude of mere subjectivities, an incomprehensible tower of Babel. To this Freud replies, "When you have attained some degree of self-discipline and have certain knowledge at your disposal, your interpretations will be independent of your personal characteristics and will hit the mark" (ibid.). Freud is arguing not only for the existence and decipherability of the heart's reasons but also for the possibility of a disciplined subjectivity.

Further, instead of following patriarchal thought's lead in excising the contamination of body/sex/female from the cultural productions of masculine reason, Freud created a system wherein each individual harbored sexual duality and wherein the relationships of reason and emotion, of concept and percept, of conscious and unconscious, were not only problematic and conflictual but also dialectical. For Freud, each male ego was hopelessly contaminated by the feminine; even the successful resolution of the Oedipus complex became more, and not less, problematic as Freud's thinking evolved and his clinical insights deepened (Freud [1905–38] 1963, 220–23).

Freud believed that every individual boy and girl starts life with an inherent bisexuality; he argued that each sex exhibits traces of the opposite sex anatomically and that each sex also exhibits bisexuality mentally by the assumption of masculine and feminine attitudes. No man or woman represents a "pure" type, Freud said; rather, all human beings "combine in themselves both masculine and feminine characteristics, so that pure masculinity and femininity remain theoretical constructions of uncertain content" (Freud [1888–1938] 1959, 197). This complex mingling of both genders from the inception of individual life is far removed from the dominant culture's rigid division of the human into male and female, masculinity and femininity. Even the Oedipus complex is, according to Freud,

twofold, positive and negative . . . that is to say, a boy has not merely an ambivalent attitude towards his father and an affectionate object-choice towards his mother, but at the same time he also behaves like a girl and displays an affectionate feminine attitude to his father and a corresponding jealousy and hostility towards his mother. It is this complicating element introduced by bisexuality that makes it so difficult to obtain a clear view of the facts in connection with the earliest object-choices and identifications. (Freud [1923] 1962, 33)

Of course, I am arguing that it is precisely this complicating element introduced by bisexuality that undermines *for the better* Freud's own version of subject/object splits.

Although in numerous contexts Freud frequently speaks of the dissolution of the Oedipus complex, he also continuously undermines the idea of its dissolution, especially in his later writings. In the above context (1923) Freud concludes that "the relative intensity of the two identifications [i.e., with mother or father] in any individual will reflect the preponderance in him of one or other of the two sexual dispositions [i.e., homosexual or heterosexual]" (ibid. 34). The idea of preponderance suggests that both sexual dispositions survive, and, indeed, Freud did write that in girls the Oedipus complex is demolished late and incompletely. Neither did Freud believe that homosexuals should be separated "from the rest of mankind as a group of a special character" (Watney in Shepherd & Wallis, 1989, 24). Freud wrote, "From the point of view of psychoanalysis the exclusive sexual interest felt by men for women is also a problem that needs elucidating, and is not a self-evident fact" (ibid.).

In 1926 Freud was declaring that although the Oedipus complex "should normally be given up, should radically disintegrate and become transformed [in men] . . . as a rule this is not effected radically enough, in which case puberty brings about a revival of the complex, which may have serious consequences" (Freud [1927] 1969, 44–45). At times Freud speaks of the resolution of the Oedipus complex by means of its repression into the id, where "ideally" it is smashed, destroyed, dissolved, abolished. In most of his pronouncements, however, Freud equivocates and writes of a "more or less" complete renunciation of the mother; he writes of the only "apparent" surmounting of incestuous desire and of the powerful resurgence of Oedipal urges at puberty, at times of crisis in later life, and in all neurotics. In both earlier and later work Freud spoke about "crippling" effects of the Oedipus complex that last into adult life.

Moreover, in an unfinished fragment published posthumously in 1940, "Splitting of the Ego in the Defensive Process," Freud appears to be reevaluating not just the dissolution of the Oedipus complex, but its entire significance. Far from being smashed by the castration complex or partially dissolved and partially repressed into the unconscious, here the

Oedipus conflict is resolved by a displacement, specifically by the creation of a fetish that abolishes for the boy the mother's castration and
therefore denies the possibility of his own. Although Freud was now
elderly and dying, Freud's system, I argue, was still dynamically evolving.
These fateful openings constitute rich clues for feminist transformations.
I agree with psychoanalyst Robert Stoller, who has cogently argued that
"bisexuality should still serve as a central theme in understanding human
psychology" (Stoller in Strouse 1985, 344). I also argue that Freud's
glimpse before his death of the indestructibility of the Oedipus complex
casts a new light upon all of Freud's ideas regarding psychosexual
development.

Freud's positing of the universal bisexuality of each human being
allows for essential overlap between female and male: Each woman
harbors masculine tendencies; each man, feminine. There exists in
Freud's system the potential for inner dialogue, as well as inner conflicts,
between these tendencies. The preconscious layer of mind allows for
dialogue and conflict between the unconscious and the conscious mind.
In the beginning is the unconscious, but the preconscious perceptual
system—the outer layer of the id—represents the transitional system
from which the conscious ego arises. In fact, Freud asserts that "all
perceptions which are received from without (sense-perceptions) and
from within—what we call sensations and feelings—are Cs. [conscious]
from the start" (Freud [1923] 1962, 19). We must retain that Freud
attributes a degree of consciousness to the body-ego from the *very
beginning* of individual development. The consciousness of the body-ego
may be characterized by Freud as lower in type and more akin to the
awareness of animals, but Freud does grant consciousness and a type of
thinking to the body-ego. It is what he calls "thinking in pictures" and, as
such, is "only a very incomplete form of becoming conscious" (ibid., 21).

Freud's assertion that the body thinks and communicates from the
beginning of life, Freud's understanding of the importance of the
development of this body language represent other important Freudian
breaks with the dominant patriarchal paradigm. Bodily acts and gestures
represent a symbolic, or metaphoric, language just as important as
spoken language and one that, like the dream and neurotic symptom,
requires interpretation in relation to the hidden wishes and desires of a
specific dreamer.

Just as Freud's originality lay in positing the Oedipus complex as the
origin, not only for the genesis of the masculine self, but for social
organization, religion, myth, and culture as well, so also is Freud's schema
of mental organization an original one that deepens the accepted definition of mind. From now on mind would no longer be synonymous with

consciousness but would be extended to preconscious and unconscious phenomena. Furthermore, Freud claims to have found explanatory principles for phenomena — dreams, neurotic states, and symptoms — that up until his time had been viewed as entirely irrational, that is, as not susceptible to systematic explanation. Freud even dared to claim that the mind's functions were enhanced by the interaction of these two differing processes, each possessed of a characteristic type of rationality.

Unique to the primary processes of the unconscious are two principles, the principles of condensation and displacement. They operate during sleep to produce our dreams, and during the formation of jokes and neurotic symptoms. The thoughts pressing for expression in dreams, jokes, and neurotic symptoms represent sexual thoughts originally repressed in early childhood, thoughts that are highly distressing to the ego. Therefore, in order to be admitted into consciousness, these thoughts must undergo transformations, Freud says, that permit them to evade the censorships set up by the preconscious ego. Since the instinctual cathexes (energy charges) of the latent thought processes are very mobile in the unconscious, the primary process can easily disguise the latent thoughts by infusing these cathexes into something whose form is similar but does not carry the same intense emotional meaning. This describes what Freud calls the mechanism of displacement. Behind the dream images, for example, of wounded animals may lurk the theme of sexual cruelty, a theme only extensive dream analysis may uncover.

By the mechanism of condensation Freud refers to the concentration of instinctual energies coming from diverse sources onto certain elements of a manifest dream or symptom; in other words, a given manifest element or neurotic symptom can refer to many elements in the latent dream-thought or hidden neurotic complex. For example, a dream figure may combine features from several persons that, when disengaged from each other, will be found to have links to several dream-thought motifs. Most important, Freud explains that "condensation is brought about by *omission*: that is, the dream is not a faithful translation or a point-for-point projection of the dream-thoughts, but a highly incomplete and fragmentary version of them" (Freud [1900] 1965, 315). In other words, during the dream-work, wholes are fractured and salient features extracted while residues and new images (symbols) are created.

Condensation, then, *concentrates* psychic energy while splitting or fracturing wholes, whereas displacement *disperses* psychic energy. The primary processes of the dream-work, according to Freud, act both to disguise and to fulfill the unconscious wishes of the dreamer. Most displacements occur at the level of the unconscious (i.e., intrasystemically), whereas condensations occur throughout the course of the dream- or joke-work and symptom formation (i.e., both intra- and intersystemically).

Although Freud is best known and most often portrayed as a strict nineteenth-century determinist (statements by Freud such as "people are unaccustomed to reckoning with a strict and universal application of determinism to mental life" are "case-closed" examples of Freudian determinism), Freudian indeterminacy plays an even more preponderant role in what Freud called his "metapsychology" (Freud [1910] 1977, 52). Besides the multiple determinations deriving from Freud's insistence upon interpretation, Freud's concept of overdeterminism also refers to the mind's primary processes of condensation and displacement, which, in effect, operate to produce the symbols and metaphors of dreams, jokes, and neurotic symptoms. These principles Freud discovered bridge the gaps between levels in the self; their nature as theoretical entities is indexical *and* nonindexical. In addition, Freud introduces the necessary analytical means by which one principle itself can be transformed into the other.

The importance of these Freudian devices — of condensation and displacement — for producing the symbolic bridges between the conscious and unconscious mind should be clear. Freud has transcended the dominant culture by discovering principles of transformation that are simultaneously principles of change and development. Unlike the dominant culture's rigid separation of hierarchically ordered and reductive (and therefore spurious) dualities, locked into categorical stasis, Freud's system provides for interaction between each polarity. Freud has constituted a logic of nonidentity and provided for open-ended transformation across levels. Freud has provided us with a model of change through a dialectics of difference. Unlike most patriarchal systems of thought wherein difference cannot effect change and is subsumed by identity, difference within Freud's system is the engine of change. Therefore, on the highest level of abstraction, Freud validates and makes central the other — which includes the differences of women.

In Freud's world view, as in that of biologist Barbara McClintock, "difference constitutes a principle for ordering the world radically unlike the principle of division of [masculine] dichotomization (subject-object, mind-matter, feeling-reason, disorder-law). Whereas these oppositions are directed toward a cosmic unity typically excluding or devouring one of the pair, toward a unified, all-encompassing law, respect for difference remains content with multiplicity as an end in itself" (Keller 1985, 163). The complexity of Freud's work affirms the multiplicity of our socialselves that can evolve only through a dialectics of difference derived from, and respecting, the differences between femininity and masculinity.

Freud's colleague and biographer, Ernest Jones, citing Freud's moral greatness, summed up Freud's apostasy: "To men of the school of Helmholtz, the idea that the mind—not the brain, not the nervous system—might itself be the cause of its own malfunction, and even the cause of the body's malfunction, was worse than a professional heresy: it was a profanation of thought" (Jones 1961, x). For this and other better-known profanations—that of infantile sexuality, for example—Freud was willing to pay the price of relative isolation and relatively late recognition. Freud's clinical experience told him that mind could act upon body, that fantasy had its own reality, that ideas were dealt with as things by the unconscious—and this not just with psychotics. He in fact demonstrated the kinship of normal phenomena such as dreaming and joking to the abnormal symptoms of the neurotic, just as he demonstrated the relationships among normal, neurotic, and psychotic types—all this while asserting that someday science would thread its way from the neuron to the instinctual impulse to the highest cultural sublimations.

At the beginning of this chapter I characterized the twentieth century as centrally preoccupied with the meaning of metaphor, of madness, and of memory. Freud understood the importance of analyzing each of these in relation to the passage of time. Freud's thought is profoundly metaphoric and he was quite aware that this was so. In fact, Freud expressed a modern understanding (today being developed in the work of French philosopher Jacques Derrida) when he explicitly spoke of the metaphorical nature of the concepts of psychoanalysis: Freud said that we are obliged

to operate with scientific terms, i.e., with the metaphorical expressions peculiar to psychology (or more correctly: psychology of the deeper layers). Otherwise we should not be able to describe the corresponding processes at all, nor in fact even to have remarked them. The shortcomings of our description would probably disappear if for the psychological terms we could substitute physiological or chemical ones. These too only constitute a metaphorical language, but one familiar to us for a much longer time and perhaps also simpler. (Rickman 1957, 165)

To state that even the languages of the physical and biological sciences are metaphorical in nature is to overthrow the identity theories at the base of most masculine thought. It is to deny the perfect correspondence of thought and object, it is to cast doubt upon the possibility of *a* reference language, upon the closure of protocol statements. If Freud had also stated, "these metaphorical languages are simpler *because* familiar to us for a much longer time," he would have thrown open wider the doors toward understanding temporal categories and cultural change.

The passage of time is also central to Freud's observation that as civilization progresses, the splits within the individual between the desexualized superego and unconscious forces and desires grow ever wider, resulting in increasing guilt and unhappiness for social individuals. Freud's *Civilization and Its Discontents* should have been translated, "Man's Dis-ease in Civilization" (Jones 1961, 476). In this book Freud boldly argues that "the sense of guilt [is] the most important problem in the development of civilization and . . . the price we pay for our advance in civilization is a loss of happiness through the heightening of the sense of guilt" (Freud [1930] 1961, 81).

Toward the end of his life Freud began speculating that the increasing guilt, neurosis, and "madness" that he observed accompanying temporal progress could perhaps be cured by a psychoanalysis of culture. This paradox of progress—the progress of patriarchal civilization that Freud saw occurring through processes of desexualization—is a paradox best explained by the deeper examination of temporal categories, an examination Freud knew was necessary, but one he was unable to carry out himself. If one understands that the civilization that is advancing is *patriarchal* civilization, and that each advance of such a civilization constitutes a step backward for women *and for the feminine selves of men*, then this paradox can be meaningfully resolved.

Finally, temporal categories form the essence of both psychoanalytic theory and therapy: As Freud asserted in several contexts, "Our patients fall ill from their reminiscences." In his early work with hysterical women Freud was impressed by his patients' memories of seductions, frequently incestuous in nature, with the father most often named as assailant. Since 1981 a controversy endemic to Freudian studies has intensified. This controversy revolves around Freud's findings that the seduction memories of adult patients are not in all cases based upon real happenings in the patients' early childhoods. Jeffrey Masson, the projects director of the Sigmund Freud Archives and a member of the inner circle of psychoanalysts given access by Anna Freud to protected Freudian correspondence, wrote a book, *The Assault on Truth: Freud's Suppression of the Seduction Theory* (1985), in which he accuses Freud of suppressing the truth of real seductions in favor of a theory of fantasy seductions that originate in patients' guilt regarding childhood masturbation and in their Oedipal desires. Masson accuses Freud of moral cowardice in the face of the disapproval of his colleagues, who were shocked by Freud's accusations against the male relatives of his female patients.

This question as to whether or not an actual seduction took place continues to surface periodically in the Freudian literature, and Masson's book is only one of the most recent examples. Some feminist thinkers during the 1970s also attacked psychoanalysis for shifting blame from a seducing adult (usually the father or stepfather) to a seductively fantasizing patient as child. This issue of fantasy versus reality provides complex keys to my reinterpretation and extension of the Freudian system because Freud's emphasis upon the importance of *psychic* reality, upon the metaphoric nature of dream and symptom, has opened to psychology the dimension of the symbolic constitution of the self and its concomitant symbolic deformation within patriarchal cultures.

That the reality/fantasy of the childhood seduction controversy continues to rage both within and outside Freudian studies is again symptomatic of the dominant culture's collapsing of complex issues into the one-dimensional either/or binary. Most scholars, even those who disagree with him, do respect Freud's fierce honesty and courageous integrity. It was Freud, after all, who first took seriously the accounts by his female patients that they had indeed been sexually molested by their fathers. In fact, he took them seriously enough to identify childhood sexual trauma as the essential cause of neurotic illness. When, in September 1897, Freud retracted this version of hysteria's etiology, it was not to deny the existence of sexual molestation.

In 1917 Freud was still insisting that seduction fantasies "are of particular interest, because so often they are not phantasies but real memories" and that "you must not suppose ... that sexual abuse of a child by its nearest male relatives belongs entirely to the realm of phantasy. Most analysts will have treated cases in which such events were real and could be unimpeachably established" (Freud [1916–33] 1966, 370). Furthermore, in his last major work published after his death, Freud said, "Our attention is first attracted by the effects of certain influences which do not apply to all children, though they are common enough — such as the sexual abuse of children by adults" (Freud [1940] 1969, 44). Freud's emphasis upon the truth of fantasies of sexual molestation, while representing a step backward from one point of view, makes possible a giant leap forward into symbolic dimensions where the covert abuse of children both male and female can be understood as occurring because only one sex has structured our sex/gender system — a system that then cripples both sexes.

Far from dismissing his patients' fantasies as inconsequential, Freud took them quite seriously and proclaimed that they must be seriously dealt with. Freud asserted the importance and reality value of psychical events. But Freud did even more than this: The important modification that Freud did make to psychoanalytic theory after 1897 was to proclaim that the causative sexual traumas missing from the real external present world of the neurotic, and missing from the real external past world of the neurotic's childhood, were once present in the real external world of the ancestors of his patients. Freud declared that children "fill in" gaps in their knowledge of sexuality with truths they instinctively know because their fantasies actually did occur in the prehistory of human families (Freud [1916–33] 66, 371).

In other words, Freud developed the theory of the phylogenetic inheritance of primal fantasies, and he related these to both the early sexual impulses of children and to their shame and guilt regarding these impulses. Because patriarchal science has dismissed the idea of phylogenetic inheritance, along with the idea of the unconscious, Freud's formulation has been stunted in its growth and development. An important contribution toward the development of Freud's ideas of phylogenetic inheritance has come from the French writers Gilles Deleuze and Felix Guattari, who assert in *Anti-Oedipus* (1982), that the dominant culture first structures the sexual desires of children and then forbids and represses these desires. In this sense, Freud's claims regarding the incestuous desires of tiny children may indeed harbor an important truth.

I submit that Freud's theory of phylogenetic inheritance makes sense on two levels: first, as a metaphor for the absorption of material by the body-ego during the very early pre-Oedipal period of development; and, second, as an actual inheritance of the patriarchal culture's structures of sexuality embedded in the structures of the cultural surround. For the dominant paradigm of sexuality in Western culture is that of *masculine* sexuality, and the transmission of these sex/gender structures during the prehistory of the early pre-Oedipal period of infancy *do* constitute a violation of the sexuality of the mother and the child — *whether the latter is female or male.*

I further submit that these hierarchical sex/gender structures are transmitted through the interaction of the child's body-ego (skin, nervous, and limbic brain systems) with the parents and the cultural surround during early critical periods of development. The primary organs involved are those of touch and taste and smell, that is, the *proximity senses*, the importance of which our Western culture vastly underestimates. That such processes of interaction do exist is supported by many new research findings accumulating in the brain sciences, in biochemistry, and in the new science of psychoneuroimmunology. Naturally, with so much that is yet unknown regarding the interactions of brain and psyche and the interactions of cultural parents and infants, much that I have to say will remain speculative in nature. Yet I believe such speculations represent much-needed theoretical contributions to the evolution of empirical research in the area of psychosexual development.

In order to fully understand the meanings of these interactions be-tween nascent self and cultural others, a new vision of early development is necessary, a vision that overcomes the dominant culture's metaphors of object (self/other) relations and of exchanges between infant and mother. This new vision demands that we comprehend that the dynamic interaction between the nascent self and the cultural parent is asymmetri-cally productive of the selves of both infant and parent. Grasping this new vision will not be easy: Everything in our Western culture, particularly patriarchal language structures, militates against this new understanding. Yet the vision persists and is pressing in upon us on all sides. New discoveries in science, new understandings of the capabilities of the newborn, new ideas regarding the importance of human relationships — all these recommend that we make an effort to see anew. Gordon Taylor has intensively studied the brain and the mind, as well as their interaction. He reports that "the cognitive nature of perception is quite a recent idea in psychology" (Taylor 1979, 200). It is an idea foreshadowed by Freud's discovery of the unique rationality of primary process thinking. I believe that it is a revolutionary idea that signals the need for a complete rethinking of early infant development.

To better appreciate some of the obstacles to these new under-standings, let us now turn to those areas within the work of Freud himself that need to be transformed before a new system, one that will include the realities of women, can be incorporated into the cultural body. Despite Freud's promising clues for a womanist psychoanalysis, there are gaps in his system over which a new theory must build.

WHERE FREUD'S BRIDGES BREAK

In a recent issue of the *American Psychologist*, Barry Silverstein en-titled his contribution to a debate on Freud "Will the Real Freud Stand Up, Please?" (Silverstein 1988, 43:662–63). With this title Silverstein emphasizes the complexity of Freud's thought and indicates that this complexity does indeed lend itself to multiple interpretations. Sil-verstein, however, correctly argues that Freud's basic position is that of a dualist who believes that the mind and body are qualitatively different and that their relationship is one of reciprocity and mutual constitution. Other Freudian scholars have found Freud to be a biological reduc-tionist, and still others have argued that he was an emergentist. Freud's work, in fact, contains elements of all three positions, but I am arguing that Freud's emphasis upon an interactive dualism of mind-body and masculine-feminine allows for the emergence of a new and subtle epistemology—which is also an ontology, one which can revolutionize our vision of the human self, female and male.

In the first part of this chapter, I enumerated the many ways in which Freud's system lends itself to furthering feminist thought because of its important interactive dualisms and its validation of difference. Now I wish to enumerate those elements that also exist in Freud's thought and that link it to the dominant patriarchal culture, in particular those elements that are ahistorical, linear, reductionistic, and nondialectical. Locating these critical lapses in the Freudian system—the points at which Freud's bridges break—will give us precisely those points that must be transformed by feminist analysis.

I submit that the dominant culture's rationalisms experience logical difficulties because they are founded upon an absolute split, a binary opposition of knower/known, subject/object, reason/intuition—and, most important, of masculine/feminine. These splits or oppositions foreclose explanations of the relationships between polarities. Aspects of these masculine rationalisms—which I will identify as Kantian—are also evident in Freud. Freud's most telling Kantian statements present the unconscious as a "thing-in-itself," as ultimately unknowable as the external world of sensory perception. For example, in *The Interpretation of Dreams*, Freud proclaims, "The unconscious is the true psychical reality; *in its innermost nature it is as much unknown to us as the reality of the external world, and it is as incompletely presented by the data of consciousness as is the external world by the communications of our sense organs*" (Freud [1900] 1965, 651) (Freud's emphasis). Freud accepts here the Kantian assertions regarding the ultimate impenetrability of "things-in-themselves" and extends this radical impenetrability to his formulation of the unconscious mind. However, in this formulation as in many of his other conceptualizations, Freud was not consistent; he punched holes, opened windows—as I have previously indicated—through which a dialectical consciousness seeped.

Kantian also is Freud's splitting of abstract and concrete, of word and image. These dichotomies, in fact, spring from Freud's split between concept and percept, a split that is almost pre-Kantian in its insistence upon the unmediated registering of raw sensation from which memory traces arise. For example, when describing the characteristics of the unconscious, Freud said that "in a primitive language without any grammar only the raw material of thought is expressed and abstract terms are taken back to the concrete ones that are at their basis" (Freud [1916–33] 1966, 484).

For Freud, the primitive, the unmediated "raw" materials upon which unconscious id energies cathected (diffused themselves into), were the memory traces or "image-presentations" of concrete things derived from perception. Freud's hierarchy begins with concrete perceptions of things directly registering upon our sense organs and then transformed into memory traces, which, in turn, give rise to images or "thing-presentations." These latter attach themselves by means of instinctual cathexes to concepts or "word-presentations," which bear the same relationship to words as the image- or thing-presentations bear to perception's memory traces. In the Freudian dream-work, that is, in the mechanisms of displacement and condensation, "all operations with words are merely preparatory to regression to concrete ideas" (Freud [1911–23] 1959, 144). From this acceptance by Freud of the "facticity" and concreteness of the world of things follows the necessity Freud met when he proposed a transhistorical, transcultural trauma, namely, the patricide that simultaneously founded culture, religion, and the individual male ego. In other words, Freud betrayed his own insights into the shaping of gender in the child's pre-Oedipal period (which he calls "prehistoric") by a displacement into the real history of so-called primitive man.

One can detect Freud's struggles with the paradoxes of the Kantian ahistorical split between knower and known not only in his unique version of the Oedipus myth but also in the ways in which he deals with the levels of his hierarchy of mind, with the unstructured dynamic processes of the unconscious mind's primary process, with the latter's unique rationality, and with the structured and bound preconscious-conscious systems Freud identified with secondary process and with conventional reason. At bottom, then, Freud is struggling with the problem of origins — always particularly difficult for patriarchal thought — and with the logical paradoxes Western reason harbors. The following quotation is a telling example of the difficulties Freud falls into when attempting to account for the difference between conscious ideas and unconscious ideas — and, by implication, also attempting to account for the origins of conscious ideas. Freud is explaining the differences between the "idea of the word," the verbal idea, and the "idea of the thing," the concrete idea:

The two are not, as we supposed, different records of the same content situated in different parts of the mind, nor yet different functional states of cathexis in the same part; but the conscious idea comprises the concrete idea [the thing-presentation] plus the verbal idea [the word-presentation] corresponding to it, whilst the unconscious idea is that of the thing alone. The system Ucs [unconscious] contains the thing-cathexes of the objects, the first and true object-cathexes; the system Pcs [preconscious] originates in a hyper-cathexis of this concrete idea by a linking up of it with the verbal ideas of the words corresponding to it. It is such hyper-cathexes, we may suppose, that bring about higher organization in the mind and make it possible for the primary process to be succeeded by the secondary process which dominates Pcs. (Freud [1911–23] 1959, 133–34)

The reader will note that Freud's above accounting for the system preconscious (which can "empty" directly into consciousness) has as origin a linkup with the "verbal ideas of words." Freud here asserts that *in the beginning was the word.* Paradoxically, for Freud Logos may indeed be rooted in Eros, as philosopher Abraham Kaplan has stated, but for the Logos of secondary process to develop, a preexisting Logos has been tautologically assumed by Freud. Here Freud's system cannot think back beyond a time before language: This preverbal time remains as mysteriously veiled for Freudian psychoanalysis as does the early averbal pre-Oedipal period in infant psychosexual development.

Contrary to what some critics have claimed, dreams and symptoms as explained by Freud are not creatures of a truly dialectical process. Freud's system describes a blocked and frustrated dialectics of dream, fantasy, and reality, of id, ego, and superego. But the fault is not entirely Freud's. The fault lies in large part with the patriarchal reality that structures and then represses and blocks not only sexual impulse but also feminine and masculine development. The development of the body-ego of both sexes is also blocked by the dominant culture because of the body-ego's close alliance with femininity resulting from the intimate interaction of both sexes with the mother in infancy and early childhood. The splits and paradoxes in patriarchal thought that I have been uncovering in Freud's system have in recent years been traced by many feminist theorists to men's denial of their origins in the mother.

The conflict between the two Freuds — the dialectical Freud and the patriarchal Freud — can be seen most clearly when one analyzes the contradictions in Freud's handling of temporal categories. Freud himself announced that although psychoanalysis had not explored as fully as it should the category of time, he personally had penetrated as deeply as he could into the problems of temporality. However, even while ostensibly accepting "the Kantian proposition that time and space are necessary modes of thought"(Rickman 1957, 153), Freud went about undermining Kant's proposition by positing a timeless unconscious and by contrasting this timelessness with the operation of the perceptual system, which "provides the origin of the idea of time" (Freud [1916–33] 1966, 540). Further, in his discussion of the ego and the id, Freud states that it is the ego that "by virtue of its relation to the perceptual system . . . arranges the processes of the mind in a temporal order and tests their correspondence with reality" (Rickman 1957, 232). Here one meets once again that familiar ambivalence within Freud: on the one hand, the desire to found his system upon the dominant Kantian rationalism of his day and, on the other hand, the demand of his own insights for a dialectical flexibility.

Note, for example, the duality of Freud's formulation of the category of time itself: In the first instance time is born with the perceptual system's body-ego. The body-ego emerges into immediate apprehension of Kantian time. But, no, in the second instance it is the ego itself that has the task of arranging "the processes of the mind in a temporal order" (ibid.). Yet if this is so, then the temporal order must develop as the ego itself develops, that is, *over time.* An analogous ambiguity is acknowledged by Freud in relation to the process of being conscious or unconscious. Whereas the body-ego's external perception is immediately conscious, consciousness otherwise develops; that is, consciousness is a process extending over time.

In relation to Freud's insistence upon the timelessness of the unconscious id, it is also interesting to contemplate that encapsulated within Freud's concept of id are both the phylogenetic heritage (the human species' biological history) and the individuals' instinctual drive structures derived from their childhood histories. Freud asserts that desires that never left the id and experiences that are repressed there are both unaffected by the passage of time; they remain unchanged as if immortal (Freud [1916–33] 1966, 538). Here Freud is declaring the relative atemporality of historical structures. And to the degree that Freud embraces the recapitulation of phylogeny by ontogeny, and reaffirms that all individuals must repeat within their early life history the great dramas and conflicts of species development, Freud is also embracing that truism dear to patriarchal philosophy, "Plus ça change, plus c'est la même chose." Almost in spite of himself, however, Freud points beyond such cyclical futility.

For Freud, the ego represents the development of time concepts, not only because it arises out of the body-ego but also because the ego forms the superego (or ego ideal) at the time of the repression/resolution of the Oedipus complex by means of both an identification with parental agency and as a reaction-formation against it. The superego represents Freud's final temporal category, since the ego takes into itself with superego formation its cultural heritage and the history of its own socialization. The superego, therefore, represents the historical experiences of the species (specifically, the parents) within the individual. Portions of the superego also are unconscious.

Freud admits that the superego has many contacts with the phylogenetic heritage of the id; that is, id and superego do interact: "The super-ego is thus proved to have known more than the ego about the unconscious id" (Rickman 1957, 229). This interaction would in effect represent an *intersection* of time with the timeless—but Freud does not specify clearly the product of this interaction (although at one point Freud does suggest that the present is changed into the past with the birth of the superego). In co-constituting itself in interaction with the outer world, the ego also co-constitutes its superego and deposits this within itself, that is, within the unconscious. Here is one point at which Freud could have carried his temporal analyses further; had he done so, he would have realized the need to posit a changing phylogenetic inheritance. Since in Freud's own system, time, represented by the ego and superego, can indeed be seen as interacting with the timeless, represented by the id, Freud should have recognized that *the categories of repression themselves change over time.* Instead, Freud chose to emphasize the ahistorical, universal, and cyclical nature of the Oedipus drama. By so doing, Freud produced another patriarchal apology for the maintenance of the status quo.

Just as we can discover structures in the id's primary processes, so also must psychoanalysis admit to the contamination of the unconscious's atemporality by time. First, the drive impulses or instinctual forces of the id give direction to ego development and therefore establish a relationship to time; second, the id contains a dual historical heritage, that of biological development and that of cultural development; and, third, the id also contains the repressions of the individual's childhood. The poet T. S. Eliot mused, "To find the intersection of time with the timeless is an occupation for a saint" (Bergsten 1960, 104) (paraphrased). Freud located not just one intersection of time with the timeless but several; he also developed the devices whereby one temporality could merge into or transform the others.

Freud also experienced difficulty in attaining consistency with his theories of identification and object-choice. The very choice of the words *identification* (to represent the boy's movement toward father during the resolution of the Oedipus complex) and *object-choice* (to represent the boy's relationship toward mother) reflect Freud's struggle with the non-dialectical elements in his work. In particular, these words reflect Freud's capitulation to the dominant culture's intellectual heritage of Kantian subject/object split. The major schools of neo-Freudianism neglect Freud's emphasis on bisexuality, on the boy's identification with the mother, and his object-choice of the father. In object relations theory, people are viewed as objects and all openings to dialectical interaction and co-constitution of selves within dialogue are thereby lost.

We should take more than passing note that Freud's writing not only is strongly metaphoric but also contains highly significant imagery. The metaphors Freud chose present images that, I contend, were designed to overcome the linear, Aristotelian limits of language. Freud uses one of his most striking metaphors when trying to convey his idea of the relationship of ego-libido to object-libido. Freud conjures up the picture of amoebas sending out "protrusions," or pseudopodia, by means of which the amoebas flow into and absorb other objects without losing the ability to withdraw these pseudopodia back into themselves. Freud compares these protrusions to the "emission of libido on to objects while the main mass of libido can remain in the ego" (note that Freud also thought of libido energy as "mass"), and he submits that "in normal circumstances ego-libido can be transformed unhindered into object-libido and that this can once more be taken back into the ego" (Freud [1916–33] 1966, 416).

Similarly, Freud visualizes libido as flowing. His usage of the word *cathexis* means, as I have noted, a charge of energy flowing into objects. Yet the loss of an object causes the cathexis to flow back into the ego, where it congeals, as it were, since Freud describes the ego as "a precipitate of abandoned object-cathexes." The ego itself is described by Freud as a "projection of a surface," yet here Freud does not mean to portray the ego as an image as the Lacanians mistakenly believe, but as flowingly attached to and grounded in the body-ego and the id. To believe otherwise would be to ignore the weight of metaphoric consistency and imagery and to reduce Freud's conceptualization to one-dimensionality—which is indeed the result of Lacan's efforts. For example, Freud compares "identification" with a cannibal-like incorporation of others (Freud [1916–33] 1966, 527). These images are evocative of the Freudian insights I will extend shortly with my development of the concept of accomplicity, which describes the production of the structures of selfhood during parent-child interaction. Accomplicity's new view upon psychosexual development is wholly consistent with the weight of Freudian imagery and, I argue, crystalizes what was only half formulated in Freud's mind and metaphors.

In Freud's process of developing his ideas of identification and object-cathexis, it becomes clear that the underlying cultural principle of organization by means of gender distinctions is at work in several respects. Since Freud uses almost exclusively the example of a male infant (he admitted that female development perplexed him), I shall follow suit here, reserving for later my explanation of feminine development: The male infant takes as his first object the mother (or very early on the mother's breast); the male infant's first identification is with his father. Freud differentiates between the two modes by explaining that an object-cathexis means the infant wants *to have, to possess,* the mother; an identification means that the infant wants *to be like* the father.

It is fascinating to realize that the whole Oedipus complex theory is already embryonic in Freud's delineation of the differences between object-cathexis and identification. The principle difference is that which an adult Western heterosexual man is supposed to feel when relating to a desired woman as opposed to an admired man. It is equally fascinating to recognize that these two modes open to the infant take on some of the character of the temporal modalities I have discussed, temporal differences that certainly reflect the differences in temporal interactions the infant has with his mother as opposed to his father. The process of sending out object-cathexes is most often pictured as continuous, or at least multiple and temporally protracted — as are the interactions typical of the mother-infant relationship. The process of identification is most often pictured as occurring over an abbreviated period of time, as most typically are father-infant interactions. However, with identification the incorporation or "introjection" of the object can be either primary and therefore timeless or dramatic and sudden, as at the time of the Oedipus crisis. Freud, of course, also elaborated upon these modes with the inverted themes of bisexuality.

The Oedipus complex itself is typically depicted as a brief period of crisis during which the male child identifies with the father, that is, incorporates him and produces simultaneously with this incorporation his superego or conscience. The mechanism of object-choice — the sending out of object-cathexes — is usually portrayed as a process involving a relatively long time; that of identification results from a sudden crisis and is usually of relatively short duration.

Here we have the essence of the Lacanian interpretation of Freud, which follows so closely the Kuhnian paradigm and repeats all the latter's logical contradictions. The first paradigm of self is that of the pre-Oedipal self presided over by the mother. The Oedipus crisis represents the interparadigmatic period of confusion and split. The post-Oedipal self represents the second — and superior — paradigm of self. In the Lacanian and other neo-Freudian versions the post-Oedipal self formed in an identification with the father is both superior to and noncommensurable with the pre-Oedipal self, which has arisen from a primary unity with the mother. Ideally for patriarchal culture, the pre-Oedipal self is abolished with the resolution of the Oedipus crisis. This scenario, of course, is understood to be that of the male child.

Freud explicitly admitted that the female child's Oedipal crisis is less readily understood. He later admitted that the transactions of the male's pre-Oedipal period also remain obscure. To his credit, Freud himself did not present the above process as starkly as I have done. Freud blurred the categories of self by introducing his important ideas regarding bisexuality and the simultaneously existing negative Oedipus complex. These latter ideas can be seen as bridging the gaps between the genders, as well as between the succeeding paradigms of self. Finally, near the end of his life Freud introduced ideas regarding "the splitting of the ego in the process of defense," which, in my opinion, totally reopen the question of Oedipus complex resolution.

Any transformation of Freud's insights must acknowledge that the secondary process cannot be separated from the primary process, which is its ground: Reason ungrounded by the modalities of the body-ego not only becomes sterile, it risks schizophrenic madness and self-destruction. Freud has a word for reason ungrounded; he calls it "rationalization." Furthermore, the Freud who in his early work could discuss the "omnipotence of thought" and call it "magical thinking" (which, according to Freud, reflected the power early "savage" men found in words), this same Freud could himself confer upon words the inestimable power of creating consciousness itself, and then go on to realize that he was wrong. Toward the end of his long career, Freud realized that the simple verbal acknowledgment of a neurotic complex by a patient was not enough to bring about a lasting analytic cure. The sudden illumination was curative only if a long period of emotional "working through" had first taken place. The sudden gestalt switch, the revolutionary paradigm switch to which Kuhn referred, cannot occur for either science or the individual without the simultaneous development of the new within the matrix of the old. Once again we must recall that at the very end of his life, Freud acknowledged in "Splitting of the Ego in the Defensive Process" (1938) just how impotent intellectual understanding can be when it comes to changing powerful structures of desire from which even scientific rationality is not immune (Freud [1888–38] 1959, 372–75).

In the final analysis, like the German philosopher Hegel, Freud has framed his system with a species of identity theory: For Hegel, it was the reasonableness of the real, the end immanent in the beginning. For Freud, it is, on one side, the unknowability of the real world beyond the incoming flow of perception and, on the other side, the atemporal impenetrability of the id giving rise to the continuous pressure of instinct-presentations. But Freud gives us more than another identity theory. Freud gives us the indeterminate, the multiple, the ambiguous, and the means by which something is simultaneously both itself and other.

Freud gives us the possibility of a logic of paradox and of a theory of becoming, along with the principles of transformation and complementarity adhering in his ideas regarding bisexuality and dream symbolization. The object-cathexes of the id are both discrete quanta of energy and flowing charges; the ego is both a secondary process of reasonable choice and "a precipitate of abandoned object-cathexes . . . [containing] a record of past object-choices" (quoted in Rickman 1957, 218). Consciousness is both the thought-pictures of the body-ego and the conceptual representations of the ego. The id is timeless, yet it absorbs the temporal constructs of both species and individual; the superego represents a rooting in the lowest depths of phylogenetic endowment and, also, "what we value as the highest in the human soul" (ibid., 222).

In the dynamic relationships of the composite and bisexual social-self, as viewed by Freud, not only is time multiple, it can be reversed in the service of regression and transformed in the service of becoming. It is, in fact, only through the different levels of the social-self, only through the existence of the self's different mental processes, and only by means of different temporal modalities that development becomes possible at all. At the very end of his monumental work *The Interpretation of Dreams*, Freud declares, "I hope to be able to show elsewhere how the compounding of the apparatus [of the mind] out of two agencies makes it possible for the normal mind too to function with greater delicacy than would be possible with only one of them" (Freud [1900] 1965, 648).

Once again, Freud affirms the potency of a dialectics of difference. While formulating his ideas regarding psychosexual development, Freud was struggling with the problem of transformations across levels (from unconscious to conscious and vice versa), with progressive/regressive changes (the ego's stages of development), with origins (the original identity of ego and id and their antagonisms), with the relationships between the individual and culture (family relationships, the sexes, and the phylogenetic heritage). Most important, Freud was struggling to overcome the limitations of patriarchal rationalisms by developing his ideas regarding the mind's primary and secondary processes and their interactions by means of symbol formation (through condensation and displacement). In brief, when developing the science of psychoanalysis, Freud expanded the categories of patriarchal thought while simultaneously founding his system upon them.

BEYOND FREUDIAN PSYCHOANALYSIS

The original Freud has much to offer feminist theory: Freud focused attention on the genesis and development of masculinity and femininity within the unequal power structures of patriarchal family relationships. By positing the original bisexuality of each human self and the Oedipal conflicts occasioned by this bisexuality, Freud provides clues to the transcending of inner and outer conflicts. Freud leads us to a recognition of the ways in which we are all constituted by the contradictions in the forces and relations of reproduction. Knowledge comes, Freud knew, from nonidentity, from differences culturally grounded in the unconscious. As I extend and transform important Freudian categories, I hope to convince readers that a reversal of the suppression of differences, beginning with those of the female gender, will bring about a cultural revolution more profound than any we are now capable of imagining.

As we have seen, Freudian metapsychology provides clues toward a bridging of gaps between levels within the divided self, as well as between the cultural heritage and the biological heritage. Freud also presents us with clues as to the ways in which our culture's symbolic structures are dissolved, reabsorbed, and precipitated into the very structures of gendered selfhood during the "timeless" times when the body-ego reigns supreme and dreams its reality with images — the images furnished by the proximity senses. For Freud's metapsychology constitutes a nonidentity theory of transformation across levels, of conflicts and mediations giving rise to compromise formations in which the instinctual fusions and defusions create a residue, so that something is always left over, left out, and, therefore, something new is produced, is created. Despite his difficulty with the problem of origins and his resulting proposal of phylogenetic inheritance, Freud's theory of the ego's becoming is not merely a theory of *re*production; it is a theory of production. It is also not a theory of self-creation, but rather one of co-creation. The ego is subject to powerful forces, but the ego has reason and self-consciousness as countervailing forces. Freud proposes that by uncovering the reasons of the heart, by making the unconscious conscious, he is forging one more weapon: Once an unconscious idea has been made conscious, it is weakened, he declares, and it is amenable to control by the ego.

Even Freud's ambiguities, inconsistencies, and contradictions can be read as a history of his struggle to free his essentially dialectical vision from the dominant patriarchal paradigm of his time. Freud failed to develop a psychoanalysis that centrally incorporates the experience of women, and he understood his failure. He urged and encouraged his women followers to develop that which he realized he himself could not develop.

Psychoanalyst Robert R. Holt's insightful essay "The Development of Primary Process" (1967) will take us far along the analytical road that women must travel in developing Freud's vision. Holt argues that the realistic and rational secondary process does not develop out of a structureless chaotic primary process as Freud proposed. Making use of Freud's own formulations, Holt points out that primary process thinking must consist of stable structures, must have had its own developmental history, and, therefore, must have grown up *along with* the secondary processes and not prior to them. As evidence for the structural character of primary process thinking, Holt cites Freud's conception that "the primary process is *not* a completely fluid, random chaos; it has a perverse logic of its own" (Holt 1967, 5:351). Meanings can be discerned in the dream-work, and the joke-work, and in neurotic symptom formation — all examples of primary process — and these meanings depend at bottom upon the *"structured network of memories: the drive organization of memories"* (ibid., 352).

The nonarbitrary use of symbols, the devices of condensation and displacement, the repetition of dreams and dream elements, the mechanisms of defense — all these characteristics of primary process are listed by Holt as reflecting the structural properties of the unconscious processes that Freud named primary. Finally, Holt quotes from later work in which Freud not only writes about the repressed memory traces contained in the id — and Holt reminds us that these imply structure — but also writes of memory traces representing the archaic symbols and experiences of our ancestors — and these, too, imply structures.

Holt skillfully and convincingly argues the case for a structural emphasis as opposed to Freud's "economic" and dynamic emphasis when viewing primary process. These stable structures for which Holt argues serve their own synthetic necessities, and Holt concludes his essay by insisting that they "must be the product of a considerable development" (Holt 1967, 5:383). I do agree that Holt's points are cogent, yet I think that in the final analysis he misses the most important point: Holt, while correct in his observations, has slipped into a typical masculine stance: *either* structure, *or* energy, *either* mechanism, *or* process.

Rather, I argue that the very ideas of change and/or development demand their own "principles of complementarity," demand that *both* structure and energy are conceptualized, and, further, demand that the moment envisioned by the philosopher Hegel when a thing is both itself and other be the essential moment of becoming, of the indeterminacy that changes structure into energy, or vice versa. Holt, like British social theorist Anthony Giddens (1979), has overlooked the need for a concept of "destructuration." Holt, unlike French theorist Jacques Derrida (1981), has not understood that the very act of definition, of cognitively focusing, confers structure — reifies, if you will — and that this becomes at times inappropriate and can reintroduce the very elements one wishes to critique.

The essential elements in Freud's discussion of the primary and secondary systems, overlooked by Holt as well as by other critics, have to do with a relativity of conceptualization, with transformations from one state to another, and with a simultaneity of process and structure, as well as with their implicit interrelationships. Specifically, Freud frequently speaks of instinctual elements "more" or "less" bound or freely mobile. In his later work, Freud also elaborates upon instinctual fusions, admixtures, and defusions. Most important of all, Freud's conceptualization of cathexes, like the dual nature of photons in physics, takes on the character of both flowing charge and quanta of energy. Also, the flow of these energetic cathexes infuse themselves into thing- and word-presentations in order to form complex entities simultaneously exhibiting both the character of structures (the more qualitative concept) and that of energetic processes (the more quantitative concept).

In fact, to describe the coming into consciousness, Freud uses the concept of a hypercathexis from the thing-presentation existing in the unconscious to the word-presentation existing in the preconscious. In other words, consciousness dawns as a *qualitative* change brought about by an additional energy flow, which represents a *quantitative* change. Where Holt complains of the ambiguity of Freud's structural formulations, I recognize unique strengths: Freud's system's very ambiguity, which permits a "principle of indeterminacy" to become operative, produces a dialectic of quality and quantity, of primary and secondary processes, of affect and reason, of percept and concept, of id and ego — of the feminine and the masculine.

Unlike the dominant culture's systems of thought, which delineate separate but parallel levels of thought, universes related by inevitably tautological correspondence rules or by indexical (point-to-point, homological) relationships which are inevitably static, Freud's gendered selves exhibit great potential for dialectical transformation. Moreover, Freud explicitly shows that where id is, ego may be, and he also indicates how over time portions of the social-ego become transformed into new ids and superegos. Behind his back, the Freudian categories themselves evolve over time.

Building upon the foregoing critique, I delineate in the chapters that follow a new angle of vision upon Freud's Oedipus paradigm of self, and I present a new theory of psychosexual development. Whether masculine maturity is seen as a sudden identification with the father or a slow emptying, a divestiture by stages of the accomplicity of the mother-involved body-ego, it remains an uneasy maturity, perched as it is over the abyss of volcanic forces eager to erupt to the surface should the ego relax but for a moment its eternal vigilance. I will demonstrate why, in the final analysis, it is neither possible nor desirable for Faustian man to disentangle himself from contamination by the body-ego, by primary process thinking, or by the feminine. I will show why Freud's intuitions in later life regarding the ultimate indestructibility of the Oedipus complex are more profoundly correct than his earlier formulations. Finally, we will come to an understanding of the truth — and the limitations — of Norman O. Brown's declaration that

Formal logic and the law of contradiction are the rules whereby the mind submits to operate under general conditions of repression. As with the concept of time, Kant's categories of rationality would then turn out to be the categories of repression. And conversely, "dialectical" would be the struggle of the mind to circumvent repression and make the unconscious conscious. (Brown 1977, 321)

But, most important, we will come to understand just what the "resurrection of the body" — Brown's solution to patriarchal neurosis and guilt — entails and why a resurrection of the body presupposes a "liberation" of those repressed and backward instincts of which Freud spoke, presupposes a liberation of the body-ego, of femininity in the persons of contemporary women, and, finally, an unleashing of the woman imprisoned in the psyche of every man.

For Western man has sought refuge in the sublimations of a reasoned faith and has placed his faith in a reason held aloof from any subjective taint, a reason he has declared totally objective and impartial. Western man's ultimate paradox is his impassioned partiality for an objective reason that refuses to recognize that the child is mother to the man.

4

Femininity and Masculinity: The Genesis of the Divided Self

Whence does neurosis come — what is its ultimate, its own peculiar raison d'être? After tens of years of psychoanalytic labours, we are as much in the dark about this problem as we were at the start.

Sigmund Freud

THE SIX MYTHS OF MASCULINE THOUGHT

Freudian psychoanalysis shines much more light into the darkness than Freud's modesty admits. Neurosis certainly has much to do, according to Freud himself, with our original "bisexuality," with traumas — especially sexual traumas — in early childhood, and with the divisions within the self that result from these traumas. In this study I am taking one small step beyond Freud: I am asserting that the original bisexuality of our species — the division of nature into two sexes — has served all cultures as *the* primordial organizing principle. In addition, I am reasserting the Freudian contention that cultural gender distinctions — feminine and masculine selves — are to be found in uneasy coexistence within each woman and man.

This division of our doubly gendered selves represents the deepest cleavage in the human species and is one that, over millennia, has become freighted with unconscious, symbolic, and traditional meanings. Moreover, for the last two millennia, the keepers of the cultural heritage — men — have seen to it that the cultural halves associated with women be those traits least desirable. Even the two halves of the body have not escaped this tendency: In all languages "left" means clumsy (*gauche*), bad, strange, or evil (sinister); "right" means right, and also straight (*tout doit*), good, and virtuous (righteous).

In the fifth century B.C., the Greek philosopher Parmenides projected the ideas regarding left and right "into the very womb itself. The origin of the sexes, he decreed, depended upon the position of the fetus in the mother. Boys were on one side, girls on the other, and it doesn't take a card-carrying feminist to guess which was which" (Fincher 1980, 33–34). British argot uses *cack-handed* to refer to lefties (*cack* is a British colloquialism for excrement — from the French *caca*); in Australia lefties are called *molly-dookers*, which translates as "woman-handed" (ibid., 36–37). Here one finds left/right added to the usual patriarchal oppositions of emotion/reason, body/mind, nature/culture — all of which are supported by that ur-division female/male. Space and time, qualities and quantities, visible and invisible — all the aspects and furnishings of nature and of our cultural surround are divided up and related to the fact of maleness or femaleness.

Unfortunately, in patriarchal cultures the relationship between female and male is not a straightforward complementarity. Most often it is an invidious hierarchy with the woman-terms less desirable than the man-terms. Whether the opposite of woman (depending upon the context) is spirit, transcendence, mind, city, or culture, the corresponding woman-terms — sex, immanence, body, countryside, and nature — are viewed as inferior and, therefore, fit only to be subordinated. The famous mind-body dualism, then, is a *spurious* dualism in patriarchal cultures because one term only is glorified, while the other is reduced to a nasty fact to be overcome, subdued, controlled, and mastered — even eliminated if possible. This is why I have declared that most masculine dualisms are actually closet monisms.

However, the problem of the status of the feminine in patriarchal cultures is more complex still. Social critic Theodore Roszak calls for an end to sexual stereotyping so that the virtues attributed to women can become *human* virtues. He asserts that "the woman most desperately in need of liberation is the woman every man has locked up in the dungeons of his own psyche" (Roszak & Roszak 1969, 101). A similar statement is made by feminist writer Coppelia Kahn when analyzing Shakespeare's *King Lear*: "A psychoanalytic feminist reading reveals that though women are excluded from the public arena, which is usually the scene of tragedy, they are present nonetheless in the character structures of its heroes, scripted here in a code derived from the structure of the family" (Kahn

1982, 12:41). How does the woman become locked away in every man's psychic dungeons? What happens to the masculinity of women? These are the questions I am attempting to answer by questioning some sacred presuppositions of patriarchal culture.

For example, the dominant culture assumes that having a divided self is a bad thing. To the contrary, I agree with psychotherapist Mary Watkins that having "invisible guests" — other selves — is not in itself sick-making (Watkins 1986). Rather, I submit that neurosis arises from the proscriptions of the dominant culture, which require us to repress important parts of ourselves, to silence what are potentially healing dialogues between the feminine and the masculine portions of the self.

I suggest that the two most important parts of each woman and each man are, first, what I call the *majority self,* constituted through the relationship with the mother during the early pre-Oedipal period of childhood; and, second, what I call the *minority self,* constituted through the relationship with the father (or father surrogate), also during this same pre-Oedipal period.

These selves are formed by a process I call *accomplicity.* Therefore, the three key concepts through which I am extending and transforming Freudian psychoanalysis are the majority self, the minority self, and the process of accomplicity. I further submit that a multitude of modern crises, including those deformations Freud called neuroses, can be explained through an understanding of how these divided selves are generated and how they are prevented from interacting with each other — except through the limited means of dream, joke, and symptom. Writer James Hillman puts the matter squarely: "The specific consciousness we call scientific, Western and modern," he states, "is the long sharpened tool of the masculine mind that has discarded parts of its own substance, calling it 'Eve,' 'female' and 'inferior' " (Bordo in Harding & O'Barr 1987, 249).

I also suggest that not only is division or duality necessary — provided the parts of the self are allowed to interact — but that spiritual progress or social maturation cannot occur without these relatively autonomous divisions within the self, the most important of which are the two selves related to femininity (majority self) and masculinity (minority self).

When he discusses the dangers (inhibition and regression) involved in a child's development through various stages, Freud uses the analogy of a migrating people who leave behind at each stopping place a detachment of their members (Freud [1916–33] 1966, 339–41). He compares this "lagging behind" of a part of the group to a child's fixation at an earlier stage of development. He also mentions that the larger the "groups" (parts of the self) lagging behind, the stronger will be the tendency of the main contingent to retreat (regress) to these sites should they come up against obstacles to their advance. I am applying a modern insight to this scenario when I affirm that in order for development to proceed, rear guard detachments are absolutely essential. Otherwise, how can the self effectively take measure of its own progress? On the path to relative autonomy, external cues are also necessary, but not sufficient.

Similarly, I have asserted that in order to measure their own progress and development, men have assimilated women to the assumed stasis of the primitive, of childhood, and of nature. Heroic men journey forth on quests; in this way, men climb to ever-higher intellectual and spiritual realms. Therefore, the greater the heights attained by men, the relatively lower the valleys assigned to women. Yet given that men also harbor feminine selves, are not then the breaches in the self dangerously widening? Freud himself commented upon this danger when he saw that his migrating group were in "greater danger of being defeated the more of their number they have left behind on their migration" (ibid., 341). So, too, men are endangering their own development by detaching both women and their feminine selves from the paths leading to greater development.

Having defined women as identical with immanence, with body, and with primitive nature and sexuality, men have been obliged to become fathers of themselves, to declare themselves self-made men, in order to avoid contamination by this feminine weakness. For this reason men have developed psychosexual models of development that exclude women as mothers, while repressing knowledge of their own feminine selves. The Freudian system, too, points toward a stalled dialectics of mind/body, power/love, and feminine self/masculine self.

Within patriarchal thought the perpetuation of gender stereotypes continues unabated. Women's needs and experiences remain as peripheral as ever to this dominant culture's calculations. Recent analyses of the psychological literature reveal that "mother blaming" is still rampant: Mothers inevitably bear the responsibility for children's deviance, whether that deviance is autism, schizophrenia, neurosis, chemical dependency, or failure at school. Nearly always found is "too much" mother, or "not enough" mother; mother is either "too distant" or she is "smothering." The most mother can aspire to is "good enough" mothering.

Psychoanalyst Karl Stern writes in *The Flight from Woman* that "estrangement from matter and the maternal has reached a point of no return" and that the maternal is somehow "a sticky, messy, oozing business which makes you vomit" (Stern 1966, 140 & 133). Sartre and the male descendents of "the generation of vipers," Stern implies, have voyaged inward and found, not nothingness, but the inescapable stickiness of a suppurating wound in the masculine psyche. Let us now turn to an examination of those crucial myths that patriarchal culture has erected to purge itself of the "sticky mess" of motherhood and feminine contamination.

The first and most ubiquitous myth concerns the nature of the infant's primary tie with its mother: Patriarchal thought is nearly unanimous in proclaiming this bond a symbiotic identity in which the mother represents the total environment of the child. Psychoanalyst Erik Erikson points out that "a stubborn tendency persists [in psychoanalysis] to treat the 'mother-child relationship' as a 'biological' entity more or less isolated from its cultural surroundings" (Poster 1978, 67). Object relations theorist Margaret Mahler writes of the symbiotic phase as one in which infants behave as if they form a common-boundaried "dual unity" with their mothers. It is no accident that the word *symbiosis* connotes a lack of cognitive awareness and is most frequently used in scientific contexts like the following: "Bacteria frequently live in symbiosis with other organisms in a way that makes both their own lives and the lives of their hosts dependent on the symbiotic relationship" (Capra 1983, 278). Along with this unthinking symbiotic merging by which patriarchal thought characterizes the early mother-child relationship, one finds a multitude of metaphors of attachment: tie, bond, apron-string, and so on. Opposing the mother-child identity of symbiosis, these metaphors call to mind the external sticking of surface to surface, a literal *attaching* of child to mother. In both the merging and the attaching, one can detect the limitations of a model based upon the subject/object split.

Although male thinkers frequently speak of early symbiotic fusion as a lost paradise to which all men long to return, they just as often couple symbiosis with a discussion of the struggle for identity, mastery, and independence. In his book on object relations, psychoanalyst Arnold H. Modell comments "The wish to abandon our identity, to give up our sense of separateness, to relinquish our unity, to again merge with other objects is always present" (Modell 1968, 135). Modell also flatly states, "We know that for the young child the mother and the environment are indeed synonymous" (ibid., 8). Erich Fromm sets up an opposition between being rooted, having an unsevered umbilical cord, and lack of individuation. He proclaims that "it is years before the child ceases to confuse itself with the universe" (Fromm 1969, 42). Of course, most men identify this early universe with mother. In fact, the dominant paradigm of patriarchal thought that posits the individual male genius heroically working alone after having won the struggle to separate himself from his matrix (mother, nature, country, or culture) explains why a fully developed concept of culture is so palpably missing from Western social thought. In essential ways, the Western male imperial ego is both preformed and self-formed. I call these phenomena the *parthenogenesis* (virgin birth) of the masculine mind.

This primary identification between mother and child is further characterized as primitive, regressive, noncognitive, unstructured, and blissful. Even Erikson traces the "universal nostalgia for a paradise forfeited" to the earliest stage of infant development (Erikson 1963, 250). Because of the unconditional love all mothers are said to feel for their children, patriarchal thought finds a lack of reality testing in this first relationship. Lack of reality testing, then, accounts for the fatality of the bond: Hereafter all other loves will have to measure up to this paradise lost of unconditional love and are therefore doomed to failure. As adults, we all try to recreate this first perfect merger, but our recreations are frustrated by the adult reality in which, as Carl Jung describes it, "man is essentially determined by spirit, woman by matter" (Glover 1957, 131).

Intimately linked with this first male myth regarding the primitive "unreal" mother-child unity is the second myth of patriarchal thought. This myth declares the passive dependency of the child upon the mother and the weakness (or nonexistence) of the child's ego. Norman O. Brown summarizes this myth when he describes what he sees as "the infant's objective dependence on parental, especially maternal, care [which] promotes a dependent attitude toward reality" (Brown 1977, 25). Brown also claims that children are not exposed to life's serious business (ibid., 26) – that is to say, to reality as male defined. Freud, too, went on record describing infant love as basically "anaclitic" or dependent: In infancy we love the hand or breast that feeds us. In addition, Freud proclaims that despite their utter dependency, there is nothing objectively present in the lives of children that might explain infant neurosis and trauma. Aside from actual molestation, which Freud admits does occur, the only other possible explanation of childhood trauma and neurosis Freud finds in the weakness of the infant ego and its resulting vulnerability to instinctual trends operating from within.

The third myth of masculine psychology declares that the child's desires are insatiable. Freud declared the nursing infant to be "altogether insatiable." Modell states, "Children's wishes know no limitations" (Modell 1968, 25). Norman O. Brown follows Freud in proclaiming the child to be more sensuous than the adult. I cannot help but note a parallel between the boundless desires of the child, as portrayed by patriarchal myth makers, and the insatiability of female sexuality, which also has been a dominant theme in patriarchal cultures. For example, when speaking of Leonardo's "Mona Lisa," Freud refers to the blending of opposites "which dominate the erotic life of women," to her "reserve" and to her "sensuality that is ruthlessly demanding — consuming men as if they were alien beings" (Freud [1910] 1964, 58). In other writings Freud declares that female libido is less demanding than male libido. Let us note that women, children, the lower classes, and minority groups perennially vacillate in the minds of dominant males between the extremes of asexuality and voracious, even perverse, sensuality.

The fourth myth of masculine psychology asserts the absolute necessity of breaking the primordial maternal bond so that maturity, progress, health, sanity, and, above all, normal adult sexuality might be attained. Fromm sums up this myth when he declares, "Man, in order to be born, in order to progress, has to sever the umbilical cord; he has to overcome the deep craving to remain tied to mother" (Fromm 1955, 44). If man fails to overcome this "incestuous desire," he quite simply vegetates and cannot develop any independence or individuality. Fromm notes that the nearly inescapable pull toward the mother tie stems from the absolute security it provides. Norman O. Brown even attributes the origin of the "death instinct," which for Brown represents "the core of the human neurosis," to "the human infant's incapacity to accept separation from the mother" (Brown 1977, 284). In Fromm's lexicon, too, an inability to break from mother symbolizes things sinister: perhaps even that unquestioning obedience and loyalty to motherland or leader essential for good fascists.

Philosopher Herbert Marcuse describes how Hegel's *Phenomenology* epitomizes the coming into being of the Western male ego. This Hegelian model holds true for many of Freud's formulations — and even more so for those of his followers and for the existentialists. This model depicts the ego's self-consciousness as depending upon the other, but only because its satisfaction demands "the 'negation' of the other, for the ego has to prove itself by truly 'being-for-itself' *against* all 'otherness' " (Marcuse 1974, 113-14). The woman as mother represents, of course, the primordial absolute other. Finally, Erikson echoes Jung's equations of man = spirit and woman = matter when he shows with approval how Freud makes separation from women synonymous with intellectual potency and draws parallels among "the turn from dependence to self-help, from women to men," and from the ephemeral to the eternal (Erikson 1964, 184). Manhood, freedom, accomplishment, immortality — according to masculine mythology, all these require a merciless, resolute, and complete severing of any connection to mother.

With their fifth myth patriarchal culture asserts that women as mothers are omnipotent in their relationship to their children, simultaneously maintaining the contradictory assertion that women as females are weak and impotent. This myth epitomizes the contradiction between the responsibilities given to women as mothers and their lack of power, respect, and authority within the wider culture. This myth thus encapsulates the principal contradiction between the forces and the relations of reproduction. The mother is said to have limitless power to shape her child, but in patriarchal societies she has neither the power of self-definition nor the power to judge and define the limits of her own success. Patriarchal cultures inevitably find that "there has been, in all instances [where there is developmental arrest], a relative failure of the maternal environment" (Modell 1968, 87). Since for patriarchal thought women represent the natural and primitive level of sexuality and mother instinct, for men, then, mothering is, quite simply, mothering: Women as mothers are impotent to do anything positive for their child; they can only fail along a one-dimensional continuum that ranges from "too much" mother care to "too little" mother care. The most that they can aspire to is D. W. Winnicott's "good enough" mothering.

To produce a happy creative adult, the mother must satisfy the child's wishes, although this cultural imperative conflicts with male myth number three regarding the insatiability of the child. Modell declares that an "absence of intuitive mothering may strengthen the negative omnipotence leading to the belief that one possesses unlimited powers for destruction" (Modell 1968, 24). Side by side with such predictions of ominous outcomes resulting from "intuitive mother absence" (translation: "too little natural mothering") are the pronouncements of the dominant culture regarding the inconsequential impact of mother-infant bonds upon the larger community. Even when the mother-child relationship is understood to have changed and "evolved," as in the work of historian Edward Shorter, it still must be explained "why the evolution of the mother-infant relationship deserves to be discussed here," since, "it has little immediately to do with the larger narrative of family ties to community" (Shorter 1977, 168). The family in the work of male thinkers like Shorter, Fromm, and others is a monolithic agency stamping society's structures and strictures upon the child.

On the one hand, the mother-child unit is portrayed as an island universe floating in the center of the family lagoon; on the other, the family, seen as monolithic, stamps the child with the character of the social land beyond the moat. Lost amid the contradictions of this myth — of the mother all powerful vis-à-vis her child and of the woman weak and requiring protection vis-à-vis patriarchal society — lost are analyses of the power relationships between Western men and Western women, and of the impact these power imbalances might have upon the developing child.

Finally, the sixth myth of masculine thought is that love, despite its glorification and idealization in patriarchal culture, represents a regression to an earlier, more primitive state: Love merely reawakens childhood's paradise of play and allows respite from harsh realities. As psychologist Havelock Ellis, Freud's contemporary, said, "In women men find beings who have not wandered so far as they have from the typical life of earth's creatures; women are for men the human embodiments of the restful responsiveness of Nature" (Harding & O'Barr 1987, 193).

Love and work are yet another set of patriarchal antitheses paralleling those of female/male and species/individual. Discussing Freud's work, historian Thomas Johnston summarizes this myth when he states, "In assisting social change, love is not a helpful factor, for love, whether it is based upon inherited traits or is learned behavior, or both, continually acts in conservative ways for the perpetuation of the species" (Johnston 1965, 52–53). Production is the natural sphere of men; nature limits women to the sphere of reproduction — at least according to all these learned shapers of Western thought. Growing up for Western man therefore requires separation from the siren's song of symbiotic fusion with mother and with all that this unity encompasses: body, emotion, nature, sexuality. Our society is permeated with injunctions to set all these "backward" aspects of life aside with childhood's toys. For example, while picking up our cat at the vet, I recently came upon a pamphlet explaining how children's attitudes toward their pets change as they enter adolescence: "Maturity is a separation from the animal part of ourselves" (Beck & Katcher 1983, 89). Unfortunately, for men as well as for women, amputation of the animal part of self also entails amputation of that which is essential to continuing development and maturity, namely, the body-ego and its roots in the processes and structures of the unconscious.

The six masculine myths described above form and deform our ideas regarding our relationship to ourselves, to our fellow beings, to our environment and to our cultural surround. In sum, these myths assert, first, that a symbiotic identity between mother and child creates for each child an early unreal, primitive paradise; second, that the infant/child is utterly and passively dependent upon the mother; third, that the infant's desires are insatiable; fourth, that each child must break with the mother in order to reach psychological maturity; fifth, that women as mothers are omnipotent in relation to their children, yet weak and dependent in relation to their husbands and to male society; and, sixth, that love is a regressive force pulling us backward toward primitive symbiosis.

These myths reinforce the patriarchal paradigm of separation for boys during early psychosexual development and of Faustian individualism for men during later adolescent and adult development. Before presenting evidence that reveals the illusory nature of these myths, and before elaborating my own theory of accomplicity, which more satisfactorily explains the psychosexual development of both male and female, I wish to demonstrate how these myths are reproduced within the heart of feminist theory itself. In this way one will acquire respect for the tenacity of these myths, if not for their veracity.

HOW (SOME) FEMINIST THEORY REPRODUCES MASCULINE MYTHS

With increasing sophistication and intensity, feminist thinkers over the last two decades have begun to challenge the dominant paradigms of patriarchal culture. Feminist thought is most vulnerable, however, when it unquestioningly accepts any or all of the myths discussed above, since these myths are suffused with a patriarchal point of view detrimental to women (and to men). By rigorously examining their own presuppositions, feminists can neutralize those patriarchal theories that serve to divide and separate woman from woman.

Male myth number one, which describes a symbiotic unreal and primitive identity between mother and child, has been accepted by many feminist thinkers. In her important article "Excavating 'Those Dim Minoan Regions': Maternal Subtexts in Patriarchal Literature," Coppelia Kahn discusses the work of Adrienne Rich, Nancy Chodorow, and Dorothy Dinnerstein. Whatever else in patriarchal thought these feminist thinkers might question, they all — including Kahn herself — accept the idea that males and females alike start life psychically merged with mother. Kahn speaks of the "primitive organization of experience which emanates from early childhood, when the child's most important relationship is with the mother" (Kahn 1982, 12:36). For Kahn, "the child's earliest experience of himself and his mother [is] as an undifferentiated dual unity" (ibid. 37). Chodorow agrees that the infant is unaware of the difference between itself and the "mothering agent" and states that "the infant's lack of reality principle — its narcissistic relation to reality — is total" (Chodorow 1978, 61). Dinnerstein emphasizes that human sexuality takes shape in what she characterizes as the *"pre-verbal, pre-rational human infancy"* (Dinnerstein 1976, 15).

Even Evelyn Keller, who has vigorously critiqued the dominant culture's scientific paradigms, speaks of "our early maternal environment" and "the rough waters the child must travel in negotiating the transition from symbiotic union to the recognition of self and other as autonomous entities" (Keller in Keohane, Rosaldo & Gelpi 1982, 119 & 120). The ubiquity of these ideas regarding the early genesis of the self derive not so much from Freud as from the school of object relations psychology, which has suppressed the dialectical elements in Freud's system that I discussed in the previous chapter.

Another feminist theorist, Susan Bordo, who has written perceptively on the "masculinization of thought," also uncritically accepts the dominant culture's idea that growing up "is primarily a project of separation, of learning to deal with the fact that mother and child are no longer one" (Bordo in Harding & O'Barr 1987, 259). Similarly, political theorist Nancy Hartsock accepts "the fact that women but not men are primarily responsible for young children [and this] means that the infant first experiences itself as not fully differentiated from the mother" (Hartsock in Harding 1987, 167). Although these feminist thinkers are working hard to change the negative valuation placed by the patriarchy upon "merging" and the early mother-child relationship, they all do accept that a symbiotic connection is factual.

From Freudian psychoanalyst Ruth Brunswick's characterization in 1940 of the mother-child relationship as "doomed to extinction" because of "its primitive, archaic nature" (Chodorow 1978, 121) to contemporary writer Lynn Caine's assertion that "for babes in arms and tiny toddlers, mom is the universe" (Caine 1985, 13), women thinkers of various persuasions have not been sufficiently critical of received doctrine regarding the nature of the mother-infant relationship. Most of them have accepted the patriarchal idea of mother and infant as constituting a primitive symbiotic universe apart.

Male myth number two emphasizes the complete and passive dependency of the infant upon the mother. Again, too many feminist thinkers have made this myth part of their own assumptions. Dinnerstein combines myths number one and number two as she elaborates upon the monopoly she thinks the mother holds on the infant's world, stating that in the beginning the mother *is* the child's world (Dinnerstein 1976, 10–34 & 108–111). Psychiatrist Natalie Shainess states in *Sweet Suffering*, a study of feminine masochism, that "a child's first experience of the inequity of power comes in its relationship with its mother, or the primary mothering person. An infant is small and helpless, a mother large and powerful" (Shainess 1984, 20). British sociologist Ann Oakley emphasizes the "massive inputs of the mother's personality" into the child, who is therefore "immensely vulnerable." Oakley thinks that "the mother must be good because nobody can cure her mistakes. They are embedded in the life of the child for ever" (Oakley 1976, 216-17). All these thinkers are one with the male world in viewing the infant as helpless, as vulnerable, and as passively accepting whatever the mother "puts in."

In male myth number three, however, some contradictions are beginning to crop up. One recalls that this myth views infant desires as insatiable, and even the "unconditional mother love" that the patriarchy claims to admire in mothers cannot satisfy insatiability. Therefore, in patriarchal terms motherhood is doomed to failure from its inception. I have already remarked upon the conflation in patriarchal thought of the woman, the child, the primitive, minorities, and the elderly (one male journalist refers to these as America's "Third World Hordes"). These groups are labeled as either asexual or insatiably sensuous. Thus, helpful as it is in other ways, the emphasis placed upon "women's inordinate sexuality" by some feminist thinkers does serve to reinforce the patriarchy (e.g., Mary Jane Sherfey in Miller 1978, 152).

The missing, yet essential, analysis is one that underscores qualitative differences in sexual as well as other desires, as opposed to a quantitative contest that seeks to prove which sex's desires are stronger. Strong desires unsatisfied can be repressed or sublimated; strong desires can remain, not insatiable, but quite simply unsatisfied when the qualitative conditions for their satisfaction remain unmet. Frustrated and unsatisfied desire has often been the lot of women in patriarchal societies.

Feminist theorist Mary O'Brien correctly critiques Simone de Beauvoir's depreciation of reproduction as "animal contingency" (O'Brien 1983, 75). Those women thinkers who accept the dominant culture's view of women and children as more akin to the animal in their appetites — even when presenting animal nature as good — are reinforcing male myths that support patriarchal institutions. Even writer Sara Ruddick, whose essays on maternal thinking begin to break away from the patriarchal paradigm, describes mothers as "objects" of their "infant-child's primitive, pan-erotic desires" (Ruddick in Trebilcot 1984, 254). However, it is significant that among women, among those very persons whom the patriarchy has charged with fulfilling infant desires, the myth of insatiability echoes more softly than the other male myths.

Male myth number four states that each child must break with the mother in order to reach psychological maturity. Chodorow and Dinnerstein accept this male myth but modify it in important ways by emphasizing the different modes of breaking away used by girls and boys and the different effects these modes have upon their mothers. Chodorow claims that mothers make of girls extensions of themselves and that girls experience themselves as such; boys, on the other hand, are too often experienced by mothers, she says, as surrogate mates and therefore boys experience themselves in relation to mother as absolute others (Chodorow 1978, 103–107). Neither Chodorow nor Keller nor Ruddick questions the idea that for both boy and girl psychological adulthood means separating from mother. Chodorow does claim that girls stay merged with mother longer because of powerful same-sex identifications, and she attempts to attribute a richer inner life to women that she thinks results from girls' prolonged pre-Oedipal periods.

Dinnerstein, who also has been strongly influenced by the psychoanalytic tradition and who, like Chodorow, wishes to critique and modify it, emphasizes the problematic nature of women's mothering. Rather than the object relations standpoint espoused by Chodorow, Dinnerstein reflects the gestalt tradition and the work of Norman O. Brown. Dinnerstein writes of the "early rage" at the mother, which she deems useful to the Oedipal boy in order that he might *"consolidate* his tie with his own sex by establishing a principled independence, a more or less derogatory distance, from women" (Dinnerstein 1976, 53). This same rage, she says, is used by the Oedipal girl "to *loosen* her tie with her own sex by establishing a worshipful, dependent stance toward men" (ibid.). Dinnerstein comments that the child cannot survive without his mother, yet he must free himself of her in order to come into his own. In all cases the results are the same: the tie with mother is loosened or broken.

Other important feminist thinkers, like Elizabeth Janeway and Carol Gilligan, have accepted the assumptions of the myth of merging/breaking away, but they do strive to critique the patriarchal judgments passed upon women in this context. Janeway says that patriarchal society expects women as mothers "to bring off something of an emotional *tour de force"* in successfully raising children (Janeway 1971, 162). Gilligan points to the exclusion of women's values and experience from the theories of male psychologists and emphasizes the importance to all human beings of the maintenance of connection, which she, like Jean Baker Miller, understands is a primary concern of women (Gilligan 1982, 28). In *The Dance of Anger*, psychotherapist Harriet Goldhor Lerner also equates mature relationship with separation (Lerner 1986, 185). In sum, the idea of separation or breaking away from mother as necessary for psychological adulthood still stands in need of critical examination in the thinking of most feminist thinkers.

Masculine myth number five presents women as mothers in omnipotent relationship to their infants and small children while continuing to view women as weak and dependent creatures in relation to the wider society of men. The patriarchal myth of female power in relation to children is that which seems most seductive to feminist thought. After all, most feminists are eager to empower women, and rightly so; therefore why argue with the one area where common sense and masculine thought do agree women *are* powerful. Few and far between are the feminist voices that note this "mother power" with irony or skepticism and are able to reason out how the myth of the absolute power of the mother over the child is indeed used against women. One such voice was that of psychoanalyst Mabel Blake Cohen, who noted in the late 1950s the "startling belief among many of us that most of the neurotic illness in our population is mother generated. Such a potency attributed to the mother can only amaze one when put alongside the theory of the female as the weaker vessel" (Cohen in Miller 1978, 156).

Almost to a woman, women analysts have accepted the idea of the omnipotent mother. Dinnerstein uses the idea of threatening and over-whelming mother power to excuse society's allocation of power outside the home to men. The allocator, society, remains an unanalyzed monolith in Dinnerstein's work. In fact, she asserts that both men and women want to keep social power out of the hands of women because women hold so much power when both sexes are young. Chodorow attributes to women the power "as mothers [to] produce daughters with mothering capacities and the desire to mother" (Chodorow 1978, 7). She also claims that the power men hold over women cannot "explain women's mothering" and that women are not only responsible for reproducing men socially and psychologically, but that they are also responsible for their own social and psychological reproduction (ibid., 33–36). This is awesome power indeed! In her sensitive and insightful study of motherhood *Of Woman Born*, even Rich assumes that "the recurrence of dreams, legends, myths, of an archetypal powerful Woman, or of a golden age ruled by women," is explained by the fact that "each woman and each man has once, in earliest infancy, lived under the power of the mother" (Rich 1981, 58).

In addition, Prof. Carol Becker summarizes with approval writer Kim Chernin's views that "the aesthetic of slenderness that women take as gospel results from the irrational fear of the overpowering and engulfing mother – a fear experienced by both men and women, a regression back to a childhood sense of being totally dependent on and physically over-whelmed by the presence of the mother. Women are afraid to become too large" (Becker 1987, 156). And, finally, the feminist writer Claire Kahane summarizes several of the myths when she states:

Certainly the prevailing social situation of female rule over infancy promotes ambivalence toward all women, as Nancy Chodorow and Dorothy Dinnerstein have so forcefully argued. As psychoanalysts describe this critical period of early infancy, mother and infant are locked into a symbiotic relation, an experience of oneness characterized by a blurring of boundaries between mother and infant—a dual unity preceding the sense of separate self. Because the mother-woman is experienced as part of Nature itself before we learn her boundaries, she traditionally embodies the mysterious not-me world, with its unknown forces. Hers is the body, awesome and powerful, which is both our habitat and our prison, and while an infant gradually becomes conscious of a limited Other, the mother remains imaginatively linked to the realm of Nature, figuring the forces of life and death. (Kahane 1985, 336–37)

All the examples above demonstrate that the assumptions regarding the nature of the early infant-mother relationship permeate not only patriarchal thought but much feminist analysis as well: The mother holds absolute power over her infant and "rules" this child with whom she shares a symbiotic unity, providing the first most compelling link to body, nature, sex, and death. She simultaneously represents the me and the not-me. It is as if the structures of the patriarchal cultural surround do not exist for the child, nor, for that matter, for the mother herself. It is as if the father and other male representatives of this culture do not step over the threshold of the nursery until the child has reached the age of three or four. Clearly, these fanciful visions of early childhood represent significant deviations from the actual experiences of infant, mother, and father, in patriarchal societies.

Along with these falsifications of family relationships one often finds the myth of the monolithic family: Writer Letty Cottin Pogrebin finds that like Dinnerstein's monolithic society, the family is "almost omnipowerful" in relation to the child (Pogrebin 1984, 35). This myth, like the ones discussed above, ignores the influence of men and their culture upon mothers and children through the unequal power structures of the family itself. For example, Pogrebin states that within the family, "a woman's power over her child is so total during infancy that our culture has evolved the ethic of maternal purity and selflessness to make it tolerable and to keep it detached from female sexuality" (ibid., 110). Writer Nancy Friday quotes a young woman who blames her mother for her "whole feeling that sex is forbidden" (Friday 1978, 170). Also, Dinnerstein agrees with Freud that "human infants receive such nearly perfect care" that they are set up for inevitable and crushing disillusionment later (Dinnerstein 1976, 60).

Psychiatrist Dr. Ronee Herrmann counters all these paeans to mother power with an astringent "Good morning, Jesus Christ." "Because," Herrmann astutely reasons, "you've got to think you are a god to believe that you have that much power" (Caine 1985, 185). In *What Did I Do Wrong? Mothers, Children, Guilt,* Caine provides the necessary moment of sanity by pointing out that mothers do not constitute the total environment of their children and that children themselves are hardly clay in mothers' hands (ibid., 233).

Unfortunately, none of these important feminist writers have developed an analysis of the contradictions between the powers and relations of reproduction as viewed by the developing infant/child, of the contradiction between the "potency attributed to the mother," as Cohen put it, and woman "as weaker vessel." Nor do Dinnerstein and Chodorow and others catch the contradictions in their own analyses: With Dinnerstein there remains an unresolved contradiction between the "nearly perfect care of her child" attributed to the mother and the "rage" the infant supposedly feels toward this threatening and overwhelming figure.

In both Dinnerstein's and Chodorow's analyses, the problems posed by mother power are presented as solvable by means of equal parenting by men. Both Chodorow and Dinnerstein admit the greater power of men in the wider society; neither Chodorow nor Dinnerstein explains how women as mothers are going to convince men as fathers to join them in equal parenting when the male dominated world devalues the pre-Oedipal period of early childhood as much as it devalues women and "their" domestic spheres. Changing the parenting patterns of men and women becomes even more problematic when one realizes that most feminists share the masculine evaluation of early infancy as "pre-verbal, pre-rational" (Dinnerstein 1976, 15).

In fact, Dinnerstein's "solutions" place us in an impossible "Catch 22" situation: To become whole we must change our gender arrangements whereby women alone mother, and this change will require much strength; however, "this is exactly the kind of strength that we will continue to lack so long as woman-dominated child care continues," she admits (ibid., 77). Once again, much feminist thought bumps its head upon the cultural contradiction between the relations and forces of reproduction: Given our present sex/gender system, reproductive forces are centered in the lengthy physical/emotional nurturing women provide, while the patriarchal culture exerts dominance over reproductive relations.

The final male myth that also reproduces itself within feminist thought is that of love as a regressive force pulling us all backward toward our first primitive symbiotic relationship with mother. Freud himself spoke of childhood as our ultimate goal. Collette Dowling in her best-selling book, *The Cinderella Complex*, proclaims a "deep desire for 'reengulfment' with the mother." "There's Safety in Fusion" is the subtitle for her discussion of the resurrection in most marriages of childhood's mother-child symbiosis (Dowling 1982, 144–46). Unfortunately, although Dowling admits that men are "partly responsible for maintaining this bind," she accuses women of what amounts to a perverse "brilliance" in keeping themselves mired in stunted and stifling relationships (ibid.). Here Dowling joins Natalie Shainess and a few other recent authors in what astute feminist thinkers have correctly labeled a "blaming the victim" stance.

Even Caine, quoted above as having recognized the limitations upon mothers' powers, has not been able to carry out an analysis of why these myths continue to recur in the writings of men and women alike. Moreover, Caine perpetuates a similar failed strategy. Caine's book *What Did I Do Wrong?* traces her journey from guilt-ridden mother to a recognition that at least some, if not most, of her guilt was unmerited and socially induced. But to say to women as mothers, "Don't feel guilty, you are not responsible," begs the question as to why it is almost impossible for women not to feel guilty. Caine also neglects to answer the question, "Just what *are* mothers responsible for?"

The myth of love as a regressive force is an especially destructive one because it undermines all human relationships while denigrating the very areas assigned to women as their strength. Yet this myth, too, is especially persistent. Chodorow states that "men cannot provide the kind of return to oneness that women [as mothers] can" (Chodorow 1978, 194). She cites with approval object relations theorist Michael Balint's ideas regarding "the possibility of regressing to the infantile stage of a sense of oneness" as "a main goal of adult sexual relationships" (ibid.). Dinnerstein goes so far as to state that women's sexuality is repressed because female "sexual impulsivity . . . recalls the terrifying erotic independence of every baby's mother" (Dinnerstein 1976, 62); further, she states that "a woman can assuage guilt about betraying her first, homoerotic, love in sex with a man by renouncing the pursuit of 'selfish' bodily pleasure with him" (ibid., 67–68). Here the long shadow of the mother's power determines the character of her children's sexual love, and that character—for the grown woman at least—is "absence," or frigidity. Adult loves can only be a repetition of what French feminist Luce Irigaray calls the "primitive lived experience of the mother-child relationship" (LeMaire 1981, 228). And in the latter the mother must walk a tight-rope between giving "too much" love or "insufficient" love. Irigaray claims that the former will produce obsessional neurotics and the latter hysterics (ibid.). Here Irigaray perfectly echoes the patriarchal culture's anxiety-inducing—because impossible to fulfill—injunctions to mothers!

A corollary to the primitive, regressive nature of the first love shared by mother and infant—often called primary love—is the idea of the transhistorical nature of early childhood. This conception of childhood can be found in masculine thinkers from Sigmund Freud to Claude Lévi-Strauss to Jean Piaget. It is equally present in the feminist thought of Nancy Chodorow, Dorothy Dinnerstein, and Juliet Mitchell.

For example, Mitchell agrees with Chodorow's and Dinnerstein's call for men's greater participation in early parenting. She argues that "the process of socialization is, in itself, invariable," although "the person of the socializer can vary" (Mitchell 1973, 119). Little wonder that until recently not much scrutiny has been afforded that which actually does occur between mothers and children in the present or that which did occur in the historical past. If mother love, nurturing, and the acts of socialization are primitive and invariable, they would also prove recalcitrant to change. Much study and observation would be redundant. This is one source of contradiction in the work of those who simultaneously argue that primary love, a paradigm for all love, is unchanging and regressive, at the same time arguing that male parenting is necessary for the improvement of adult love relationships. If the primary love between infant and caregivers is everywhere and at all times the same, what difference will it make if fathers parent alongside mothers?

For example, in "The Traffic in Women," Gayle Rubin argues that men and women should equally care for children so that the "primary object choice would be bisexual" (Rubin in Reiter 1975, 199). Instead of analyzing in what ways early parent-child relationships already do contribute to the production of a bisexual self, Rubin accepts Lévi-Strauss's ideas that women have always been exchanged between groups as a means to promote social peace and cohesion. Rubin calls for a "revolution in kinship" without providing the analytical openings for such a revolution (ibid.). Rubin assumes with Freud's followers (and Chodorow) that mother care induces love of mother, which, in turn, creates an original homosexual love object for the girl. This patriarchal assumption ignores both the original bisexuality of the mother herself and collapses all love and sensuousness into an adult genitality projected backward upon the child. Therefore, this assumption reinforces the masculine split between subject (child) and object (mother). It ignores the ways in which the processes of interrelationship constitute the child's structures of selfhood.

Also, it is worth noting that the very acceptance of the idea of a "primary" object choice reestablishes patriarchal hierarchy. The patriarchy attempts to establish a perfect one-to-one relationship between men and masculinity, between women and femininity, between each sex and their respective gender roles, and then subordinates femininity to masculinity. Only in Freud's system are emphasized both the original bisexuality of the sexes and nonlinear — that is, interactive and constituting — relationships between the developing self and the cultural parents. A closer examination of these aspects of Freudian psychoanalysis will permit feminist theory to pass beyond object relations theory and the myths of patriarchal culture. Let us next consider the arguments that will help us to crystalize this new vision of early psychosexual development.

CRITIQUING THE MYTHS

In the beginning of this chapter I set about analyzing and deconstructing the patriarchal culture's principal presuppositions regarding the genesis of the self during the first months and years of life. Next, I indicated the ways in which much feminist thought reproduces what I have identified as masculine myths, and I suggested that feminist theory must unmask and eliminate these myths. A closer examination will reveal how these myths reinforce the dominant culture's hegemony and, more important, will permit us to view early psychosexual development from an angle of vision closer to the truths of women's — and children's — experience.

The idea of early mother-child symbiosis, or unthinking identity fusion, presupposes the usual subject/object split of patriarchal theories and contains all the logical contradictions of this split. Freud struggled mightily with the problem of the child's primary merging with the mother versus the child's separate existence, and he produced multiple contradictions in the process. The idea of symbiotic relationship strips the early mother-child interaction of the dignity of reason and cognitive import and reduces it to the level of pure unthinking reflex or, at best, motherly feeling and intuition. The idea of the utter dependency of the child upon the mother negates the powerful cultural constraints to which the mother is subject. It sets the mother up for absolute blame should anything go amiss in the child's early development.

The idea of the child's insatiability assumes the unreasonableness of children's needs and desires and justifies the patriarchal culture's ignoring of "childish" demands. The idea that the child needs to break from the mother in order to reach maturity in effect negates the mother and situates her sphere below the father's in the cultural hierarchy. The idea of the absolute power of the mother vis-à-vis the child again ensures that any fault of the child's derives from faults in the mother, while the contradictory assertion regarding the weakness of women vis-à-vis patriarchal society ensures that women will be viewed with scorn and pity by all. The idea of love and nurturing as regressive, as the lost paradise of the nursery, ensures that what women do will continue to be seen as worthy — provided mothers see to it that children fast outgrow the need for them and leave them behind. All these myths taken together reflect the dominant scientific paradigm of patriarchal psychology and culture, which have ordered their world around these spurious dualisms of subject/object, reason/emotion, mind/body, culture/nature — and, subtending all, masculine/feminine.

Yet, as Dr. Larry Dossey has pointed out in his seminal book *Space, Time & Medicine*, ". . . both the modern view of science and the aspect of consciousness that sustains it, rational thought, have themselves come to seem almost mythical" (Dossey 1982, 200). Dossey's book sets out to demonstrate why, "as a demythologizing power, modern science is effete" (ibid.). For, Dossey agrees, we are living not only in the midst of multiple crises, but in the middle of multiple revolutions. The old paradigms, based upon the splits of subject/object, mind/body, and objectivities/subjectivities, and that between a superior masculinity and an inferior femininity, are in the process of being deposed. However, it is with great difficulty that the entrenched institutions of the dominant culture recognize these changes, and it is with great ferocity that those in power cling to the ideas that maintain their status.

Within science itself quantum physics has abolished the rigid separation between matter and energy and introduced the living observer into the heart of objective reality. The mathematician Kurt Gödel has demonstrated the incompleteness of logical systems of any complexity and shown the tenuousness of their consistency. Nature is now understood to be a part of us, as we are understood to participate in the evolution of the universe. Even the debate over monism versus dualism is beginning to be understood as spurious, since dualism's positing of a third substance only unleashes yet another infinite regress. The physicist Werner Heisenberg, the sociologist Theodore Adorno, the anthropologist Ashley Montagu, the medical researcher Norman Cousins, the psychiatrist Jean Baker Miller—to mention only a few advanced thinkers—all believe in the paradigm of emergent interactionism. This new paradigm asserts that humans create their own realities in interaction with their biological *and* their cultural heritage; that mind and body interact equally, one upon the other, with the body providing its own "wisdom," its own memory connections with unconscious dimensions of reality.

Sigmund Freud's system has foreshadowed, in the ways I enumerated in Chapter 3, many of these emergent understandings. In Freud's system, as in that of the new paradigm, indeterminacy and ambiguity are built into the essence of relationships because the new emerges from the interaction of differences produced by the unexpected mingling of marginalized aspects of reality. These aspects of reality derive from a culture's emerging systems of myth, scientific theory, and symbolic language, all of which are rooted in the metaphoric power of our minds, conscious and unconscious (Pagels 1988, 150).

Recently, writer Sam Keen explained the dominant myths of a culture in this way: "Myth is the cultural DNA, the software, the unconscious information, the program that governs the way we see 'reality' and behave. . . . A myth involves a conscious celebration of certain values."

And, Keen went on to explain, "it also includes an unconscious, habitual way of seeing things, an invisible stew of unquestioned assumptions" (Keen 1988, 22:44). Keen points out that while a system of myths — what I have called a paradigm — may be visible to those outside the culture, this system remains "nearly invisible to those inside" (ibid.). By existing outside the myths of the dominant culture, women are best able to become aware of the contradictions within these myths.

However, the new paradigm now dimly visible upon the cultural horizon is arising as much from the contradictions and discoveries within masculine disciplines as from within the feminist movement. This new paradigm presents to women the opportunity to crystalize their own myths and to integrate their stories and their lives and their powers into those of the dominant culture, transforming it forever. Although we may construct our realities through our interaction with nature, culture, and our fellow beings, this construction of reality by means of the stories we tell ourselves — our scientific theories, our myths, and our metaphors and symbols — this construction is no less true for our having participated in it. To the contrary, the suppression of women's stories has distorted human reality to the detriment of each and every one of us — man, woman, and child.

The telling of women's stories requires new language in order to communicate new ideas. The concepts I use in order to critique the myths of the dominant culture are only three in number: First, throughout the rest of this book I will be speaking of the multiple processes of interaction between infant and parent, and between individual and culture, as the processes of accomplicity. Second, through the emergent interactions of mother and infant, the processes of accomplicity produce the infant's majority self. This is true whether the infant is female or male. Third, the processes of accomplicity produce, through the emergent interactions of father (or father surrogate) and infant, the infant's minority self. Again, this occurs whether the infant is female or male.

Accomplicity is the process by means of which the culture's *selective systems* — that is, its myths, metaphors, and scientific theories — pass through the unconscious social membrane and become individual body by incorporating themselves into our very nervous systems during the critical period of pre-Oedipal childhood. As Montagu has so eloquently stated under the heading "The Myth of the Individual," all evaluations of human beings as social organisms should make clear that they are "as organically bound to others as if [they] were one of a number of cells comprising a colonial organism," (Montagu 1981, 111). I suggest that this "social membrane," this "colonial organism" is none other than the Freudian unconscious through which psychosexual development becomes psychosocial evolution. (For further supporting arguments, see Dossey 1982; Winson 1986; Lynch 1985; Pagels 1988.)

The importance of these new concepts will become apparent as we further analyze the myths of the dying patriarchal paradigm. First, the myth of the unreal, primitive, symbiotic unity and primary fusion or identification between mother and child during the child's earliest years must be critiqued on three levels: the level of theory, that of empirical evidence, and that of women's experiential realities. On the level of theory: One more subspecies of the split running through the patriarchy is the masculine idea that the pre-Oedipal period of childhood is mother dominated and characterized by symbiotic fusion, subjectivity, and lack of a reality sense, as opposed to the post-Oedipal father-dominated period seen as the age of reason and objectivity. This study identifies the source of all these divisions as that biological division within the species between male and female and that cultural division of labor between the masculine and feminine genders. The relationship between these two divisions — the biological and the cultural — must be understood as *indeterminate* because of their interaction and intermingling over the course of millennia. Biological sexuality itself is also culturally mediated.

The feminine halves of the split in patriarchal cultures are inevitably found on lower rungs of a hierarchy. I have suggested that the power to define — monopolized by men — has brought about these hierarchical relationships and, paradoxically, has also resulted in men's desire to distance themselves from that which they themselves have over generations defined as inferior. Of course, what is so often overlooked in nondialectical linear analyses are the extensive temporal periods during which patriarchal culture established these cultural divisions with all their symbolic and economic ramifications. At no one time did a group of men once and for all conspire to consign women and woman-terms as a whole to inferior rank; there was no one world historical defeat of the female sex. Our present dilemmas are rooted in our species' biological dimorphism and in the historical circumstances leading to masculine hegemony, which, in turn, has accentuated gender differences. Biological sexuality and cultural gender roles have interacted over long periods of time. In fact, it is only very recently that modern genetics has begun to permit us a glimpse of the ways in which our history becomes, in part, our biology.

Western culture has increasingly moved away from explanations that make sexual drives the primary force behind all human motivation. Returning to the original Freud, my theory of accomplicity transforms the idea of sexual drives into that of *gender drives* and asserts that gender drives represent the manifestation of the contradictions between the cultural feminine and the cultural masculine, the contradiction between the forces and relations of reproduction. I submit that these contradictions are the primary motive force driving human beings today.

At the center of these gender contradictions stand the tremendous advantages that have accrued to men over recent centuries. These advantages range from the augmentation of masculine economic power to the enormous growth of masculine cultural, or defining, power because culture has become progressively more influential than nature — and progressively more masculine. The disadvantages and harm done to men by their own power (especially the power of some men over others) has been obscured by the cultural myths of heroic masculinity.

The logical weaknesses in the linear analyses of patriarchal thought, discussed in relation to the paradigm model of Thomas S. Kuhn, have counterparts in the idea of symbiotic fusion between mother and child during the primitive pre-Oedipal period of early childhood, a period inferior to the later post-Oedipal period when the father-child relationship becomes salient. If masculine psychologies merge the early self with mother, then they have to describe how the self emerges from mother; above all, they must explain how the male self can emerge untainted by maternal qualities. Freud's writings, of course, are a monumental contribution toward the solution of these masculine theoretical dilemmas. The contradictions that remain in Freud's work are testimony to his ultimate failure to resolve these problems, which, indeed, are not resolvable from a patriarchal, linear, monological perspective.

Freud himself was honest enough to note many of the shortcomings of his work: He realized that he had not penetrated deeply enough into the mysteries of time and temporal categories; he admitted to understanding little regarding the psychology of women; he acknowledged being puzzled by what he saw as the "more intimate relationship of sadism to masculinity and of masochism to femininity"; and, finally, he saw that his solution for bridging the pre-Oedipal period and the post-Oedipal period, that is, his theory of the Oedipus complex, grew more problematic with increasing psychoanalytic knowledge.

In Chapter 2, I stated that patriarchal thought struggled with the problem of origins, that masculine solutions to the problem of origins collapsed under the weight of tautology and infinite regress; opposites fell back into identities, which, in turn, sprang forth inexplicably reborn full-grown. This can be clearly illustrated by Freud's (and other masculine psychologies') simultaneous positing of infant-mother identity and the total narcissism (self-identity) of the infant — who then "chooses" as love object the hand or breast feeding it.

The same logical errors are repeated by feminist thinkers like Chodorow who are trying to transform Freudian psychoanalysis from an object relations standpoint. Chodorow, like Freud, sees the infant totally submerged in mother, yet she sees "all aspects of psychic structure" in the child as social because "constituted through a 'history of object-choices'" (Chodorow 1978, 50). She claims that the infant cannot differentiate between itself and its mother, but that the infant simultaneously remains totally narcissistic, that is, wrapped up in self. The question is, of course, if the child begins life in a submerged identity with the mother, who is doing the choosing that determines the mother as object? Does the child really have any choice, since it is by definition (Freud's and Chodorow's) totally submerged in mother identity? A close reading of the work of Freud and of the various schools following him, and of many in partial opposition to him, will reveal a constant vacillation between the poles of this unresolved dual positing of subject-object, of being-for-the-other and of being-for-the-self, of identity with the other and of total narcissistic self-involvement. Nowhere is the relationship between these two modes clarified, nor is the jump from one to the other standpoint ever satisfactorily explained.

As early as 1913 Freud's disciple Sandor Ferenczi understood that one could not separate "object relations" development from the ego's development of a reality sense (Modell 1968, 99–100). Expanding upon this insight, Melanie Klein, a British psychoanalyst of children, proclaimed that object relationships begin developing at birth; in this way Klein validated the cognitive powers of the newborn (ibid., 148–49). Indeed, it is precisely in the recent explosion of knowledge, subsequent to empirical studies of the newborn and of young children, that the link between the "object relations" theorists' critique of Freud and my own theoretical critique is forged. The dialectical theory of accomplicity, which describes the process through which each infant's feminine (majority) and masculine (minority) selves are formed, is consonant with women's psychology and with women's existential realities; it agrees with new empirical research asserting infants' early cognitive development; and it succeeds in overcoming the logical dilemmas endemic to patriarchal accounts of early development.

The theory of accomplicity explains that, upon the birth of the child, the mother and infant neither constitute an identity nor are they separate from each other. Their relationship is determined by the realities of the processes of pregnancy and parturition as experienced by women; their relationship is also regulated, as O'Brien has stated, by the patriarchal culture's "denial of creativity, historicity and intellectual significance to human reproduction" (O'Brien 1983, 18). However, the interrelationship of mother-infant is also imbued with an element of indeterminacy stemming from the activity and creativity of newborn babies themselves. This aspect of accomplicity agrees with Eleanor Maccoby's emphasis upon the "self-socialization" activities of the child. For it is as impossible for the mother to identify perfectly with her newborn and anticipate all of its needs ("Good morning, Jesus Christ!"), as it is impossible for the infant to be submerged in or perfectly identified with the mother. They are separate and individual from the moment of birth (although asymmetrically so); they are also united by the cultural surround that penetrates them and by the unconscious social membrane through which complex constituting communications take place.

The process of accomplicity represents the complex growing together-apart, apart-together relationships that constitute the child's selves. Accomplicity is always mediated by the culture, and, I must emphasize, it is qualitatively and quantitatively different as undertaken by mothers as opposed to fathers (or masculine surrogates). Ambiguities introduced at this point will resolve themselves somewhat as I proceed, but I cannot promise that they will entirely disappear. In order to move away from the linear and quantitative analyses of the dominant culture's "too-much mother, too-little mother" toward more qualitative analyses of the mother-child (and father-child) relationship, I find it necessary to embrace ambiguity and eschew the simplistic formula. So deeply embedded is the patriarchal formula of the critical importance of infants' attachments to mother in a hermetic symbiotic merging that any new vision can only come into focus slowly and with difficulty.

Earlier, I stated that Freud failed to resolve these theoretical problems of origins and tautology, of symbiosis and splits. Yet Freud did move the discussion creatively to a level at which openings can be glimpsed, and Freud never strayed from his conviction that the problems of bisexuality were key. One of the important openings created by Freud stems from his assertion that the body, the infant's body-ego, *thinks*. Here one has in embryo the new vision emanating from modern empirical science, a vision that affirms the rational powers of the newborn as well as the wisdom of the body.

Montagu has championed the rediscovery in the Western world of "our neglected senses," in particular those proximity senses of touch, smell, and taste. Montagu declares that "to shut off any one of the senses is to reduce the dimensions of our reality.... The one-dimensionality of the world becomes a substitute for the richness of the multidimensionality of the senses" (Montagu 1986, xiii). Montagu also emphasizes that although infants' nervous systems are unfinished, infants' senses are all very well developed, that infants "can hear, see, taste, smell, feel, and even think, as well as make fine discriminations of various sorts" (Montagu 1981, 101). Montagu indicts the patriarchal culture's single-minded exclusion of nonverbal communications of the sort I believe form the nucleus of mother-infant accomplicity.

Montagu argues convincingly for the "mind of the skin" and reminds us that the skin is "our first medium of communication" (Montagu 1986, 3); he further reminds us that the ectoderm gives rise to both the skin and the nervous system, that the "nervous system is . . . a buried part of the skin . . . [and] the skin may be regarded as an exposed portion of the nervous system" (ibid., 5). Freud, of course, made body memory central for his therapeutic insights by describing how repressed feelings "speak" through the body, a process he called "conversion."

Prof. James J. Lynch has also discovered in *The Language of the Heart* (1985) stunning evidence that confirms our modern loss of body memory, our culture's literal splitting of mind from body. Lynch says, "It is not simply that these patients have 'no words for feelings,' but rather that they have no words to describe what they cannot feel in their own bodies: they are fundamentally deaf to the language of their own hearts" (ibid., 240). Lynch discovered the astonishing phenomenon of elevated blood pressure — even in babies — during speech or other vocalization. Even more astonishing is that these dramatic changes in blood pressure with attempts at communication were not registered by the subjects. Lynch has established the medical reality — nearly a century after Freud — of the importance of "talking cures": "Patients can gain insight into their problems," Lynch writes, "if they are first taught to listen to their own bodies by therapists who can hear and decode the messages spoken by those bodies" (ibid.).

Through such careful decodings Lynch has been able to help put individuals suffering from a wide range of "psychosomatic" complaints in touch with their own bodies. Lynch theorizes that the specific complaints — migraine, colitis, high blood pressure — are subtly communicated to children by parents during very early childhood. I suggest that it is just such "communication" via the proximity senses during the critical periods of early infancy that produces not only psychosomatic illness but also the dual — majority and minority — selves of each of us.

In order to visualize the production of these selves we must overcome all of the deeply ingrained prejudices of the patriarchal culture. Foremost among these is the prejudice that separates mind from body and grants intelligence only to the former. "Can we," Dossey asks, "go beyond our traditional cause-and-effect habits in assessing our body function? Can we transcend our tendency to put the brain in charge, to impute intelligence only to the brain, and to relegate the rest of the body to the status of dumb organs?" (Dossey 1982, 220). We must be able to do this if we are to understand what happens in early infancy during mother-infant and father-infant accomplicity – during the times when these dual selves in conflict are in formation.

It is now well accepted that there are critical periods of development during which nonreplicable events produce nonreplicable changes in our nervous systems. There appear to be critical periods for the acquisition of certain motor skills and certainly for language skills. Neuroscientist Jonathan Winson also uses the idea of critical periods in developing his brilliant hypothesis regarding the brain mechanisms that may underlie the repression of unpleasant experiences into the unconscious. Winson has discovered that it takes one-half second for sensations to register themselves consciously and that during this brief interval brain mechanisms exist in the preconscious that can prevent these thoughts from ever reaching consciousness. In addition, Winson postulates that "early misimpressions may be fixed and not available for correction later in life" – at least not available without the use of Freudian decodings of body memory (Winson 1986, 220).

Those vague ideas concerning the "wisdom of the body" that are now being given precision, shape, and substance by the research of people like Montagu, Dossey, Lynch, and Winson have manifested themselves in earlier writings of philosophers and psychologists. In philosophy the work of the French theorist Maurice Merleau-Ponty also attempts to "force us to form the idea of an organic thought through which the relation of the 'psychic' to the 'physiological' becomes conceivable" (Merleau-Ponty 1965, 77). Also, although his work on gender identity embraces the ideas of symbiosis and identification, psychiatrist Robert Stoller does explicitly recognize the need for other mechanisms, which he calls "nonmental . . . (i.e., not motivated by the individual) by which the outside reality also is emplaced within" (Stoller in Strouse 1985, 354). These are only two examples that demonstrate that the patriarchal culture, having separated mind from body, subject from object, and the feminine from the masculine, is now struggling to put them back together again, to visualize the ways in which these polarities truly are related to each other.

In sum, just as patriarchal culture has collapsed the erotic into the genital – most specifically into the male genital, the penis – so also has it collapsed the intellect into the brain – most specifically the (white) adult male brain. The body has been disinherited. However, as Norman O. Brown so clearly saw, the body, like the Freudian repressed, will continue to return demanding a restitution of its lost estate.

If scientific observation finds gender awareness and cognitive growth occurring during periods when masculine thought previously found only an undifferentiated mother-infant identity, empirical studies that demonstrate differential treatment of infants according to sex by both parents further explode the tenacious myth of mother-child symbiosis. We have seen how, on a purely theoretical level, mother-child identity is untenable. The increasing weight of observational studies renders this concept even less tenable.

Chodorow, one recalls, claims that a perfect identification between mother and child energized the mother's perfect anticipation of her child's needs. Chodorow herself undermines this premise when she discusses the qualitative differences in the love a mother gives to her girlchild (narcissistic) as opposed to that given the boychild (anaclitic) (Chodorow 1978, 195). She argues that this qualitatively different mother love shown to girls and boys, "beginning in the earliest period," results in the infants' differing attitudes toward objects (other people), cutting off or curtailing "relational possibilities for parenting in boys, and [keeping] them open and [extending] them in girls" (ibid., 90–91). For if the mother were perfectly identified with her infants, would she not extend the potentialities of both sexes equally instead of cutting them off or extending them as the Procrustean bed of the patriarchy dictates?

Similarly, Joanna Rohrbaugh reports that "parents treat male and female newborns differently, encouraging gross motor behavior in males while viewing females as littler, cuter, cuddlier, and generally more fragile" (Rohrbaugh 1979, 77). Rohrbaugh further reports that cross-cultural research turns up similar findings, with most cultures giving greater independence and self-assertion to males while keeping females dependent and responsive to the needs of others. Oakley cites a study showing that "mothers differentiate between boys and girls in their behavior towards them. . . . At three weeks of age mothers held male infants 27 minutes more per eight hours than females: at three months, 14 minutes longer" (Oakley 1972, 173).

There are enormous differences in parental attitudes toward girl and boy babies, the latter being far and away the preferred addition to a family. Shainess reports on an article appearing in the Journal of the American Medical Association in which a pediatrician notes the "disappointment in the faces of fathers, and even mothers, when they learned their child was a girl" (Shainess 1984, 26). Other studies have revealed that the infamous postpartum depression some mothers experience is more likely to follow the birth of a girl-child. The self-conscious differential treatment mothers accord girl and boy babies undercuts the myth of one type of natural, intuitive mothering.

In brief, the myth of perfect mother-child symbiosis and identification is subject to grave theoretical difficulties, to contradiction by recent empirical studies, and to refutation on the level of the experience of women as mothers. As to the latter, Oakley has written a book, entitled *Becoming a Mother* (1980), designed to meet the lack of empirical data collected from mothers themselves. Her principal findings reveal the emptiness of the mother-child symbiotic paradise myth: Most of the new mothers interviewed by Oakley were totally unprepared for how difficult mothering would be; their experience clearly shows natural intuitive mothering as the product of masculine fantasy life.

One can readily see that the foregoing critique of male myth number one also provides material for a critique of male myth number two, the idea that an infant or young child is completely and passively dependent upon the mother. By thus denying agency or subjecthood to the child and locating agency exclusively in the mother, the untenable subject/object split is reproduced. Erikson was nearer the truth when he stated, "Parents who are faced with the development of a number of children must constantly live up to a challenge. They must develop with them.... Babies control and bring up their families as much as they are controlled by them" (Erikson 1963, 69). Erikson's affirmation of dialectical reciprocity on the part of parents and children is consonant with the theoretical foundation of accomplicity, and it underscores limitations in the exercise of power by both parents. Recently, studies of infants with depressed mothers suggest that these infants' "depressed styles of inter-acting" are capable of eliciting depressedlike behaviors in nondepressed adults (Field et al. 1988, 59:1577). This is a remarkable example of infants influencing adults. Clearly, as Prof. Mary Ainsworth has written, "despite recent research into mother-infant bonding [note ubiquity of word *bonding*], remarkably little is known about the processes involved in the formation and maintenance of the bond, or even of the criteria that mark its establishment" (Ainsworth 1989, 44:712).

I submit that "remarkably little is known" about the mother-infant "bond" because the presuppositions of patriarchal myths and theories, "bonding" among them, have blinded us to the ways in which processes of interaction (accomplicity) build the structures of self-hood. Left to emphasize are the mediations of the cultural surround that by means of the body-ego and the unconscious also influence the interactions of mother-child, father-child, and mother-father-child. Unfortunately, modern science has ignored the many links between our bodies and our social relationships. These links are central to the theory of accomplicity that in emphasizing the action of babies upon their parents, further modifies Erikson's statement by taking into account the asymmetry of parent-child interactions. The most potent influences reside, of course, with the adults and with the culture. This said, however, it must be noted that mothers experience the individuality of their children from earliest infancy, even though the patriarchal culture imbues mothers with certain attitudes depending upon the sex of their infants. The great child psychologist Jean Piaget also understood that the mother does not exist as an independent variable, but interacts with and is influenced by her child (Piaget 1969, 27).

In fact, it is *as mother* that the controls upon women are most rigid in patriarchal societies. Patriarchal motherhood with its mythical "unconditional love," "symbiotic paradise," and "perfect identifications" requires superhuman — if not inhuman — efforts on the part of women as mothers, who are punished with excruciating guilt if they should deviate in the slightest from these prescriptions. Mothers who do not seek custody of their children in divorce, mothers who abuse children or abandon them, these mothers elicit feelings of horror and are branded as "unnatural" or "monstrous" in the popular press. Indeed, the lack of latitude in patriarchal ideals of mothering creates a perverse kind of "baby power" that gives the lie to the male myth of the helpless infant. Furthermore, studies completed in recent years regarding the influence of fathers (a much-neglected topic) are beginning to reverse the prevailing view that fathers' influence on small children is negligible (Hamilton 1977, 145). Indeed, the patriarchal vision of a mother-child island isolated in the middle of the family lagoon is revealing itself as deceptive mirage.

The myth of the infant passive and dependent upon mother is theoretically inconsistent; it ignores existing cultural and paternal mediations; it also ignores the experience of women as mothers. Recent empirical studies bear witness to the competency of the youngest infant. "The Competence of Babies" (Quinn 1982, 249:54–62), "Born Smart: Imitation of Life" (Miller & Greenberg 1985, 127:376), and "Baby Talk: The Babble Has a Message" (McCann 1984, IB:7) proclaim typical headlines and articles in innumerable magazines, newspapers, and journals from the *Reader's Digest* to professional newsletters. Newborn babies are making news: From being considered "little more intelligent than a vegetable" in 1895 to being considered only a "bundle of organs and nerves" by no less than Dr. Benjamin Spock in 1946, the modern infant has become a "competent" individual even at birth, able to respond with "26 behavioral and 20 reflex activities" (Quinn, ibid., 55). As we get smarter, so do they! Unarguably, baby cannot fight off with a karate chop an abusive parent of either sex, but the new understanding of early childhood reveals a little individual from the first moments of life, competent and even in some respects controlling its environment, including its parenting figures.

Since the infant/child is now understood to be far from helpless, the myth of insatiability, which stems in part from a presumed complete dependency, can also be laid to rest. Nursing mothers know the profound joy of a satiated baby who quietly dozes at the nipple. "Desire" in the Freudian and neo-Freudian lexicon (particularly in that of the French neo-Freudian Jacques Lacan) is insatiable because founded upon a lack, upon the impossibility of ever possessing the first love, the mother. To the contrary, I affirm that desire is structured by means of accomplicity and that which is perceived as lack or absence to the patriarchal culture viewing the infant-mother relationship through its mythic lenses can mask fulfillment on hidden levels. The mother (or other) may leave the child, but the presence of mother (or other) remains in the form of the full stomach, lingering body perfumes, body warmth, and kinesthetic sensation, and in the structures of selfhood formed during accomplicity.

Let us clearly understand that accomplicity constitutes self and desire simultaneously and that the symbolic level of culture and paternal metaphor mediate this self and this desire from the earliest beginnings of life. However, I am not proclaiming a perfect correspondence of infant desire and mother response. On the contrary, one aim of this study is to reveal why in patriarchal cultures both infant desire and mother response are inevitably frustrated. But please note that the myth of infant insatiability fulfills the theoretical prediction of Chapter 2 that masculine thought harbors opposing dualisms that reduce to the same untenable identity. The counterpart of perfect unconditional mother love creating symbiotic paradise lost is the insatiable desire of the infant and the overwhelming power of a terrifying mother figure: These pairs are identical in the final analysis because both conceptions are equidistant from the reality of mother-child interactions.

The fourth myth of the dominant culture claims that each child must break away from the mother in order to attain adulthood and psychological maturity. Fromm, quoted previously, expresses this myth most concisely when he states, "Man's sense of identity develops in the process of emerging from the 'primary bonds' which tie him to mother and nature" (Fromm 1955, 62). Feminist thought echoes this myth when Chodorow explains that "children wish to remain one with their mother, and expect that she will never have different interests from them: yet they define development in terms of growing away from her" (Chodorow 1978, 82). This myth is also present when Chodorow quotes psychoanalyst Joan Riviere's statement, "It is by turning away from our mother that we finally become, by our different paths, grown men and women" (ibid.).

Yet once again it is the differential treatment given boys and girls in patriarchal societies by both parents that undermines this myth. Whereas boys are helped by the culture and by both parents to attain, however precariously, the masculine gender prescriptions, girls often stumble along the road to womanhood and to motherhood by default. Far from binding their daughters close as alter egos and resisting their breaking away, mothers are all too often eager to be rid of responsibility for their daughters; they remain hopeful that suitable husbands will arrive early on the scene, sparing them and their daughters from the patriarchal limbo reserved for women in transition from father to husband. Feminist writer Phyllis Chesler agrees that "the way in which female children grow up – or learn how not to grow up – is initiated by the early withdrawal or relative absence of the female and/or nurturant body from their lives" (Chesler 1973, 19-20). Lacking a nurturant body, lacking that which Montagu has called "a basic behavioral need" – affectional touch – it is little wonder that women in patriarchal cultures are stunted in their development (Montagu 1986, 46).

Freud thought that all human relationships, except that of a mother and her son, were fraught with conflict and ambivalence. For Freud, the mother-son relationship, among all relationships, exhibits the least ambivalence and brings "unlimited satisfaction" to the mother (Freud [1916-33] 1966, 597). Although most mothers undoubtedly will agree that Freud overstates his case, it is true that in patriarchal cultures only as a mother of sons can most women at least vicariously develop their own full potentials as human beings. Therefore, far from being the most unselfish and "disinterested" of relationships, as Freud claimed, the relationship of mother to son holds the promise of the greatest rewards possible for a woman in a masculine society and is, for this very reason, the most "interested" of relationships.

Since the paths to immortality have been barred to her personally, a woman's surest monument to self has been – and to a great extent still is – erected only indirectly as she becomes the force behind a "great" man. When husbands become great men in patriarchal cultures, they usually trade in their wives for younger models. In fact, clever Don Juans know how to capitalize upon women's Faustian hungers and may attempt seduction by convincing desirable females of their masculine "genius" and inevitable fame. All these facts account for the "comment on the social evaluation of femininity in our culture [which] is that 44 per cent of the women who had girls were disappointed to have daughters (compared with the 93 per cent who had boys and were pleased)" (Oakley 1980, 118).

As for the need to break from father, recent research into the nature of the father-child relationship has revealed that the quality of the mother-father relationship and socioeconomic factors are more important than the absence or presence of the father in the home when predicting delinquency in boys (Hamilton 1977, 21-23). For girls, successful heterosexual adjustment has been linked with father identification as opposed to identification with feminine mothers (ibid., 85). This latter finding, especially, confounds the traditional psychoanalytic and psychological wisdom regarding the development of femininity.

The only light cast thus far upon these anomalous findings has come from feminist thinkers who are beginning to question the patriarchal idea of breaking away. Gilligan, cited earlier, has determined that women's morality and values are very different from those of men, which constitute the cultural norms. It is only in relation to norms based entirely upon masculine values that women's concern with maintaining relationships instead of breaking away appears deviant, dependent, and immature. Psychoanalyst Jean Baker Miller astutely argues that something is amiss in theories urging independence and separation as norms and then finally presenting the attainment of intimacy and creativity and generativity as ultimate goals of mature adulthood (Miller 1986, 83–114).

The contradictions of the dominant culture's separation-and-independence model render it one-dimensional and incapable of explaining the complex reality of early psychosexual development. This complex reality requires a dialectical theory like that of accomplicity, which takes into consideration quantitative development (i.e., degree of separation or independence along one dimension) *and* qualitative development (i.e., the kind of growing together along other simultaneously existing dimensions). For example, I assert that one never entirely breaks with parents – or, for that matter, with anyone to whom one has been close. Relationships change and develop along several dimensions simultaneously, and the interaction between individuals lays down "precipitates," as Freud has said, that constitute not only the "history of object choices," but also the very substances of the selves.

There is much that we have yet to learn regarding the interaction between mind and body and precisely how cultural understandings are communicated to infants during their first months and years of life. However, an astonishing amount of scientific evidence has appeared within the last decade which lends support to feminist theories like that of accomplicity. These theories all assert that the self can grow only within relationships; that without human contact and communication, human development will not occur. Montagu has collected evidence that "infants deprived of their accustomed maternal body contact may develop a profound depression with lack of appetite, wasting, and even marasmus leading to death" (Montagu 1986, 97). Montagu further reports, "At Bellevue Hospital in New York, following the institution of 'mothering' on the pediatric wards, the mortality rates for infants under one year fell from 30 to 35 percent to less than 10 percent" (ibid., 99).

There are no theories at present, however, that model the ways in which the processes of parent-child interaction — what I call accomplicity — produce the very structures of selfhood. Many feminist theorists, among them Jean Baker Miller, Carol Gilligan, Eleanor Maccoby, Carol Nagy Jacklin, A. G. Kaplan and J. L. Surrey, have emphasized models of women's development in which the "self-in-relation" is central. Some of these theorists have extended this model to include men's development and have speculated that "we are the company we keep," that is, that interaction with specific individuals elicits specific types of behavior (Jacklin 1989, 44:131). Drawing upon new research findings within psychoneuroimmunology, cardiology, and psychology, the theory of accomplicity explains that the very substances of self — our minds, brains, bodies, and nervous systems — are laid down through processes of interrelationship of which we are only now becoming aware.

In addition, the theory of accomplicity asserts that due to the nature of parenting within Western cultures, *two* substantive selves are generally produced: The processes of mother-child accomplicity constitute the majority self, while the processes of father-child accomplicity constitute the minority self. These selves are produced principally by means of differential proximity sense interactions. Montagu points out that children respond to parents' inner states by means of messages from parents' "muscle-joint behavior." Montagu emphasizes that a babe in arms may be able to "read" its mother's state of mind more correctly than others who see only the outward appearance (Montagu 1986, 141). Moreover, Montagu reminds us that "there can be little doubt that in tactile stimulation electrical changes are transmitted from one individual to the other" (ibid., 183). Montagu sums up the central idea behind the theory of accomplicity when he states:

To touch means to communicate, to become part of, to possess. Whatever I touch becomes part of me, I possess. When I am touched by another, that other transfers part of himself to me. When I touch another I transfer part of myself to them. (Montagu 1986, 389)

The theory of accomplicity would modify Montagu's account simply by noting that it is the process of interaction (accomplicity) that produces new self substances for both child and parent. For it is not a question of an exchange whereby each gives the other unchanged a part of self, but a far more complex interchange whereby new structures are laid down for both. The idea of the production of the structures of selfhood, of the constitution of our divided selves, is one that must be explored in all its complex ramifications if humankind is to reach the higher levels of spiritual development necessary for our survival as a species. The patriarchal culture has analyzed the self in terms of space and to some extent in terms of processes of interaction that represent exchanges. Now it is necessary to set aside these either/ors and to analyze the self in terms of dynamic self substances formed by gender divisions during critical periods of pre-Oedipal infancy. We must begin to think of our selves, as psychologist Rollo May has suggested, in terms of time as well as space.

Dr. Larry Dossey reminds us that "bodies do not stay put; they are alive in space and time. The boundary of our physical self, our skin, is an illusion. It is no boundary at all, being constantly regenerated in only a matter of days" (Dossey 1982, 143). The new model of relationship emanating from the physical sciences of quantum physics, biochemistry, and medicine envisions a web of interconnections, linking us with each other, social universe to physical universe. In this new paradigm, "life is not the property of single bodies," states Dossey; it is, rather, "a property of the universe at large, connected, as are all living bodies, to all other things" (ibid., 144).

Both Dr. Dossey and Professor Lynch emphasize the need human beings have for each other; they recognize that physical, psychosexual, and spiritual development can occur only by means of human interrelationships. Lynch's research findings have dramatically underscored the vital physiological consequences of human dialogue. These findings cause Lynch to speculate, as have many feminist theorists, that "we are far less distinct and separate than we have been led to believe" (Lynch 1985, 179). Lynch asks, "What if all our bodies are part of a much larger body — the communal body of mankind?" (ibid.).

The theory of accomplicity suggests that this "communal body of mankind," which both unites and divides us, is the Freudian unconscious. Precipitated by the processes of accomplicity, arising from this social body are the dual structures of gender consciousness. Specifically, they are precipitated by means of the body dialogues of mother-infant and father-infant during the critical period of pre-Oedipal childhood. Lynch describes what he calls a "social membrane" that simultaneously separates and connects us to the world. Just as Freud claims that the unconscious is both social and individual, so, too, Professor Lynch speculates that the distinguishing characteristic of this social membrane "is that it belongs neither to the individual alone nor to the surrounding environment. Rather the membrane is two-sided, a filter that inextricably unites each person to the rest of the living world, while simultaneously keeping one separate" (Lynch 1985, 181).

This image of the "social membrane" describes the silent means by which human body dialogue produces human selves; it describes, I believe, the truth of the unconscious, simultaneously social and individual, the unconscious that simultaneously unites us and keeps us separate, providing the intersection of the timeless with time. In the next chapter, I further discuss the importance of temporal categories and relate the times of bodily cognition to the production of our divided selves by means of pre-Oedipal parenting practices. Here, I must note that there is some truth in the masculine myths I have been analyzing in order to unfold their hidden dimensions: These myths accurately describe an alienated reality; they describe the repression of part of the self that occurs during the Oedipus crisis, which I explain as a paradigm change of self in Chapter 5.

The fifth myth of masculine culture claims that women as mothers are omnipotent in relation to their children, yet weak and dependent in relation to their husbands and to male society. I have characterized this myth as best illustrating the contradictions prevailing in the patriarchy between the relations and forces of reproduction. The theory of accomplicity I have been describing is a theory of the production of the divided social-selves of girl and boy infant through proximity sense interactions with parents across a selective unconscious social membrane. The processes of accomplicity counter the myth of mother power/women's weakness by revealing hidden dimensions of power and weakness: There are ways in which women as mothers are not powerful vis-à-vis their children; there are ways in which women as competent human beings are not weak and dependent vis-à-vis men and masculine society.

I have discussed the patriarchal culture's stringent limitations upon the powers of mothers: Each mother is held to impossible ideals of unconditional love and perfect identification with her children's needs. I have suggested that it is as a mother that woman is least powerful and least free, given the present economic and cultural structures and norms. Oakley's study, *Becoming a Mother*, stresses that *"economically a woman with a baby is dependent in a way that a woman without a baby is not"* (Oakley 1980, 262). This lack of economic power in a money-is-power culture often renders mothers increasingly impotent. Having lost their own means of support, or hampered in economic competition by the time-consuming responsibilities of motherhood, women lose self-esteem and find it difficult to defend themselves from criticisms made by fathers in front of children. "Like it or not, power is what children learn to respect, and someone who is without it sinks very rapidly in their estimation," psychotherapist Natalie Shainess proclaims (Shainess 1984, 124).

Recent studies point clearly to economic factors as most determinant of power within the family, and of course men are the monopolizers of economic power in Western (and other) societies. As Oakley notes, "The father who earns money appears more powerful than the mother who spends it" (Oakley 1972, 181). To these "normal" power imbalances caused by the economic dependency of women with young children upon husbands must be added the abusive exercise of power by men in the form of wife beating and mental/emotional abuse. The topic of violence in the family, aside from that of child abuse, was virtually nonexistent in the family literature before 1970. Since 1970 an explosion of research and investigation into family violence of all kinds has demonstrated that wife battering has reached epidemic proportions in America (Berardo 1980, 42:143-55; see also studies by Straus & Hotaling 1980 and Straus et al., 1980). Lack of economic means and lowered self-esteem leave many women defenseless against their husbands' attacks. Through accomplicity children absorb into their divided selves the power conflicts of their parents.

Because until recently the patriarchal culture had succeeded in promulgating the myth of absolute mother power, it had also succeeded in spreading the idea that faulty children are the mother's fault. In fact, over recent years psychiatric and popular literature has been bulging with indictments of mothers, blaming them for everything from juvenile delinquency to autism and schizophrenia. Indeed, in the spring of 1989 in California, a mother was even arrested and held responsible for the gang-related crimes of her teenage son. (She was eventually released.)

Fortunately for many mothers, recent discoveries in the medical sciences have begun to uncover biochemical bases for autism, schizophrenia, and certain types of severe depression that have typically been blamed on faulty mothering. Other research points to the influence of the father (or of father absence or abandonment) in the production of juvenile delinquency, homosexuality, and other so-called deviant behaviors. Yet the consequences of power imbalances within patriarchal family structures need to be explored more fully. To some extent, however, recent empirical research within masculine psychology and medicine has drained the moat isolating the relationship of mother-child from the impact of the father, the environment, the culture, and biochemical anomalies.

Although the myth of absolute and perfect mother-power has been weakened, women as mothers do hold considerable power, both in relation to their children and vis-à-vis the patriarchal culture. This power is not the usual masculine hierarchical power — power over — but it is the kind of power women value, the power of relationship, the power of accomplicity. Feminist theorist Mary O'Brien focuses upon the potential power of women as socializers of young children. She emphasizes the revolutionary possibilities that would evolve from women's consciously seizing this power to shape the consciousness of their children, thereby creating new values (O'Brien 1983, 86–87). Again, I must qualify O'Brien's valuable insights, as I did those of Chodorow and Dinnerstein, by insisting that in order to effectively carry out a change of consciousness in their children, women must simultaneously develop what I call their minority selves. This would entail women's increasing their competence as economic providers and as producers of cultural symbols. Women must also change their own consciousness by becoming aware of the ways in which they form and develop the cognitive abilities of their infants.

And, finally, women theorists must develop the new models of psychosexual development that will demonstrate to men the need to cooperate with women in bringing about a revolution in the structuring of gender. If, as the theory of accomplicity asserts, children become the company they keep, then fathers as well as mothers have an interest in keeping company with their children. Fathers also have an interest in furthering egalitarian relationships with the mothers of their children, since the nature of children's developing selves centrally depends upon the nature of the relationship between their parents. Feminist theorist Sara Ruddick joins many other women thinkers in arguing for equal child caring on the part of men: "If men were emotionally and practically committed to childcare, they would reform the work world in parents' interests" (Ruddick in Trebilcot 1984, 226). Ironically, I believe it is women's attainment of greater economic and cultural power that will most effectively involve men in the nurturing of children.

I am convinced that greater parental involvement with cognitive growth from the earliest age will reveal that children's potentials have been underestimated. By pointing to the transmission of the cultural heritage via the proximity senses, the theory of accomplicity also reveals to us that cognitive development has been too narrowly conceived. Early education of sensory and bodily modalities (taste, touch, smell, and the kinesthetic senses, as well as hearing and sight) will certainly accelerate what have been more narrowly defined as intellectual abilities. Recent evidence from work with brain-damaged children, Glenn Doman's work in particular, and recent evidence regarding the very early growth and plasticity of the brain point toward a reevaluation of the mother-dominated period that patriarchal thought has characterized as primitive and emotional. Finally, evidence from historical studies of childhood suggests that early precocity is sensitive to cultural influence. When, between the seventeenth and the nineteenth centuries, the precociousness of young children began to be considered an anomaly, the child prodigies prevalent between the fifteenth and seventeenth centuries slowly disappeared (Ariès 1962, 193–231).

Thus, on the frontiers of several disciplines evidence is accumulating that demonstrates the considerable cognitive abilities of infants and toddlers and also, in turn, dignifies the work mothers and their surrogates do with young children. In fact, patriarchal civilization is beginning to understand that the early development of children is too important to be left in the hands of only one individual, of whichever sex; the job is too demanding, the expectations are growing too rapidly, the opportunities for positive results are too far reaching. As Montagu has noted, "The extent to which the child has played a role in the development of humanity has been severely neglected" (Montagu 1981, 81). In sum, women hold an enormous potential power to shape and develop their children, a power that has too often been short-circuited by the patriarchy. This hidden power of accomplicity also reaches into the psyches of adult men because, whether or not mothers realize their powers as producers of self-conscious fifth columns within male society, the dynamics of accomplicity currently do produce the conflicts and contradictions between our divided selves. These conflicts threaten to destroy not only social-selves, but as Dorothy Dinnerstein and Norman O. Brown have argued, patriarchal civilization itself.

THE THEORY OF ACCOMPLICITY: OUR SECRET SELVES

Finally, to deepen our insights into the true powers of women, in relation to their children and vis-à-vis patriarchal society, let us explore the meaning of love as a force in its relation to accomplicity. The last masculine myth presents love as a regressive force pulling everyone backward toward primitive symbiosis. By deconstructing the myths of mother-child symbiosis, of infant dependency and insatiability, of the child's need to break from mother, and of maternal omnipotence and feminine weakness, I have laid the ground from which, at last, the myth of love's retrogressive attraction will reveal its phantom character. We must understand that far from representing the call of the past and of the primitive, love — in the form of care and interrelationship — represents a potent progressive force that builds and produces the very structures of selfhood of every individual. There are differences both qualitative and quantitative in the care and time spent by mothers with girls as opposed to boys. These differences will be examined in greater detail in the next chapter. For now I must emphasize that the extended period of time spent by the mother with both sexes means that the majority self of both sexes — the child's dominant self — is mother-accomplished.

However, as I have demonstrated, the child's developing social-self is *not* merged in an isolated mother-child identity; rather, it interacts also with the father and with father figures, with the majority and minority selves of the mother (and father), and with the cultural surround. Because all these complex interactions give rise to "precipitates" of self, the child simultaneously develops a minority self that represents the patriarchal heritage of the father. This occurs with both girls and boys. Girls and boys alike simultaneously build up via the processes of accomplicity a social-self both divided by the contradictions between the relations and forces of reproduction and united by the heritage embodied in environmental structures, in nurturing figures, and in the unconscious social membrane.

The primary contradiction between the relations and forces of reproduction I have already characterized as that brought into existence by the contradiction between the responsibilities given to women as mothers and their impotence and lack of power as women culturally defined by men. I have suggested that women possess less power as mothers than the patriarchy has assumed and that, similarly, they possess more power vis-à-vis patriarchal society than is realized. These qualifications of current attitudes converge upon the theory of accomplicity.

On the highest level of abstraction, accomplicity as it applies to the interactions of individuals is a theory that explains the productions of processes. Therefore, it is a theory that overcomes the spurious dualisms endemic to masculine thought; that is to say, the theory of accomplicity helps to resolve the splits of subject/object, agency/structure, and reason/intuition, and most important, feminine/masculine. By developing in his metapsychology the intra- and intersystemic bridging devices of condensation and displacement, and by asserting the bisexuality of each individual, Freud has provided intellectual tools and clues that contribute to my theory of accomplicity.

Freud describes forces operating within the ego that bring about splitting and repression. Contemporary events reawaken these split-off and repressed elements, which gather strength thereby and try to force themselves to the surface of consciousness. When they do, the resistance of the censorships on the frontiers between the unconscious and the preconscious and consciousness brings about the compromise formations that neurotic symptoms and dreams represent. The elements of indeterminacy, and overdetermination, which characterize dream/symptom formation and the bridging of levels by means of the preconscious, are some of the dialectical elements I have identified in Freud's system.

As the schools of neo-Freudianism influenced by structural linguistics would say, the dream and the symptom are metaphors; they symbolize the self and its conditions of being. In fact, Freud's devices of condensation and displacement can be read as mechanisms of symbol and myth construction. These mechanisms bridge the levels within the self as well as the gaps between self and society. The symbolic structures thus produced are the filters operating within the social membrane. Furthermore, the idea of metaphoric knowledge points beyond the self to the culture in which self is grounded. Metaphors regulate the cultural paradigms; they are the symbolic filters by which wholeness is carved from infinite possibility. Metaphors regulate and open up possibility, just as they tend to cut away possibility. To understand the nature of cultural metaphor is to understand the nature of culture as tragedy. These ideas will be given greater definition in Chapter 6 as well as in future work.

Other dialectical elements are represented by Freud's understanding of the transformation of quantity (as in quantities of cathexis or of time) into quality, and vice versa, and by his simultaneous positing of ego as a precipitate of object-cathexes and as formed by processes, by instinctual forces and counterforces. Now, to these Freudian insights I add the concepts of the majority self formed by processes of accomplicity with the mother (or surrogate) and that of the minority self formed by processes of accomplicity with the father (or surrogate). The processes of accomplicity themselves must be visualized as the asymmetrical activities of interaction on the part of *both* the infant/child and parental figures; these interactions give rise in an indeterminate (because partly unconscious) manner to precipitates of substantive self that are mediated by the cultural surround. By introducing the idea of indeterminate (because unconsciously overdetermined) transformation, Freud has supplied us with the conceptual tools needed to overcome the subject/object split and the infinite regress that accompanies it.

The conceptual model Freud's system suggests is a complex one to visualize, accustomed as we are to one-dimensional modeling of sameness and difference. Here we must recognize that the sameness against which differences are measured is of another logical order and represents the possibilities of the cultural surround that mediates all interrelationships. The theory of accomplicity can be understood only by holding in mind two complementary, and contradictory, models, namely, the model of parent-child interaction and that of child-culture interaction. Ralph Waldo Emerson has wryly noted that such an intellectual feat is the mark of a superior mind.

The cultural surround and its unconscious counterpart, the social membrane, act as filtering paradigms, as selective systems of metaphors, which regulate and limit the number of possibilities available. In its operation the social membrane acts much as does the visual apparatus: Gordon Rattray Taylor explains that "the eye does not make absolute judgments of colour.... *[I]t makes only relative judgments* — and then treats them as absolute" (Taylor 1979, 207). This is what I have referred to as production by means of a dialectics of difference. Progress on both individual and cultural levels occurs only by means of differences that over time are precipitated into paradigms of culture and gender, which then function as absolutes against which new differences are measured.

Acting individuals do have limited choice, since some aspects of the culture's selective systems have been overdetermined. A given mother and child in patriarchal culture are more like other mothers and other children than one might wish to admit. Any particular mother and child, however, at some moments in time have the possibility of creating the unique through their interaction. For example, let us consider the problem of infinite regress: Does the child interacting with the mother's bisexuality — with her majority/minority selves — also interact with the bisexuality of each half ad infinitum? No. Infinite regress is halted because the interaction, the accomplicity, does give rise to precipitates, which build self structures that then function as anchors or absolutes. Note that this is the same concept on the level of social-self formation as the concept of the cultural reification of ideas in language. These reifications — these self precipitates — halt regress by acting as "unconditioneds," that is, as absolutes. They are also the necessary foundations for progress against which movement is measured. These difficult philosophical concepts can only be touched upon in this context. I will return to them briefly in Chapter 6 — and in future work.

In brief, when patriarchal philosophy eschews dialectical thought, criticizes reification, and condemns deconstruction, I would explain these prejudices psychoanalytically, that is, as reflective of masculine thought's desire to remain uncontaminated by what it *itself* has defined as feminine and, therefore, as inferior. In Faustian fashion the dominant culture has frozen time for all time in order to assure its own immortality and the immortality of those men who have fashioned it. Is this not the meaning of "eternal" truth in patriarchal religion, science, and philosophy?

Here, then, is the reason why even Freud could not push further his temporal analyses, although Freud had intimations of the rich insights that might be forthcoming. Earlier I mentioned that Freud had identified the id with the timelessness of the unconscious, with the transhistorical categories of phylogenetic inheritance of the primal deed of patricide. He also identified the superego with the inheritance of the historically determined moral values of the parents. He thought that the id and superego interacted, but he did not specify the fruits of this interaction. In Chapter 3, I drew attention to Freud's discovery of this intersection of time, or linear masculine history, with the timeless, that is, with that cyclical time associated by the patriarchy with reproduction and the feminine. I indicated that temporal categories are key to my transformation of the Freudian categories.

Now I suggest that instead of positing the opposition of the categories of time and the timeless, we instead contemplate the idea of various temporal modalities, some of which are more intimately linked with women and some with men. Theorist Mary O'Brien states, for example, that "female temporal consciousness is continuous, whereas male temporal consciousness is discontinuous" (O'Brien 1983, 32). O'Brien reaches this conclusion through her belief that the differing temporal modalities involved in the act of reproduction for female and male have far-reaching psychic ramifications for femininity and masculinity. She calls this "reproductive consciousness." I agree with her but again wish to emphasize that this is true, not because of any innate or natural valuations that are inevitably attached to the acts of insemination and parturition, but because of historical circumstances interacting with biology. These former have allowed men slowly to obtain the greater economic power and, with this, the power to define women and the feminine negatively. The discontinuous time sense of men is based, in my opinion, less on the biology of the inseminatory moment than on the act of separation, of avoidance, of rupture: Masculine discontinuity stems from a need to deny feminine connection — and contamination.

Edward Hall has demonstrated in *The Silent Language* (1973) that each culture constructs its own time sense and that each culture's time sense is multiple, as is the sense of space appropriate to occasion. So, too, Hall stresses the differing time senses of men and women within each culture. Robert Levine and Ellen Wolff in "Social Time: The Heartbeat of Culture" also insist that "to understand a society you must learn its sense of time" (Levine & Wolff 1985, 19:29). Far from being a rigid, clear-cut, monolithic category built forever into the functioning of our senses as Kant thought, Levine and Wolff present evidence that the pace of life varies considerably from culture to culture. Our rules of time are quite informal, they report. Furthermore, "the world over, children simply 'pick up' their society's time concepts as they mature. No dictionary clearly defines the meaning of 'early' or 'late' for them or for strangers who stumble over the maddening incongruities between the time sense they bring with them and the one they face in a new land" (ibid.).

Robert R. Holt, whose arguments for the structuring and development of primary process were discussed earlier, also speculates regarding "a cultural transmission of ways to dream, to fantasize consciously and unconsciously, even to construct delusional systems and other kinds of symptoms, ways that are culturally viable because rooted in certain kinds of world views, as Erikson's studies of some American Indian tribes have so beautifully shown" (Holt 1967, 375). In short, Holt theorizes that there may be *"cultural styles* of primary process" (ibid.). Of course, in so theorizing Holt is buttressing by implication and extension the notion of differing cultural temporalities as well. One finds, then, in all cultures not just a sense of "time lived" and "time by the clock," as French philosopher Henri Bergson would have it. Rather, one finds multiple senses of body time (in fact, the processes of accomplicity centrally depend upon the circadian rhythms of the heart, lungs, brain, and organs of secretion); and one finds multiple social times that change from culture to culture (work time, leisure time, times when young, middle aged and old, as well as the time of atomic physics and the time of paleontology). That the rhythms of the body are deeply affected by the rhythms of the culture is a logical extension of the research of both Holt and Hall and their research supports a central thesis of the theory of accomplicity: The most important times are gendered.

Masculine time, for example, is deceptively dual: Masculine time separates the continuous from the discontinuous (another objection to O'Brien's formulation: It uncritically repeats the masculine formula). Masculine time separates the time of the mother (pre-Oedipal period) from the time of the father (post-Oedipal period). During the time of the mother, according to masculine thought, nothing authentic can occur: The ego is either an identity (symbiosis with the mother) or narcissistic (self-identical); or it exists in an "imaginary" state, seeing itself reflected in the (m)other. If masculine thought recognized that the interacting continuities and overlapping of various temporal modalities in the processes of accomplicity result in precipitates of self (i.e., the triangulations of nonidentical modes of sensing/knowing constitute being), masculine thought would have to admit to the inevitable and everlasting contamination of (male) self by the feminine.

The crisis of Oedipus would then be understood, not as the choosing of masculine identity on the part of the boy (or of feminine identity by the girl), but as the impossible repression of the majority self (the mother-accomplished self) by the minority self (the father-accomplished self). In addition, patriarchal society would be forced to recognize that the only way that unique and individual selves can develop is in accomplicity with others, an accomplicity always mediated by the unconscious social membrane. Therefore, the very substance of each social-self partakes of the social-self of woman via the mother. The core of the masculine (and feminine) self is, in modern patriarchal cultures, mother-accomplished, that is, it participates in the mother's social-self via accomplicity.

Just as Freud's disciple Ferenczi noted that the character defenses *are* the self, so also is the majority self of the young child — of both sexes — a *feminine* self. This is true because of the nature of accomplicity as described and because of the extensive periods and intensive qualities of time in children's early affective/cognitive development during which the mother is lending herself to them, particularly through proximity sense interactions. Far from being a regressive force pulling us backward to primitive symbiosis, love exemplified by care and interrelationship (accomplicity) is the only means by which the human being is realized and can progress. If the love of woman for man and man for woman (or, woman for woman and man for man) recapitulates elements of the relationships of child to mother/father, it is not because of love's transhistorical phylogenetic nature. It is because the self-fulfilling forces of patriarchal definition and economic power have stalled the development of woman and, through her, stalled that of the masculine self sitting on the lid of his majority self. Patriarchal culture collapses the multiple dimensions of time and the multiple dimensions of our bigendered selves into a one-dimensionality that cripples our material, cognitive, and spiritual development.

Although loving interrelationships are essential for human survival and growth, we must avoid the dominant culture's one-dimensional model that blames conflict and neurosis on too much mother care or too little mother care. We must understand that accomplicity is always carried out by more than one person and that it may be evaluated along several dimensions, both quantitative and qualitative. It is especially important to remember that the minority self is produced by the father-child (or father surrogate–child) relationship and that this self is formed simultaneously with the formation of the majority self. Furthermore, since accomplicity includes cultural mediations, one must also evaluate the nature of the culture in which a child is being raised in order to evaluate the quality of a given accomplicity. Patriarchal cultures, for example, provide a degraded ideal of femininity for female children and an impossible masculinity for male children.

With the theory of accomplicity, we can begin to understand better why it is that children who have been abused, sexually or otherwise, often become abusers of others. The processes of accomplicity ensure that abusing becomes part of self. It is a fact that those individuals suffering from multiple personality disorder have been shown, almost without exception, to have suffered sexual abuse. In these extreme cases, the power of accomplicity appears to produce multiple selves, each cut off from the others, just as in "normal" cases the power of accomplicity produces the divisions of our feminine and masculine selves, along with the repressions, conflicts, and alienations from which they suffer.

The problem is not that we are all dual or multiple selves; the problem is that the abusive nature of patriarchal power structures – abusive to both boy and girl – divides us from ourselves and silences healing dialogues. Health and wholeness, Freud has taught us, lie in remembering, in the recovery of our lost selves.

Why is it that the majority self of both boys and girls is mother-accomplished? After all, if one wishes to abandon one-dimensional thought for more qualitative analyses, one could reasonably argue that although the mother does normally spend more time with infants and young children, the father may spend more quality time with them. To some degree, this indeed may be the case. And, as Caine points out, the "now, children, I can fit five minutes of quality time for you into my crowded schedule" syndrome afflicts working mothers even more than fathers (Caine 1985, 75). In fact, the idea of quality time is often the last thread by which harassed working mothers cling to a relatively guilt-free conscience. Quality time is usually mentioned in the same breath as "good enough" mothering, and "adequate" care.

However, the dialectical truth of accomplicity is that length of time spent often translates into quality of time spent: Programmed periods of five or ten minutes will not usually produce quality times. Unfortunately, most fathers spend neither great quantities nor great qualities of time with their infant/toddlers. The patriarchal socioeconomic system militates against it, even when fathers might be willing. The six masculine myths already discussed give fathers six reasons why spending time with very young children is not necessary – and maybe not even desirable. Men become the victims of their own mythology: By believing that mothers best know how to care for infants, they cripple their children's development as well as their own.

Fortunately, some modern fathers are discovering, as Pogrebin puts it, their "other selves"; they are rediscovering what I have been calling their majority selves, long ago repressed, if not totally extinguished. However, studies of father-baby (or father-child) accomplicity still produce dismally low estimates of their quality time together. Pogrebin cites one famous study showing that "the average father interacts with his baby for less than 38 seconds a day. In 38 seconds, you cannot change a diaper or sing three verses of 'The Farmer in the Dell.' The *most* time any father in this sample devoted to his infant in one day was 10 minutes, 26 seconds – barely enough time for a bottle and a burp" (Pogrebin 1984, 201). Other studies have discovered that many fathers spend as much as twenty to twenty-six minutes per day with children under five; less with children six to seventeen years old. This is barely enough time to produce the child's minority self.

In *Psychoanalysis and Women* Jean Baker Miller summarizes my point when she states: "The child is led to believe that he or she has a father, and in essence, he or she does not. Rather, the child has a legal relative who says, in effect, 'I am dominant and do the important things. I leave the major interaction in your development to your mother because it is a lesser matter.' The inevitable conclusion is that dominance and important affairs do not include involvement in the growth of another human being" (Miller 1978, 396).

More than the majority self of each child participates in the selfhood of the mother through accomplicity. When the lack of status of the mother is fully realized by the child, the child's substantive self (comprised of both the majority and minority selves) is wounded. Freud called this realization and this wounding the Oedipus crisis.

Freud avoided the understanding of how the mother's very self is implicated and woven into that of the child's. He avoided this insight because of his masculine prejudices, which determined his handling of temporal categories. If the boy's substantive self is in some sense implicated in the mother's self, this would represent too much contamination by femininity, too much even for Freud with his theory of human bisexuality. But Freud was also constrained by the dominant patriarchal philosophy with its subject/object split. I submit that this split itself grew out of the separation of masculinity from femininity in the patriarchal culture's sex/gender divisions of labor.

The subject/object split is represented within the Freudian system by Freud's theories of identification and object-choice (discussed earlier in Chapter 3), and by Freud's ideas regarding introjection and projection. Once subject is split off from object, then the question must arise, how are subjects and objects related to each other? How does the outside get "in," and the inside, "out"? Moreover, how indeed are these inner and outer realities related to each other? These are the problems patriarchal social theory spawns; introjection/projection, and identification/object-choice represent Freud's solutions to these problems.

The theory of accomplicity overcomes these divisions and by so doing opens up a totally new vision of psychosexual development. Freud does attempt to overcome these dichotomies (subject/object, self/other, inner/outer) by means of the metaphor of incorporation. "Identification," he explains in various texts, is like an "oral, cannibalistic incorporation of the other person" (Freud [1916–33] 1966, 527). With these images Freud tries to illustrate an inextricable mingling of subject and object and the production of new portions of the self, such as the superego. My theory of the processes of accomplicity, resulting in the production of majority and minority selves, transforms and expands upon this neglected Freudian objective.

To differentiate what is meant by accomplicity from that which the term *identification* has come to mean, one must be able to visualize the difference between an incorporation that creates a new synthesis — new individual self substance — out of the selves of mother and infant, for example, and the merging or fusion that symbiosis represent: here all individuality is extinguished by identity. To avoid a common confusion, please note that the idea of attaining an identity is popularly used to mean finding one's unique self and becoming "self-identical."

Freud implicitly understands that we are *never* unsplit, or self-identical. For Freud and for patriarchal culture, identification with father or mother at the time of the Oedipus complex in order to attain a masculine or feminine identity is, as Mannoni states, to lose one's uniqueness. Therefore, sexuality — femininity and masculinity — exists in the minds of men, not to further individuation and the progress of the individual toward greater maturity, but to service reproduction of the species. Although masculine mythology assigns individuation only to the spheres inhabited by men, it is indeed a paradoxically desexualized individuation.

Jean Baker Miller, like Carol Gilligan, has recognized the need for theories that take into account women's unique values and women's existential realities. In this context Miller emphasizes the importance to women of the maintenance of relationship and that "for many women, the threat of disruption of an affiliation is perceived not just as a loss of a relationship but as something closer to a total loss of self" (quoted in Gilligan 1982, 16:77) Miller and Gilligan also believe that "the boundaries between self and others are less than they sometimes seem" (ibid.).

The theory of accomplicity provides an explanation for these facts and feelings. Women's gender consciousness and the truths of accomplicity are exemplified in anthropologist Susan Harding's description of women in a Spanish village: "Her role requires that she identify [note ubiquity of term *identification*] with her charges, especially her children, to such an extent that she may experience insecurities about them as insecurities about herself. Given her position, and as a result of her worldly inexperience and primary cultural formation, a woman becomes unusually vulnerable to fear. [She imagines the worst if child is lost.] ... It is as if she had lost track of a part of herself" (Harding in Reiter 1975, 292). Harding attributes these responses to the provincial nature of these women, yet, I assert, these responses are not at all uncommon among Western women; they testify to the power of accomplicity to lay down the structures of selfhood for both mother and child.

In fact, it is common enough to hear references to a man's or boy's "woman within" (Chodorow quoted in Thurman 1982, 11:36). Social critic Theodore Rozak speaks of the woman locked in men's "psychic dungeons"; Coppelia Kahn, of women's presence in the character structures of men. Adrienne Rich debates whether men's selves include a "ghostly woman." My theory of accomplicity explains that the man's "woman within" is an inalienable portion of each man's self.

Modell, the object relations theorist who, far from solving the subject/object split in his work, appears to declare this split a solution, has gone so far as to comment, "It is as if the process of loving consists of the mingling and sharing of psychic substances" (Modell 1968, 62). This indeed is one way of viewing accomplicity. And Erikson gives this interesting account: "Fathers ... function somewhat like guardians of the child's autonomous existence. Something passes from the man's *bodily presence* [my emphasis] into the child's budding self — and I believe that the idea of *communion*, that is, of partaking of a man's body, would not be such a simple and reassuring matter for so many were it not for that early experience" (Erikson 1962, 124). That to which all these different accounts allude is given substance by the theory of accomplicity.

In sum, the theory of accomplicity overcomes important dilemmas of patriarchal psychological theory; it fits more closely recent empirical evidence accumulating regarding the nature of early development and the pre-Oedipal mother-child, father-child, and mother-father-child relationships. It is also consonant with the experiential reality of women as mothers and the intuitions of some patriarchal theorists, including Freud.

In addition, accomplicity casts light upon the "hidden connections" within Western culture, between the "processes of knowing and loving ... that have not as yet been fully appreciated" (Modell 1968, 58). Sociologist Richard Sennett once commented upon the modern quest for self by means of the genitals (1978, 7), and French philosopher Michel Foucault similarly remarked that "sex was constituted [for Western man] as a problem of truth" (Foucault 1980, 56). These intimations become perfectly intelligible when, by the light of accomplicity, one recognizes the dialectical implication of the other in the constitution of the self, when one understands the dialectical interrelationship between being and knowing, between caring and being.

Writer Meg Campbell recounts how "my best friend in high school used to theorize that the reason you missed somebody was because you missed the side of yourself that only that particular person was able to bring out. You missed part of yourself" (Campbell 1984, 13:140). Accomplicity explains that this "bringing out" can be more precisely described as co-creation, and that this co-creation is the essence of human interrelationship.

The theory of accomplicity states that the mother, in a seemingly paradoxical manner, co-constitutes the majority selves of both sexes, and that in early childhood the majority self is, as the name implies, the dominant self of both girl and boy. The denigration of the feminine in masculine cultures, then, comes to be experienced by both boy and girl as a denigration of self. This double bind is handled differently by girl and by boy, since the culture makes available (or nonavailable) different resources to each of them. The products of the processes of accomplicity are children's dual social-selves. It is in this sense that Freud was correct when he claimed that psychoanalysis is a social psychology because an other is always implicated in the constitution of the self.

The theory of accomplicity explains not only how the other is implicated in the substance/structures of selfhood but also how this process creates the substance/structures of culture and community. Upon these tacit and unconscious social structures, social contracts are erected. Patriarchal civilization misapprehends accomplicity, a process that explains that the denigration of femininity results in repression of majority selves in boys and the alienation of majority selves in girls. Finally, the theory of accomplicity also explains the paradoxical crises of majority and minority selves, which I describe in the following chapter.

In conclusion, I have presented the six persistent myths of masculine thought and patriarchal culture and demonstrated that these myths also underlie much feminist thought. Through my critique of these myths I reveal a new vision of the production of dual selves within each woman and man through processes of interaction that I call accomplicity. The conflicts and contradictions between these selves are caused, I suggest, by family power structures that reflect the power structures of the wider culture. The relative lack of cultural power of the mother as opposed to the father brings about what Freud calls the Oedipus complex. Freud believed that all later neurosis traced its seeds to this period of crisis.

Freud posits a pre-Oedipal time of the mother as constituting one paradigm of self, and a post-Oedipal time of the father as constituting another. The period of Oedipal crisis represents for Freud that inter-paradigmatic period during which the self must dramatically change allegiance. Earlier I critiqued this dominant model of change as it presents itself in the work of Kuhn. I pointed out the logical contradictions of this model in which two succeeding paradigms are seen to represent both change and progress. Where the succeeding paradigm is seen to be incommensurable (noncomparable) with the preceding paradigm, I have pointed out that there can be no grounds upon which to declare one or the other superior. The reading of Freud dominant today, which parallels the Kuhnian model, reveals the same logical weaknesses. The motive force behind this model is to keep the masculine ego free from contamination by the feminine (mother).

The theory of accomplicity opens up a new vision of the production of the self. Differential processes of interaction with mother and father (or father surrogate) produce two selves. The boy's, as well as the girl's, majority selves are produced by means of accomplicity with the mother. Therefore, contamination of the boy by the feminine is unavoidable: All boys develop a feminine majority self.

Although the Freudian system has reinforced in ways previously mentioned most of the prevalent masculine myths as well as the subject/object split, Freud's greatness consists in his having simultaneously opened doors to the transcendence of these myths. Because Freud stubbornly refused to abandon his *shibboleth* of childhood bisexuality, he kept alive the problematic of the female sex and of the woman as mother. Freud insisted upon the coexistence in each self of what he called the negative Oedipus complex. Therefore, despite Freud's difficulty with the problem of origins and his resulting proposal of phylogenetic inheritance, Freud's theory of the ego's becoming is not a theory of *re*production, but rather a theory of production. It is also not a theory of self-creation, but one of co-creation. The self is multiple for Freud and is the product of family relationships, as well as the product of relationships with the biological and social heritage via the unconscious. By means of his symbol- and symptom-producing devices of condensation and displacement, Freud also supplies the theoretical openings whereby levels are bridged within the self and between the self and the culture.

Conceptually, Freud has presented us with dialectical openings that permit us to envision the theory of accomplicity and the participation of the mother's social-self in producing the majority selves of her children. In this theory loving/caring, especially through the proximity senses, is transformed from a regressive state and activity to that ultimate progress without which there can be no spiritual development. Freud was correct, however, in many of his formulations, which describe a stalled process of social-self formation, a self divided against itself without the means for healing dialogues. Freud describes the modern condition wherein "the story of humanity has stopped." In both Freud's time and our time, neither sex is whole: Mermaid and minotaur, satyr and sphinx, women and men remain equally arrested half-selves; they are equally trapped living half-lives in "Flatland."

At present, the structures of selfhood are a repressed duality, masquerading as identity. The selfhoods of the future will be multi-dimensional. The fact that all dimensions cannot be equally and simultaneously present to consciousness will have a qualitatively different impact upon future imaginations than the concept of the unconscious has upon us today. Human beings will be ever ready to summon and entertain the invisible; abstract and concrete will meet in the pulse of accomplicity and in the asymmetrical halls of time.

In the following chapter I further clarify the issues of sexuality, of the mother's body, and of the concept of accomplicity. I discuss why Freud was correct in rejecting Jung's suggestion of an Electra complex for the girl that would symmetrically balance the boy's Oedipus complex. In Chapter 6, I show why Freud's intimations of the closer relationship of sadism to masculinity and of masochism to femininity remain correct and also why he was correct in asserting their coexistence in each social-individual. The theory of accomplicity, of the production of majority and minority social-selves, casts new light upon sadomasochistic phenomena and helps to explain Freud's puzzlement regarding these phenomena; it also clarifies the impetus behind some forms of homosexuality.

5

Big into Small: The Repression of the Majority Self

Deeper than the problem of the relation between the sexes is the problem of the reunification of the sexes in the self.

Norman O. Brown

DOING THE IMPOSSIBLE: BECOMING A MAN

I have discussed logical inconsistencies in prevailing patriarchal systems of thought: Where absolute identities are proclaimed and where a monolithic block universe is equated with Unitary Truth, no change or development is possible. Origins are not only obscured, they become unthinkable. I have suggested that the dominant culture's abhorrence of duality, complementing its insistence upon identity, stems from the anxiety-producing nature of sexual dimorphism. Aeons ago men defined women as identical to nature. Centuries ago this masculine equation caused men to view women as inferior because, like nature, women were viewed as locked into cyclical time and therefore unable to evolve. In the sexual division of labor, women were charged with responsibility for biological *re*production and men with cultural production. The value of cultural production could only be measured against the undeveloped and purportedly static worlds of nature, women, children — and the impoverished.

Furthermore, patriarchal culture made women identical with material life, with sex, and with the body. These dilemmas of masculine thought and life are epitomized by philosopher William James's emphatic pronouncement, *"The intellectual life of man consists almost wholly in his substitution of a conceptual order for the perceptual order in which his experience originally comes"* (James 1953, 77). Of course, what really counts for man is intellectual life, that is, reason and objective facts. In James's statement the famous subject/object, mind/body split of the seventeenth century achieves its modern avatar as the split between concept and percept. Few patriarchal thinkers have addressed themselves to puzzling out the relationship between these poles.

Within the dominant culture the problem of transition from one level to another remains unexplained, and the questions of progress, development, and origins are left unanswered. The very recent glimmer of an understanding that percepts also develop — and develop in dialectical reciprocity with concepts — has not yet penetrated and broken down these compartmentalizations within patriarchal thought. However, it bears repeating that these divisions are spurious dualisms. I call them "closet monisms" because one half of the duality is viewed as reducible or inferior to the other half. Each half is hierarchically and rigidly cordoned off from the other half; no dialogue is permitted.

In fact, the one theme that unites modern intellectual giants such as Nietzsche, Freud, Husserl, and Whitehead is that of the "widening chasm" that they document within the Western psyche. They all warn about the divisions increasing between reason and the affective life. In Thomas S. Kuhn's seminal book *The Structure of Scientific Revolutions*, discussed in Chapter 2, I stated that humanity is experiencing a paradigm change upon a vast scale. In support of this idea, I quoted Roger Walsh, who describes the changes now occurring. "The classical Greek concept of the universe as essentially atomistic, divisible, isolatable, static, non-relativistic, and comprehensible by reductionism, is in the process of replacement, not just for physics . . . but for all sciences" (Walsh & Vaughan 1980, 222).

I also drew upon the work of physicist Werner Heisenberg, who, in *Physics and Philosophy*, clarified the ways in which knowing determines being, in which our universe is a "participatory" universe. Heisenberg believed that much time must pass before Western cultures absorbed the meaning of his principle of indeterminacy which leads to the conclusion that the knower is inextricably involved with the constitution of the known. This involvement raises chance and choice to ontological validity. Heisenberg thought that the spirit of an age was as real as any other hard fact. Heisenberg drew out the implications of quantum mechanics for philosophy and psychology: The most important implication for this study is the need for a disciplined subjectivity.

Building upon these new insights, I called for a theory of cultural indeterminacy that will respect the reality of interactive dualisms and of the dual existential realities of the sexes. I noted that the gaps between levels, between paradigms as well as between conscious and unconscious structures, are suppressed by patriarchal thought through theories of identity and correspondence which completely close off potentials for change. Principles of indeterminacy and models of complementarity are ignored. Only by means of such principles, which dignify difference and validate disciplined subjectivity, can new life-enhancing consciousness be born.

In addition, I noted that Kuhn's failure to account for cultural progress during scientific revolutions stemmed from the logical paradox inherent in his implied comparison of what he claimed were noncommensurable (and therefore noncomparable) periods of normal science. For if structured periods alternate with periods of no structure, and if the structured periods are totally noncommensurable, then upon what basis can progress or development be claimed? Further, what are the principles that determine – or regulate – the new formations out of the structure-less interregnums? Here again patriarchal thought has developed an equation wherein absolute difference (the noncommensurable paradigms) is identical to absolute sameness; that is, all paradigms must be equally valid, since there are no bases presented for preferring one paradigm to another; therefore, they are all equivalent. Progress, development, origins, and transitions are all negated.

Unfortunately, this paradigm of progress has been the archetypical model of patriarchal culture. I further noted that this model can be found in the Freudian system: The pre-Oedipal mother-dominated period equals one paradigm of self; the post-Oedipal father-dominated period equals another. These two noncommensurable periods of paradigmatic normalcy are separated by the period of personal crisis and chaos represented by the Oedipus complex. Kuhn's – and patriarchal thought's – logical dilemmas are also reflected in Freud's Oedipal schema: The post-Oedipal period is supposed to represent a progression, since the Oedipus crisis is resolved by the male through an identification with the superior father. (Freud admitted that he could present clearly only the developmental crisis of the male child.) Yet the idea of identification and becoming the same as, like that of absolute difference (incommensurability), negates the idea of progress. For Kuhn, each paradigmatic period of scientific normalcy was simultaneously different from that which preceded it and yet was superior to that which preceded it. For Freud, the paradigmatic period of the father is superior to that of the mother; that of the mother, related to the natural, never changes; that of the father also is transhistorical in so far as the attainment of masculinity is dependent upon the primal deed of patricide. However, Freud does admit that some evolution takes place: What was once an actual murder is now a symbolic one. And what was once an incestuous seduction or rape of the female now has become — at the least — a symbolic rape. Yet, paradoxically, Freud asserted that the evolution of civilization was bringing about ever-increasing guilt for the modern individual. Freud's presentation of these ideas is contradictory and ambivalent. As in Kuhn's model, it is impossible to account for progress where differences (each individual's masculinity) are simultaneously rendered absolute and identical.

With the Oedipus complex Freud reduces the individual (father) to his sexual identity — to his masculinity. When the son identifies with his father in order to obtain an identical masculinity, all change, evolution, and progress are foreclosed. To quote the French neo-Freudian O. Mannoni once again, "Identity is nothing but the socially accepted form of lost uniqueness" (Mannoni 1974, 185). Carrying this line of reasoning to its logical conclusion, masculinity, then, as male culturally defined can have nothing to do with the uniqueness of the person, with originality and creativity. Men have "murdered to create" but their creation is death — the death of their own uniqueness.

Freud does not, however, rest content, like Kuhn and others, to present a model of a monolithic noncommensurable self collapsing into a chaos from which another monolithic self is somehow constituted. Freud breaks the monolithic self apart: From the very beginning, Freud proclaimed that the individual is not identical with his conscious mind. Moreover, Freud's noncommensurate levels of consciousness, the conscious and the unconscious, are related not only via the transitional layer of preconscious mind but also by means of the bridging devices of condensation and displacement, which construct and deconstruct images and symbols. The Oedipus crisis, which represents a progression, also precipitates a loss: Part of the self is repressed or split off.

Today we see in the work of neo-Freudians, in Jacques Lacan's work especially, a denial of reality to the pre-Oedipal mother-involved period. This denial represents patriarchal culture's solution to the problem of contamination by the feminine. We see in the work of other thinkers, and to some degree in Freud himself, that this contamination by the feminine is avoided because an object-cathexis is regarded as exchanged — like an object external to self — for an identification. This identification is reified in words and concept into objectlike obduracy. For object relations theorists object-cathexis represents a cord, or apronstring, which can be cut; it is a bond that can be dissolved, like glue holding exterior surfaces together.

Despite this neo-Freudian emphasis upon exchange, I have emphasized that Freud describes the processes of interaction between mother and child as doing more than effectuating an exchange: Freud also describes these processes as precipitating the very structures of selfhood. Freud is important on an epistemological level because his is the only influential masculine system that has centrally incorporated a dialectics of power and nonidentity, a dialectics of difference. Being—the structures of selfhood—is constituted through difference within a cultural matrix. My critique of Freud's metapsychology revealed the mingling and mutual checkmating of elements both Kantian, that is, based upon subject/object splits, and dialectical, that is, based upon principles such as condensation and displacement, which can account for transitions, and bridge levels and explain origins, change, and developing structures of selfhood.

Although Freud's system, like most patriarchal models, does not contain a well-developed theory of culture nor fully explains feminine development, Freud does provide valuable clues toward such theories. Freud's concepts of bisexuality, of the unconscious, and of the Oedipus complex are in fact essential for the construction of such theories.

I discussed in Chapter 4 the ways in which children in patriarchal cultures develop two selves arising out of interactions with their mothers and fathers (or surrogates). I preceded this discussion with a critique and destructuring of the six masculine myths that have prevented us from understanding our origins and development. Logical analysis, recent scientific studies, and the testimony of women as mothers all support my argument that the infant's early world is neither merged with the mother's nor entirely separated from hers; that the child is not totally passive and dependent; that the child's desires are not insatiable; that children never entirely "break" from their mothers or fathers, but that the relationship changes qualitatively. Finally, I discussed the ways in which mothers are not omnipotent in relation to their children and are not weak in relation to patriarchal culture. The last two assertions depend, I stated, upon a clear understanding of love/caring—especially as manifested through the proximity senses. I call the productive forces that form each individual's dual selves the power of accomplicity.

The task of this chapter is to further clarify the nature of accomplicity by analyzing its part in the production of masculinity and femininity during early pre-Oedipal periods of infant development. Since Freud spoke most often and most confidently of the boy, I will consider the boy's development first. This order of presentation will permit the girl's Oedipus crisis to be thrown into sharper contrast. Therefore, in the sections that follow I will first discuss the Oedipus complex of the boy;

next, that of the girl; then, I will speak about how patriarchal culture, by forcing a paradigm change of social-self in the boy and by preventing one in the girl, cuts both off from further development. I will conclude by clarifying the concept of accomplicity itself. An understanding of this new model of psychosexual development will bring into sharp relief the difficulty, if not the impossibility, facing a boy when he attempts in modern patriarchal cultures to "become a man."

Freud's Oedipus theory is a theory of the genesis of the nearly mature masculine self in an identification with the father. One of Freud's classic statements explains that

the Oedipus-complex offered the child two possibilities of satisfaction, an active and a passive one. It could have put itself in its father's place and had intercourse with the mother as he did, so that the father was soon felt to be an obstacle; or else it had wanted to supplant the mother and be loved by the father, whereupon the mother became superfluous. . . . If the gratification desired in consequence of the love is to cost the child his penis, a conflict must arise between the narcissistic interest in this part of the body and the libidinal cathexis of the parent-objects. Normally, in this conflict the first of these forces triumphs; the child's ego turns away from the Oedipus-complex. . . . The object-cathexes are given up and replaced by identification. (Freud [1906–24] 1959: 272–73)

Freud goes on to assert that the superego is formed at this time because the identification with the father causes his authority and severity to be "introjected into the ego." The superego so formed acts as a barrier against mother-son incest and prevents "a recurrence of the libidinal object-cathexis. The libidinal trends belonging to the Oedipus-complex are in part desexualized and sublimated, which probably happens with every transformation into identification; in part they are inhibited in their aim and changed into affectionate feelings. The whole process, on the one hand, preserves the genital organ, wards off the danger of losing it; on the other hand, it paralyses it, takes away its function from it" (ibid., 273). By this "paralysis" Freud means to signal the beginning of the latency period, that period between the boy's Oedipus crisis, occurring at approximately three to five years of age, and puberty. Freud thought that the Oedipus complex, resolving for the boy his castration complex (and thereby ensuring the health and welfare of his penis — read "masculine prerogatives"), caused a repression of sexual instincts and a boy's renouncing of masturbation.

In Freud's account of the Oedipus complex, I note the following essential points: First, Freud's account is based on his assumption of early bisexuality: The boy can assume a feminine or a masculine position in relation to the father. Here I agree with Freud, although I will offer another angle of vision upon this bisexuality when I elaborate the theory of the majority and minority social selves. I have already noted and critiqued the dual relational modes of object-cathexis and identification Freud employs. It is at this point that Freud slips back into the Kantian mode of subject/object split and offers up yet another exchange theory. According to Freud, the boy exchanges his object-cathexes (the latter primarily attaching to the mother) for an identification with the father. The theory of accomplicity explains why this is impossible: The object-cathexes (read "interrelationships producing substantive self") *are* in a special sense the boy's self, specifically, his majority self. The identification-with-father aspect of the Oedipus complex represents what I call the boy's minority self. Therefore, the Oedipus complex itself is not an exchange of objects or of object relationships: It is a paradigm change of self. Most important, the dominant self — the mother-accomplished majority self — becomes repressed as the boy struggles to make his minority self dominant.

I will discuss this momentous revolution in the social-self in greater detail shortly. At this point, note that Freud claims that the identification with the father also causes desexualization and sublimation of the boy's libidinal trends. It is important to understand that Freud describes the attainment of masculinity through father identification by the boy as a partial desexualization and sublimation because Freud himself tacitly understood that the destruction-repression of the object-cathexes to mother (i.e., the boy's majority self) meant the destruction-repression of the boy's feminine self — that which masculine culture defines as equaling primitive and undeveloped sexuality and sensuousness.

Freud compounds the contradictions in his account when he later defines a hero as "a man who stands up manfully against his father and in the end victoriously overcomes him" (Freud 1939, 9). We must ask the question, just where is the heroism in the partial resolution of the Oedipus complex when it requires that the boy give up his love for his mother (read "his majority self") and adopt the defensive mode of identification with an aggressor? For is it not true that, according to Freud, fear of the father's wrath and of the consequences of it, namely, castration (read "cultural impotence") motivate the boy to resolve the Oedipus complex by "joining the winner," namely, the parent with the greatest economic and cultural power?

Freud had theorized that both boys and girls first view their mother as phallic, that is, as possessed of a penis, and that this view permitted them to consider her as powerful. The castration complex that initiated the Oedipus complex for the boy represents that moment when the boy discovers the shocking truth that his mother lacks a penis, or, as Freud puts it, is "already castrated" (read "culturally impotent"). In modern times this aspect of the Freudian system has undergone various transformations. Some scholars, John and Beatrice Whiting among them, explain masculine aggression and violence as a reaction on the part of boys who discover as they reach young adulthood that their powerful mothers, those with whom they have a primary identification, are weak in relation to the patriarchal world outside the domestic spheres (Sanday 1981, 182).

Here we recognize again one of the popular masculine myths discussed in Chapter 4. Many women thinkers from Chassequet-Smirgel and Karen Horney to Dorothy Dinnerstein explain masculine contempt for women as a defense against the overpowering and frustrating mother. Nancy Chodorow states that mothers, lacking nurturing from their own mothers and from their husbands, sexualize their relationships with their sons and thus bring about the boy's Oedipus crisis earlier than the girl's. Like Norman O. Brown, she implies that human beings are *self*-repressed when she states, "a boy represses those qualities he takes to be feminine inside himself" (Chodorow 1978, 181).

The theory of accomplicity explains why feminine qualities do not exist inside the boy to be self-repressed. The boy's Oedipus complex is not a result of the shock of viewing his mother's or other females' penis-less genitals. The processes of mother-infant accomplicity have produced the boy's majority self which in this special sense *is* in part the boy's self and cannot be said to exist inside the boy. However, because the boy does not grow up in a dual relationship with the mother but has some direct contact with the patriarchal culture and with the father or other males, the boy simultaneously develops a minority self by means of father-accomplicity. Indeed, shock and trauma do come to the boy: The boy does discover that his mother is weaker than he had realized, that his mother does not have great economic or cultural power, and that the traits defined as feminine are not respected by patriarchal culture. He also begins to understand that further development leading to greater power, to money, prestige, and possible immortality (cultural powers of creation) are possible only by means of the development of his minority self. The Oedipus crisis represents for the boy a conflict between his two developing selves, which are interrelated, mediated by the culture — specifically through the proximity senses — and relatively autonomous from each other.

The central drama of the Oedipus crisis for the boy is not, as Freud supposed, a repetition of the primal desire to murder the father (ending with capitulation in identification), although the crisis does constitute a rupture of the self no less dramatic. The resolution of the Oedipus crisis is more closely akin to a matricide as the boy "murders" his mother-accomplished majority self by means of a repression. This paradoxical paradigm change of self in which the minority self replaces the till now dominant majority self would scarcely be possible were it not for the collusion of the mother, the father, and the patriarchal culture. Freud's version notwithstanding, the mother-son relationship *is* a highly motivated and "interested" relationship, and therefore the mother all too willingly betrays her own sex. Ann Oakley explains, in patriarchal terminology, that "the mother pressures the male child to sever the bonds of mothering and he learns to reject feminine identification" (Oakley 1976, 197).

Boys enter early into the Oedipus situation because at the age of three or four or five their encounters with the patriarchal culture multiply and they grasp more fully the scorn reserved for the feminine. Ironically, they also frequently absorb these understandings from females — mothers, grandmothers, teachers, aunts, neighbors — who take their job of socializing any "sissy" traits out of him very seriously indeed. Beginning from the boy's infancy, these women are eager to produce the little men in whose reflected glory they expect to bask. Besides, they are quite aware of the absolute contempt in which they will be held by all should their boy children exhibit the slightest "effeminate" characteristics. One source quotes a writer who points out that "a father may say of his young daughter, 'Yes, she loves sports. She's our little tomboy,' but no one would dare say of a small boy, 'Yes, he's our little marygirl' " (Abbott & Love 1978, 21).

The ubiquitous world of sports, which becomes salient to children at least by grammar school, has been, and despite Title IX still is, a world dominated by men, a distillation of masculine qualities. A not untypical sports column reads: "In the National League, they're tough. Chest hair and deep voices. Get hurt, you stay in the game. Break a bone? Rub some pine tar on it and get back to your position" and "In the NL (Nail-eaters League), with slashing cleats you attempt to sever the legs of the opponent's pivot man to bust up the double play" (Ostler 1984, III:3). New York psychiatrist Dr. Natalie Shainess has commented that "sports are selling murderous aggression and fantasized superiority" (Siegel 1984, III:3). Yet in a society where sports are a metaphor for patriarchal life (the businessman, the doctor, the president's men are, after all, part of a "team" developing "game plans" designed to "win" or make them appear as "winners"), who can blame the young boy who decides to play baseball rather than practice the piano. Still, one should not underestimate the difficulties inherent in this Oedipal revolution, which I characterize as the paradoxical suppression of the boy's majority self by his minority self. It is no simple matter of exchanging an object-cathexis for an identification as one might exchange a pitch-pipe for a baseball cap. And neither is the outcome simple, clear-cut, and conflict-free.

Freud was reported to have been panic-stricken when he wrote about the murder of the father at the end of *Totem and Taboo* (1913). Mannoni contrasts Freud's great agitation anticipating the reception to his theory of patricide with Freud's relative calm when baring his atheism in *The Future of an Illusion* (1927). Freud theorized that the original sin for which Christ gave his life was indeed this patricide, this murder of the father; and, on the symbolic level of religious belief, Freud noted that "a son-religion displaced the father-religion" (Freud [1913] 1950, 154). Mannoni attributes Freud's greater emotional involvement in *Totem and Taboo* to Freud's realization that "the murder of the father was the very knot of the feeling of guilt and, so to speak, the place where it could be untied" (Mannoni 1974, 165).

Freud might well panic over the untying of this knot, since deeper than the father murder and the son religion lie the mother murder and the great mother religions. With the theory of accomplicity, I am reinstating the centrality of matricide which is the murder by repression of the boy's majority self. This reinterpretation of Freud's Oedipus complex explains its longevity as a theory and should redirect the fervent controversy that still surrounds it by clarifying its partial truths.

I agree with Erik Erikson when he asserts that "underneath his proud sense of autonomy and his exuberant sense of initiative the troubled American (who often looks the least troubled) blames his mother for having let him down" (Erikson 1963, 296). In the same context, Erikson continues, "But wherever our methods permit us to look deeper, we find at the bottom of it all the conviction, the mortal self-accusation, that it was *the child who abandoned the mother*, because he had been in such a hurry to become independent" (ibid.). The striking new vision is that the castration complex does exist: The boy and girl discover the weakness of the mother, specifically, her cultural impotence, and it is this discovery which causes the infamous narcissistic wound to the child's self. The child is wounded not because, as Chassequet-Smirgel, Brunswick, Lampl-de Groot, Chodorow, Dinnerstein, and others believe, the pre-Oedipal phallic mother holds omnipotent power over them. The child is wounded because the child's own majority self is a mother-accomplished self, and therefore the mother's cultural castration is the child's cultural castration.

Sex researcher Shere Hite's study of American men has uncovered facts supportive of this interpretation. Hite states flatly that "most men did not admire their mothers" (Hite 1985, 118). Hite discovered that many men were angry at their mothers and that they hated them for being submissive to their fathers. It is an anger caused not by the mother's abandonment, nor by the mother's omnipotence, nor by her frustrating the child in infancy. It is, as Freud first indicated, an anger born out of the child's resentment upon discovering the mother's castration, and this castration is cultural, that is, symbolic. This interpretation finally makes comprehensible Lacan's claims that the mother must recognize the father's law-giving function, and respect his speech (word), so that the child may accept "symbolic castration by the father" (Lemaire 1981, 234). This "symbolic castration" performed on the son by the father is none other than the father's amputation of the son's majority self by means of repression. The son's anger-guilt ambivalence toward the mother reflects his own accomplicity in the act of murder, in the matricide, by means of his minority self.

The paradox of the boy's own minority self murdering his own mother-accomplished majority self can be solved only when one understands that the boy has powerful allies in the act: the mother herself, the father, and the patriarchal culture. It is within this context that Freud's assertion regarding the stronger superegos of men becomes cogent. It is not that boys develop stronger superegos in the sense of more powerful consciences so that they can give up their sexual feelings for mother and thereby obey the incest taboo. (Why, then, for example, are little girls more obedient? Chodorow presents not implausible arguments for girls' stronger superegos. Why, then, is most incest perpetrated upon girls by men?)

Rather, the Oedipal task facing the boy is even more gargantuan: The boy must give up a part of himself — namely, his majority self — which up until then constituted his dominant self. More difficult yet, with this renunciation must come a repressing of all the temporal and sensory/bodily modalities associated with the majority self. One also must understand that this tragic deed, once accomplished, is not over and done with: The mother-accomplished majority self lives on uneasily and starved for development, like Persephone below in darkness nourished by a few seeds and longing for redemption.

Therefore, from the viewpoint of accomplicity, at least three different outcomes of the Oedipus complex are possible for boys: First and most common, the minority self, aided by the mother, the father, and the patriarchal culture, succeeds in repressing the majority self more or less completely; the majority self remains sunken and slumbering in the unconscious. Its development suspended, the majority self is partially awakened only by contemporary traumas of illness, death, separation, and crises of sexuality, during which moments it surfaces in dreams, neurotic symptoms, and psychosomatic illnesses like alcoholism, drug addictions and sadomasochistic behavior.

A second possible Oedipal outcome occurs when the minority self cannot repress the majority self, having not enough help from mother, father, or patriarchal culture in various combinations, but continues in more or less open conflict with it. This state of affairs can result in the development of some types of homosexuality. Last and most rare, the boy's majority self represses his minority self (the minority self is weakly developed or weakly supported); here result the few cases of men submitting themselves to genital mutilation and hormonal treatment in an attempt to match up their body morphology with their psychic morphology (the Christine Jorgenson syndrome).

I cannot too strongly emphasize that along with the repression of the boy's majority self are repressed those proximity sense and temporal modalities that are the foundation of cognitive intelligence and adult creativity. Dinnerstein has remarked that "this deep-rooted tendency to renounce the sensuous-emotional world of our early childhood, to seal off the layer of personality in which the primitive erotic flow between the self and the surround has its source, is a puzzle with which psychoanalytic social philosophers keep trying to come to grips" (Dinnerstein 1976, 32).

I believe that my account of the genesis of the self in pre-Oedipal developments as well as during the Oedipus crisis finally assembles the far-flung pieces of this eternal puzzle. Like Chodorow, Dinnerstein thought that the solution to these problems lay in breaking "the female monopoly over early child care" (ibid., 33). Breaking the female monopoly over child care would certainly change the relative powers of a child's majority and minority selves. However, without a concomitant revalorization of women, mothers, and the feminine, it would not necessarily resolve the fundamental conflicts between these selves.

The repression of the boy's majority self at the time of the Oedipus crisis casts new light upon what Dinnerstein describes as "the mother-raised boy's sense that the original, most primitive source of life will always lie outside himself, that to be sure of reliable access to it he must have exclusive access to a woman" (Dinnerstein 1976, 43). Heterosexual boys and men must attempt to access those qualities lost to them with the repression of their majority selves by ensuring themselves of access to women. In addition, my model supports Jean Baker Miller's statement that "men struggle not against identification with the female *per se* . . . [but] men do indeed struggle to reclaim the very parts of their own experience that they have delegated to women" (Miller 1986, 46).

My interpretation of Freud's Oedipus complex also helps to explain the common masculine neurosis noted from Freud to present-day psychologists and often encapsulated under the appellation goddess-doormat syndrome. With women whom they "love" some men are physically impotent; only with women whom they do not "love" are these men potent. We can now recognize that in these men the desexualization, or the repression of bodily/sensory and temporal modalities, that occurs with the repression of the majority self is threatened by the confluence of "love" and sexual expression. At the root of this masculine impotence we will not find sexual love for the mother, but the problems caused by the repression of the boy's sensuous majority self built up by intimate interaction with the mother during infancy and early childhood.

Also less obscure now is Otto Rank's contention that the unconscious is feminine: In so far as it is the mother-accomplished majority self that is repressed into the unconscious, the unconscious *is* feminine. Similarly, Karen Horney's characterization of "masculine castration anxiety... [as] very largely the ego's response to the *wish to be a woman*" can be understood as the male's longing for his repressed feminine majority self (Horney 1973, 144–45). In sum, I suggest that this paradigm switch from majority to minority self produces the one-dimensional social-self of the average adult patriarchal male by causing a loss of temporal and proximity sense body modalities. This loss, in turn, results in a diminution of creativity and cognitive potential.

The pre-Oedipal age of the mother — the age most closely associated with the body-ego, with affect, and with instinctual strivings — constitutes one paradigm of self; that of the rational, cognitive, "speaking," post-Oedipal age of the father constitutes another. Both paradigms of self are simultaneously divided and united by Freud's critical interparadigmatic period of Oedipal crisis. Again, this change of self in the Oedipus crisis is like a paradigm change because it represents a revolution in the self. However, Freud's paradigmatic self is not a monolith like each of Kuhn's periods of scientific normalcy; unlike Kuhn's linear scientific progress, Freud's multiple social-self can both progress and regress.

In what other ways does Freud's myth of origins and change differ from Kuhn's explanation of paradigm change? Does my transformation of Freud's story succeed in overcoming the logical paradox and the vitiating contradictions inherent in Kuhn's story?

The first important difference is that the majority and minority social-selves grow up together. However, like Freud's ego and id (with which they are *not* coincident), they grow up asymmetrically. The mother-accomplished majority self is the dominant self due to the quantitatively greater and qualitatively more intense times she spends with the infant/child. Also unlike Kuhn's periods of paradigmatic normalcy, the majority and minority selves have points of similarity as well as difference, just as do masculinity and femininity, because they are mediated by the same patriarchal culture by means of the body-ego and unconscious social membrane. Finally, I have pointed to condensation and displacement, the Freudian principles capable of bridging the levels of unconscious, preconscious, and conscious self. I also account for transition from majority- to minority-self dominance. Kuhn, as we saw in Chapter 2, was unable finally to account either for transition from one period of paradigmatic normalcy to another *or* for his assertion that the revolutionary proceeding from one scientific paradigm to another constituted progress. In brief, my reinterpretation of Freud's Oedipal change of self does indeed succeed in overcoming the logical paradoxes and contradictions inherent in Kuhn's account of paradigm change.

Borrowing from Freud the intrasystemic bridging devices of condensation and displacement, I do indicate how the moving from one level of self to another, or from one paradigm to another, occurs by means of the construction and deconstruction of cultural symbols and mythic images. (I shall be presenting further details of just how these transitions occur in future publications.)

Finally, my theory of accomplicity transforms Freud's concepts of object-cathexis and identification—again with the aid of Freud's own bridging devices—into the means by which psychic energy precipitates *as* the structures of self. Here, too, it must be understood that a principle of indeterminacy is operative. The moment of structural dissolution, of destructuration, and that of precipitation cannot coincide precisely, nor can they be precisely described. At this time I can only call attention to the fact that the act of focusing attention binds psychic energies and creates the structures of self. These structures become our substantive selves because they are reified into our neural structures by habit. I believe that many of these structures are also hard-wired into the nervous systems of infants during critical periods of development occurring before the age of two.

The qualitative differences between the attention-awarenesses focused in accomplicity with the mother as opposed to those focused with the father make up the differences between the majority and minority selves. Yet similarities also exist: They are constituted by the interaction between habit and memory and by the possibility of destructuration of habit. In the end everyone is made and unmade by cultural habits.

Ann Oakley has claimed that the Freudian insistence upon early bisexuality of both female and male has been empirically disproven by the core gender identity that establishes itself before the age of two. This is to conflate two different issues. Knowing one's gender assignment and the manner in which substantive selves are built up upon disparate modes of sensory/cognitive awareness are phenomena existing on different levels of analysis. However, Oakley is entirely correct in emphasizing the influence of relative mother/father power upon the infant. She is misled when she uncritically accepts the concept of children's gender identities: A child by age two may say, "I am a girl," but this does not invalidate the existence of schisms within the self, or the existence of bisexuality, that is, of majority and minority selves (Oakley 1972, 164–65 & 180–81). Empirical studies have demonstrated that each sex actually learns the behavioral repertoire of the opposite sex and can carry out that repertoire if called upon to do so (Hargreaves & Colley 1987, 34).

Finally, as Adrienne Rich points out, all too often critics, both women and men, neglect to mention "the possibility that a return to the feminine may actually involve pain and dread, and hence active resistance, on the part of men" (Rich 1981, 63). The pain that caused the repression of the majority self is also reactivated with the lifting of the repression.

A mid-1980s movie entitled "Starman" sums up the last masculine myth, gives some indication of how far apart men believe masculine and feminine to be, and, for this reason, indicates just how resistant to change most men must be. In this movie the starman, a visitor from a far-away galaxy, responds to Voyager's invitation to visit Earth. First seen only as a brilliant disembodied silvery-blue light, this super-intelligence clones a human body as a temporary abode and medium of social and sexual intercourse with the primitive humans, represented primarily by a bereaved widow whose husband's form the visitor has appropriated. By the movie's end, the beautiful young widow has fallen deeply in love with her teacher/captor, who in fact reciprocates her love and, in tender recognition of her species' redeeming qualities (which appeared minuscule to me), gets her with child. Before departing, this wise and powerful being gifts her with a magical energy marble, about which she questions him. In essence, he tells her: "Don't worry, just give this to our son; he will know what to do with it. He will grow up knowing everything that I know and he will be a great teacher."

Although the visitor professes to reciprocate her love, it is clear that for him "'tis a thing apart," whereas for her, " 'tis her whole existence." He cannot stay with her on Earth; if he does, he will die. "Take me with you," she pleads. "I cannot. You would die," he replies. This parting is strangely moving. Little wonder: It remains a parable of the astronomical distance growing between our cultural definitions of feminine and masculine, female astronauts notwithstanding. Consider this: With whom will the men in the audience most closely identify? With whom the women? That most men secretly long to be starmen poses the problem for our gender conflicts; after all, who wants to give up a chance at being the starman-messiah?

But men and women alike can empathize with both starman and his earthbound love and this poses a possible solution: Both men and women have undeveloped oppositely gendered selves and potentials—inner resources that are both bridges to the other sex's reality as well as fifth columns within it. The problem for women and for men is to understand how social-self conflicts were produced over generations and to self-consciously set about creating new processes of accomplicity and the new consciousness that must accompany them. Because of the greater advantages accruing to men at present, the major burden of changing gender arrangements, sexual power structures, and gender definitions resides with women and with their male feminist accomplices. This burden is lightened by the understanding that the accomplicity model of psychosexual development and psychosocial evolution makes available: Wholeness and spiritual evolution are within reach only of he who is willing to voyage within and release his own feminine self.

THE CONSTRUCTION OF WOMEN'S SELVES

Throughout this study I have clearly stated my reasons for considering Freudian psychoanalysis a masculine psychology. Nonetheless, I suggest that a *transformed* Freudian psychoanalysis is indispensable for an understanding of the relationship between women and men in patriarchal cultures, and that a *transformed understanding* of the intellectual tools Freud has placed at our disposal will go far toward explaining how womanhood is formed and deformed in patriarchal cultures.

Freud's first theories about girls' development were symmetrical complements to his theories about boys' development. Freud said that the girl enters the phallic phase at about age four or five, when she begins to feel rivalry with the mother and to desire the father as a sex object. Later, Freud realized that the mother represents a sexual object for the girl as well as for the boy. According to Freud, the girl's discovery that her mother lacks a penis assists the girl in her renunciation of the mother as sexual love object. She blames the mother for her own "organ inferiority," and her original love for her mother becomes mixed with contempt, anger, and hostility. Freud finally realized, however, that any Electra theory must be rejected; under the influence of his women disciples, Freud continued to modify his thinking in order to take into consideration the great importance of the pre-Oedipal period for women's development. Of course, I am emphasizing this period's importance for *both* sexes because it is the period during which the majority self is formed in accomplicity with the mother while the minority self is *simultaneously* formed in accomplicity with the father (or father surrogate).

Very early Freud claimed that a further difference exists between the girl's and the boy's Oedipus complex: Whereas the boy is helped to overcome his Oedipus complex by means of the castration complex (that is, he renounces his mother in order to avoid castration by his father), the girl's Oedipus complex is *set in motion* by the castration complex because the girl is, Freud remarked, "already castrated." At first Freud reasoned that the boy had the more difficult conflict to overcome, since he had to renounce his mother as sex object and identify with his threatening father. Later, through his women colleagues, Freud gained a better appreciation of the "very circuitous path" that the girl's feminine attitude must take just to arrive at the Oedipus complex (Freud [1905–38] 1963, 199).

In addition, Freud claimed that women's development is complicated by the girl's need to change her leading genital zone from the "masculine" clitoris, to the "passive," "receptive," and "feminine" zone of the vagina (Freud's characterizations). Freud said that the girl's castration complex does not destroy her Oedipus complex, but instead prepares her for it. The girl's "penis envy" allows her to detach from her mother and to experience her Oedipus situation as "a haven of refuge." Because girls do not fear castration, Freud thought that they are not motivated to overcome their Oedipus complex and that they "remain in it for an indeterminate length of time; they demolish it late and, even so, incompletely" (Freud [1916–33] 1966, 593). Let me now submit Freud's account to the necessary transformations consonant with my new model of accomplicity and of the majority and minority social-selves.

I believe that Freud is correct in assuming a longer pre-Oedipal period for girls and also in emphasizing that girls "demolish" the Oedipus complex late and, even then, "incompletely." In fact, I suggest that the girl's Oedipus crisis does not occur until puberty, that is, not until between thirteen to fifteen years of age. Keeping in mind that the girl's majority self, produced in accomplicity with the mother, represents a woman's point of view and that the girl also is a father-accomplished minority self, one can readily see that the girl's problem—unlike the boy's—is not to renounce her mother as a sex object. In so far as language permits, this new account of social-self production has in fact done away with the subject/object split which Freud's dual relational modes of object-relation and identification represent. At the same time, I have eliminated Freudian exchange theory (wherein the boy or girl exchanges an object-cathexis for an identification) for a genuine theory of social-self production. These transformations of Freudian theory entail three understandings, which I detail below.

The first understanding is that of the unequal power relationship between mother and father wherein the father controls orchestration power (the power, based upon economic dominance, to decide who does what) and the mother controls implementation power (the power to do domestic work and to work in low-level public spheres) (Berardo 1980, 42:115). The second understanding is that those who live in patriarchal cultures live in civilizations essentially controlled by men. And, the third understanding is that the castration of boy and girl is not a story of potential genital mutilation (although girls and women in many cultures have been and still are today genitally mutilated via clitoridectomies and infibulation). Rather, castration must be understood as symbolically referring to the *cultural impotence of the female gender.*

Although the young girl of three to five discovers, just like the boy, the cultural impotence (castration) of the mother—and therefore of her own majority self—she is not forced, as is the boy, into an Oedipus crisis by the pressures of father, mother, and patriarchal culture. Girls are allowed to be "tomboys," for example, and this permits the individual girl to assume that she will escape her mother's fate, that she will be allowed to retain her majority self with its powerful body-ego understandings, and that she will be allowed to develop the potentials of her minority self as well.

Chodorow has commented that the major task of girls is to figure out how not to be like their mothers. And the patriarchal culture, and often the mother and father as well, allow the girl until puberty the luxury of believing that she will be able to avoid her mother's fate. Authors Sidney Abbott and Barbara Love perfectly express this phase of the girl's development (the phase between the boy's Oedipus complex at ages three to five and her own at ages thirteen to fifteen) when they point out that "in our society a girl who is assertive and rebellious is sometimes granted a period of immunity before she must acquiesce to the endless restrictions and conditions of the female sex role. This is the tomboy phase, a period of grace, a free time before rules of femininity are enforced" (Abbott & Love 1978, 21). This "period of grace" has been reinforced by the ideology of sexual equality, which rests uneasily on the present-day surfaces of patriarchal culture.

Freud believed that "not until completion of development at the time of puberty does the polarity of sexuality coincide with *male* and *female.* In maleness is concentrated subject, activity, and the possession of a penis; femaleness carries on the object, and passivity" (Freud [1905–38] 1963, 175). The truth of Freud's observation resides in the girl's becoming a sex object only with sexual maturity; it is only then that the full force of male cultural sanctions, along with those of mother and father, begin to make themselves felt by the young woman-to-be. Only then does she become fully aware of the passive role to which her femininity condemns her; only then does she begin to sight the full strength of the forces aligned against her.

In *The Cinderella Complex*, author Colette Dowling describes this new phase of a girl's existence: "Before they turn twelve or thirteen, girls are more or less free to behave as they like. With puberty, however, the trap door begins to swing shut. New and quite specific behavior is now expected of the young girl. Subtly (and often not so subtly), she will be rewarded for her 'success' with boys" (Dowling 1982, 113). Indeed, I myself have heard some mothers urging their daughters to "make yourself a bait if you want to catch a man." Mothers, fathers, teachers, peers, all begin to pressure the adolescent girl to trade in her vocational and intellectual ambitions for concern with dates and appearance. Girls at puberty learn that male acceptance is withheld if they dare to be too assertive or too competitive. Many girls also discover that outstanding intellectual success puts their budding womanhood in jeopardy.

As Carol Gilligan has discovered, Johmann reports, girls entering their teens "become increasingly vulnerable to society's attitudes. 'At about age twelve,' Gilligan says, 'girls begin to become aware that bringing in their own values is going to cause trouble. So they start waiting and watching other people for clues as to what their values should be.' The result: by their mid-teens many girls have abandoned their own approach to moral reasoning and taken on the accepted — male — norm" (Johmann 1985, 7:20 & 80). This abandonment translates into the girl's forced (partial) abandonment of her majority self.

Reinforcing girls' moral isolation in patriarchal cultures is the fact that many more girls than boys are unwanted children. An American public television program (part of the *Nova* series) was reviewed by critic Paul Galloway, who reported that this program emphasized "the markedly different way boys and girls see themselves and how their behavior is influenced by the expectations their mothers and fathers have for them." Girls cannot help but be influenced by the bald fact that parents prefer boys. Galloway notes, "Two of three expectant mothers say they would rather have a boy; for the fathers, the preference is even greater. This preference, sets into motion a pattern of treatment that continues through childhood and probably into adult life." Galloway quotes findings reporting that these different perceptions of girls and boys and their different conditioning remain "largely unconscious." In sum, "daughters receive more pressure to be obedient, kind and unselfish, attractive and loving" (Galloway 1980, V:24). These "unconscious" pressures are applied, I suggest, primarily by means of parent-child accomplicity.

Although most of my teaching experience has been at the university level, the years I did spend teaching young children were especially enlightening: I frequently heard mothers admonishing their young boys not to cry "like a girl." Some mothers expressed an astonishing indifference to their daughters' development by telling me when I enquired into their plans for their daughters, "Oh, she leads her own life," or, "She'll make some man a nice little wife someday." In the latter case, many years later this same mother was surprised when she learned that her daughter had arrived at the conclusion that her own education was not as important as that of her brothers. "Now why would she feel that way?" this mother mused to me!

Margaret Mead noted a phenomenon that is particularly discouraging for girls in American society: Teachers in the lower grades are almost all women, usually low paid, and they often reinforce sexual stereotypes in their students. True, they do sometimes encourage their female pupils, but women teachers often prefer their girl students because the girls are frequently more obedient and more industrious than the boys in the lower grades. A good part of the young boy's insubordination undoubtedly can be directly traced to his Oedipal paradigm change of self. However, in patriarchal cultures "boys will be boys" the masculine culture not only allows boys wider latitude, it positively encourages certain rule-breaking behaviors not permitted to girls.

Middle childhood coincides with the period that constitutes a "period of grace" for the would-be tomboy. A girl's culture-shock is all the greater, therefore, when upon entering high school her situation dramatically changes. Now the ratio of women teachers to men teachers begins an abrupt reversal until, arriving at the college or university levels, girls find themselves in a world almost entirely dominated by masculine authority. In high school and college, girls and young women find that they are more apt to be discouraged than encouraged by men teachers, especially when attempting to study "masculine" subjects such as mathematics, science, and engineering. When girls do manage to excel, they find that they are given credit, not for superior intelligence, but for the ability to work hard.

In an article entitled "Sexism in the Schoolroom of the '80s," researchers Myra and David Sadker report that "things haven't changed. Boys still get more attention, encouragement and airtime than girls do" (Sadker & Sadker 1985, 19:54). The Sadkers cite studies that have proven that classroom participation increases positive school attitudes, which in turn reflect in greater learning and higher test scores (on SATs, for example). The Sadkers' own three-year study proved that boys participate more in class and are called upon more frequently. They also illustrated sex bias by showing administrators and teachers a classroom discussion film and then asking them which sex talked the most:

The teachers overwhelmingly said the girls [did] . But in reality, the boys in the film were out-talking the girls at a ratio of three to one. Even educators who are active in feminist issues were unable to spot the sex bias. . . . Stereotypes of garrulous and gossipy women are so strong that teachers fail to see this communications gender gap even when it is right before their eyes. (ibid.)

Furthermore, the Sadkers report that they found "at all grade levels, in all communities and in all subject areas, boys dominated classroom communication. They participated in more interactions than girls did and their participation became greater as the year went on" (ibid., 54 & 56). The Sadkers' study is one more example of how boys and men are being found to control and dominate communication in spheres both within and outside the home. Many studies have already proven that women's communications and work must be of a much higher quality than men's in order to receive equal recognition.

When, during his earlier Oedipus crisis, the young boy is faced with the task of repudiating and repressing his dominant self—his mother-accomplished majority self—he receives much help and support. Without the help and support of the patriarchal culture, of the boy's mother especially, and of his father, the boy's weaker father-accomplished minority self would never be able to repress his dominant majority self. It is important to understand that the minority self is weaker due to the lesser quantity and quality of time spent by the father and other males with infants and children during their early years of development. I have already mentioned the incomplete and precarious nature of the boy's repression of his majority self.

During the tomboy years of grace, that is, during the years between the ages of three to five and thirteen to fifteen, the young girl lives under the illusion that she, too, will be able to develop her minority self, that she, too, will be able to do all that her brothers do. Therefore, the young girl maintains an uneasy distance from her majority self, ambivalently regarding it as a possible source of knowledge and pleasure—specifically, the pleasures and awarenesses of the body-ego. Depending upon her particular family constellation and upon changing circumstances as she grows older, the girl may consider her majority self a handicap with which she can dispense.

When the tomboy reaches puberty, she begins to understand more fully the feminine fate and life plan her culture has mapped out for her. Limited to cultural areas defined in terms of immanence and *reproduc-*

tion, she cannot help but feel rebellious. She envies her brothers, whose lives the patriarchal culture has scripted in terms of transcendence and creative production. The ensuing periods of female adolescent turmoil, and of mother-daughter conflict, have become infamous within the dominant culture. Now the girl's genuine Oedipus crisis explodes into full consciousness. The adolescent girl stretches out her hand to the culture as represented by teachers, by religious and youth group leaders, by the media models and stars, and, above all, she reaches out to her parents . . . but no hands respond to catch and steady her. She expects her mother and, especially her father, to assist her, as they did her brother, in making dominant her minority self. But they are now strangely absent in her life. The young adolescent girl stretches out her hand and grasps . . . thin air, nothingness.

Colette Dowling characterizes the parental attitudes the young girl then discovers as "the betrayal of the father," and "the betrayal of the mother" (Dowling 1982, 117–24). In what do these betrayals consist? That of the mother most often can be characterized by sins of omission. The mother may not overtly discourage her daughter from developing talents, competencies, intellectual skills. More frequently the mother simply is not there for her daughter; she does not show up at her daughter's school functions, she does not encourage her daughter to attend college, she hesitates to spend money on lessons or equipment, which she eagerly supplies to her son. If she does venture to make career suggestions to her daughter, they are for typically feminine jobs, jobs that will not interfere with her daughter's marriageability or make demands upon the family's resources.

With one eye on high divorce rates mother may tell daughter that she should learn to "stand on her own two feet," but specific vocational and money-making skills are not provided. Instead, mothers too often instill fears in their daughters by dwelling on the difficulties and disappointments facing women in a man's world; or, daughters observe the frequent depressions and unhappiness of traditional homemaker mothers, or the exhaustion of dual-role mothers, and they draw conclusions as to the hopelessness of finding fulfillment as a woman in patriarchal cultures. Chodorow is right: All adolescent girls observe their mothers' lives and begin planning how they will avoid their fate.

Unfortunately, the fears that girls have absorbed from their mothers by means of accomplicity — fears of male sexuality, fears of the difficulty of making one's own way in the world, fears of not being able to meet the competition, whether for a job or for a man — these fears often lead to a paralysis of their powers or an escape into the endless search for perfection, of which eating disorders are but one symptom.

Instead of arming her daughter with knowledge, skills, and insight, instead of making family resources available to her, the mother communicates to her daughter her own fears and anxieties. As an unnurtured nurturer, the mother too often looks to her daughter for the parenting she herself did not receive from her own mother and for the companionship she is not presently receiving from her husband. Not accepting of herself, the mother can only be accepting of the daughter when she is conforming to prescribed feminine roles, when the daughter is perfect. Above all, mothers fervently hope that their daughters will not do something foolish (get drunk, or high on drugs, or become pregnant) and bring disgrace upon them, since mothers are held accountable for all the failings of their children.

Feminist psychoanalyst Robert Seidenberg sums up the mother's "betrayal" when he writes, "It is this depreciatory attitude toward their daughters that largely accounts for the hostility that daughters feel toward their parents — especially their mothers. The mother, characteristically looking to her son for the fulfillment of her own frustrations, relegates the member of her own sex, her daughter, to second-class status. This is felt by the daughter as a horrible betrayal and disloyalty" (Seidenberg 1970, 127). In fact, girls are given far more time-consuming domestic duties than their brothers; in this way the academically ambitious girl is further handicapped in her drive to remain competitive.

Why should mothers respond to daughters in this manner? I suggest that for all mothers the entry of their daughters into that sex-objecthood that female adolescence represents in patriarchal cultures reawakens memories of their own conflict-ridden puberty. Yet instead of helping their daughters to understand the bases for their confusion and conflict, mothers for the most part have sided with the patriarchal culture. Yet one cannot blame them: The stakes are too high for them as well as for their daughters. The contradictory situation of women in patriarchal cultures is not yet well enough and widely enough understood. Moreover, daughters do face very real and growing dangers, the dangers of sexual violence, of unwanted pregnancy, and of deadly diseases such as AIDS, all of which await the incautious innocent. Above all else, mothers fear reliving their own sexual victimization, frustration, and traumas through their daughters, and these fears often prevent them from helping their daughters confront the objective threats to feminine health and safety that fester in the patriarchy.

Some feminist historical studies suggest that mother-daughter antagonisms have grown increasingly bitter since the turn of the century. I think that further investigation would reveal an intensification of these antagonisms since World War II. As more opportunities open up for each succeeding generation of women, mothers have more real grounds for envying their daughters' lives and for resenting their daughters' greater future possibilities. Feminist scholars have recently noted that nineteenth-century mother-daughter relationships appear to reflect more warmth, genuine closeness, and mutual support than do these same relationships today. Frequently cited as contributing to mother-daughter alienation is the daughter's entry into puberty, which often coincides with the mother's approaching middle-age, if not her menopause. The mother is beginning to feel her own sexual obsolescence as it is defined by the patriarchal culture, which frequently depicts in advertisements, in movies, and on television the successful middle-aged man exchanging his aging wife for a barely post-pubertal girl. She knows that real life frequently imitates art as the middle-aged husband and father uses the power he has attained economically and culturally to rejuvenate himself by means of the "purchase" of a younger wife. For the daughter's part, it is far easier to displace frustration with father onto the culturally weaker parent, onto the mother.

A daughter's feminine adjustment is more often jeopardized by identification with a feminine mother than with a masculine mother (i.e., one working outside the home) or with the father. Chodorow cites a study that found that "all forms of personal parental identification (cross-gender and same-gender) correlate with freedom from psychosis or neurosis except personal identification of a daughter with her mother" (Chodorow 1978, 177). Chodorow concludes that "for a girl, just as for a boy, there can be too much of mother" (ibid.). I think the problem is not "too much of mother" but, rather, that a feminine identification — given the inbuilt patriarchal definition of femininity as primitive, regressive, and inferior — is dangerous to anyone's health. Those girls who have succeeded in identifying with their father may have that unusual father who is assisting them in resolving their Oedipus crisis through the development of their minority selves. Unfortunately, these favorable circumstances are, even today, all too rare for adolescent girls.

The absence and betrayal of the father, rather than the helping hand of the father, is more frequently the experiential reality for the adolescent girl. There are many reasons why this is so. I have already emphasized that fathers in patriarchal cultures, even more than mothers, prefer sons. Neither fathers nor mothers take their daughters and their daughters' ambitions as seriously as they do their sons' ambitions, and for culturally obvious reasons. It is the sons' duty to be responsible for cultural production, for immortality through achievements. The daughters are destined for the culturally devalued spheres of reproduction. That reproduction is in fact actually production of the highest order is a secret long repressed by patriarchal cultures.

If mothers physically hold, emotionally nurture, and economically support their sons far more than their daughters, this is true in spades for the average father in relation to his sons and daughters. Even when fathers are proud of their daughters' accomplishments, and praise and support them, this support can be abruptly withdrawn and turned to criticism should daughters show any sign of equaling or surpassing the fathers' accomplishments. Fathers are intolerant enough of sons' superior achievement; it is totally unacceptable to be outshone by daughters, who as females are by cultural definition inferior. So it is that women have many sources of anxiety in regard to their own success. Patriarchal culture has already taught them that feminine women (read "sexy, attractive to men, dependent, passive") are not too bright, nor too competent, nor too independent. Now their achievements have made their fathers unhappy, and they have yet another source of guilt.

The prevailing cultural wisdom is that a father's primary duty toward his daughter is to help her attain her feminine identity by being mildly flirtatious and gallant as she blossoms into womanhood. In fact, the literature available on father-daughter relationships suggests that the scarce father too often becomes even scarcer as his daughter reaches physical maturity. Daughters complain that fathers who used to be affectionate and demonstrative now seem strangely reticent. It is in this way that the father unwittingly signals to his daughter that she has ceased to be the person she was and that now all of her humanity has been collapsed into her sex-objecthood. I suggest that a stronger father-daughter accomplicity would cancel out the unconscious sexual temptations that produce father's full-flight reaction formation. That her father, too, sees her as a sex object just when she is becoming more fully aware of the uses and abuses of sex objects in patriarchal culture appears to the sensitive adolescent as the greatest betrayal of all. That closer and more continuous father-daughter accomplicity correlates with fewer instances of sexual abuse by fathers has been documented in the psychological literature (Parker & Parker 1986, 56:531–49). Stepfather-daughter sexual abuse, for example, has been found to be seven times more frequent than biological father-daughter sexual abuse, and uncle-niece sexual abuse occurs more frequently than father-daughter sexual abuse (Russell 1986, 388–89).

All of the betrayals detailed above, namely, that of the patriarchal culture, that of the mother, and that of the father, have a rapidly accumulative effect upon the girl that, at puberty, triggers the girl's Oedipus crisis. As Freud describes it, "When the universality of this negative character of her sex dawns upon her, womanhood, and with it also her mother, suffers a heavy loss of credit in her eyes" (Freud [1905–38] 1963,

202). Of course, the mother's debasement is not, as Freud thought, the debasement of the girl's primary love object; it is instead felt as the debasement of that dominant part of the girl's self, the girl's majority self, produced through mother-daughter accomplicity.

At puberty all elements of the cultural surround begin to limit and confine the girl who for so long was allowed the freedom of tomboyhood and the free reign of her aspiring minority self. This confinement intends to imprison her in her majority self, to make her identical to it. However, the irony and paradox for the girl is that she, too, like her brothers, has become alienated from her own majority self. Now the patriarchal culture's fetishization of the time-conquering feminine body—forever youthful, slim, and beautiful—threatens to freeze her like a fossil in amber in what is only a parody, a ghostly reflection of her full-bodied joyous majority self. To the detriment of women's physical health, the ideal of feminine beauty has become even more decorporealized since the 1950s. For example the finalists in the 1988 Miss Universe competition and those in the 1990 Miss America pageant are painfully thin as compared with finalists of a couple of decades ago.

The tragedy of the stunted Western woman is that she is trapped between her two selves and at home in neither. Her majority self has been alienated from her by the definitions, structures, and relationships of the patriarchal culture, just as the boy's majority self has been repressed. But, whereas the boy has enormous cultural and parental aid in helping him to effect this paradoxical paradigm change from majority self to minority self, the girl turns to face a void. Development of her minority social-self is barred to her in several ways: First of all, the adolescent girl is discouraged from developing her minority self (her more intellectual and vocational competencies) because to do so would be to deny her femininity as male-defined. Ironically, with the debasement of her majority self, male-defined femininity *is* all that remains for her. Note that the radical split in patriarchal culture is at work here: The feminine is identified as the inferior, primitive mother *or* the feminine is identified as virgin madonna, as goddess. The girl flees the former definition in the form of her majority self; what remains for her is to become that contradictory icon of patriarchal culture, the sexy virgin goddess.

Second, the essentially "minority self" categories of the patriarchal culture have already been desexualized, that is, stripped of body-ego awareness and the sensuousness of the majority self. Further, since the cognitive and sensory categories of the minority self have been elaborated by men over generations, they bear little relationship to the existential realities of women of any age. Adolescent girls hereby find themselves again trapped in a fundamental contradiction: If they aspire to the full fruits of patriarchal cultures, to economic power, to creative power, to cultural immortality, they must work within masculine categories and become "honorary" men. But to do so, women once more must compromise their femininity—both that femininity of the mother-accomplished majority self and that debased and deformed femininity defined by men. In this way, the Oedipal girl also becomes castrated (feminist theorists deny that she began that way.) The Oedipal girl is castrated in the symbolic fashion Lacan revealed as the boy's fate. Many an adolescent girl is led to renounce even the alienated ghost of her majority self.

The only viable alternative for women today is to create new categories of thought and being that express women's realities; women must help create a new cultural consciousness that will permit a fuller existence to both men and women. This fuller existence can be made possible by body-ego awareness, particularly by awareness of the proximity senses, brought into dialogue with the attributes of the minority self. Note that the boy's minority self is the majority self of the patriarchal culture.

Given the monumental difficulties inherent in cultural creation, what, then, are the usual Oedipus crisis outcomes for the adolescent girl? The adolescent girl in Western culture resolves her Oedipus complex most typically in one of three ways: First, and most common, the Oedipal girl partially abandons her majority self; it is partially repressed (although far less than that of the boy), and she continues to live her multiple half-lives as a partially repressed majority self, as an undeveloped, masculine majority self, and as an underdeveloped minority self. It is the complex interactions among her fragmented social-selves that make for the normal masochism and partially repressed sadism of women. (These interrelationships of women's social-selves will be discussed further in Chapter 6.) The femininity produced in this way is that most typically identified as normal femininity: It is a femininity shattered and divided against itself.

The second common outcome of the girl's adolescent Oedipus crisis results in an ongoing and unresolved conflict between the girl's unsuccessfully repressed majority self and her own undeveloped minority self. In this case, circumstances have permitted the girl to reject the definitions of the patriarchal culture partially, but not enough to afford her respite from the contradictions and conflicts among her majority self, the alienated majority self of patriarchal definition, and her minority self.

One sees in these descriptions some of the problems of change and development creeping in because of the subject/object, male/female split as well as because of the linear characteristics of language. The concept of an alienated majority self for the girl, one that is masculine-defined, is introduced in order to communicate the progressive split in the girl's consciousness as she grows older and becomes more aware of the patriarchal culture and its attitudes toward her as nubile woman, as sex object. Of course, these selves are all social, they overlap, and they have some degree of communication with each other by means of the body-ego and the unconscious social membrane. In this second Oedipal outcome, girls and women live in an eternal checkmate that manifests itself in anorexia-bulimia and in depression; in short, in angry self-destruction.

The third possible outcome for the Oedipal girl is much rarer because it depends upon social circumstances not frequently found. These girls follow the masculine paradigm change of social-self and attempt a more or less successful repression of their majority self and development of their minority self. These women usually have supportive fathers who are secure enough to remain magnanimous in the face of their daughters' worldly success. These are the women who become "honorary" men and who cannot understand why there is a feminist movement. They usually remain childless or hire someone else to raise their children (in effect, they are hiring a wife). At times it is the widowed or abandoned mother who, lacking sons, focuses her attentions upon her daughter, helping her to develop her minority self. From among the latter types, particularly when support from the father is lacking and the mother is perceived as especially down-trodden, come those women who are able to find ways to develop their minority selves and to repress their majority selves.

Fortunately, with the cultural support of the latest women's movement, some women are painfully struggling to develop their minority selves *in dialogue* with their majority selves. They are creatively integrating their masculine and feminine selves and producing what will become the femininity of the future.

None of the usual outcomes of the Oedipus complex for either girl or boy is highly desirable; some are only less destructive — to self or, ultimately, to society — than others. In male-dominated cultures we all pay an exorbitantly high price for whatever happiness and adjustment we achieve. None of us is whole; none of us escapes deformation: Most of us, like mermaid and minotaur, like satyr and sphinx, remain divided against ourselves, cut off from healing dialogue, ignorant of our unknown selves and the true scope of human possibility.

CONFLICTS OF THE MAJORITY AND MINORITY SELVES

Chodorow claims that "women's sense of self is continuous with others and [that] they retain capacities for primary identification, both of which enable them to experience the empathy and lack of reality sense needed by a cared-for infant" (Chodorow 1978, 207). My theory of the different ways in which the dominant patriarchal culture deals with the girl's and boy's majority selves explains more satisfactorily, I believe, the "relational capabilities" supposedly maintained in women and suppressed in boys. The girl is not permitted to develop her minority self, that self which the dominant culture has made the locus of individuation for the male. Nor, ironically, is she permitted to develop her majority self. The girl's majority self, like the boy's, is stunted at a low level of development. The real secret of woman's famed intuition and empathy for others lies in her situation: Women learn how to care for children by caring for them (and for dolls and younger siblings when growing up). This caring becomes a mother's reality as well as the baby's reality; it is the shared reality of accomplicity that occurs primarily by means of the proximity senses. Recent studies of small children reveal that young boys also show themselves capable of nurturing behavior toward babies. Majority self accomplicity appears to lack a "reality sense" only because it is not a reality for the men who define the relationship without sharing in it.

Most women do manage to retain a tenuous hold upon their majority selves, and by means of body-ego awareness this gives them greater insight into themselves and others. Women are not any more continuous with others than are men, but they are more closely in contact with those proximity sense modalities that communicate a great deal of knowledge through both the body-ego and the unconscious social membrane. Ashley Montagu cites Alexander Lowen's findings (*The Betrayal of the Body*), which demonstrate the relationship between schizophrenia and children's early deprivation of tactile experience (Montagu 1986, 261). I am suggesting that the development of our divided selves, of the majority self and the minority self, occurs along similar, although not so dramatic, lines. Instead of a complete failure of bodily contact there are differentiated contacts with mother and father. The boy's Oedipus crisis, marking a partial repression of the majority self, entails a later deprivation than that which occurs in schizophrenia. However, as with schizophrenia, a dissociation from the body-ego does occur and the two selves become more sharply divided. As in schizophrenia, "one of these identities is [relatively more] based on the body, the other is [relatively more] based on the ego image" (ibid., 262). I further suggest that the former identity represents the majority self and the latter the minority self.

Women's special sensitivities can also be explained by their vulnerability and subordination within patriarchal culture; women must learn to know their oppressors if they are to survive, let alone prosper. Women's "double consciousness," the whispered dialogues between their majority and minority selves, permits them to live simultaneously in the realities of masculine society and in their own realities. Neither reality, neither consciousness, is less real than the other, but it is far more difficult for men to perceive and understand the reality of women than for women to understand that of men. The boy's earlier Oedipus crisis and the earlier repression of his majority self make it far more difficult for the boy to recapture lost categories of being/knowing. In addition, the girl has experienced some of what the boy experiences during her tomboyhood. Also, many girls today experience higher education and most young women go through the motions of career choice, experiencing, at the least, apprentice-level jobs. The ex-tomboy is permitted to penetrate much further into masculine realities than is the boy into feminine realities: Remember, no one permitted his "marygirlhood" even to get off the ground.

Toward the end of his career, Freud began to develop a new line of thought or, as I would characterize it, deeper insight into old lines. In a 1938 essay, written about a year before he died and entitled the "Splitting of the Ego in the Defensive Process," Freud said, "I find myself for a moment in the interesting position of not knowing whether what I have to say should be regarded as something long familiar and obvious or as something entirely new and puzzling. But I am inclined to think the latter" (Freud [1905–38] 1963, 220). I am inclined to think that Freud was right.

What Freud had discovered was the possibility of two contradictory ideas or attitudes existing in the ego, that is to say, on the level of consciousness, while the emotional impact of the contradiction and its sources in unconscious conflicts are repressed. Freud had already elaborated in manifold ways during his long career the side-by-side existence in the unconscious of contradictory ideas — thus his ambivalence regarding the novelty of this idea. I think that Freud sensed, and sensed truly, that this idea of the split in the ego held other fruitful connections to previous formulations, but Freud died before he could consummate a synthesis.

In brief, Freud is referring to the ability of the ego to produce a fetish, that is, a concrete obsessive symbol. In his example, Freud describes a young Oedipal boy who discovers the "castrated" female genitals and simultaneously is told that he, too, will be castrated by his father if he continues to pursue his wicked masturbation. Freud remarks that the usual outcome of this typical series of events is the destruction, or at least the repression, of the Oedipus complex. The latter event marks the arrival of the latency period during which the prohibition against touching his genitals is obeyed, at least in part, by the developing boy.

Freud then goes on to describe what he calls an "artful" solution arrived at by this particular patient. This patient, Freud explains, has discovered a method whereby he can resolve the demands of his instincts (i.e., to masturbate) and the commands of his cultural reality (i.e., not to masturbate). By inventing a fetish, by transferring "the importance of the penis to another part of the body," which is usually by displacements related to the female body instead of to his own, the boy can continue his masturbations in tranquility, since the fetish he has invented symbolizes the missing female penis (Freud [1905–38] 1963, 222). The boy was only threatened by the possibility of castration as long as reality forced his attention upon the castrated female. Having thus supplied a symbolic penis to the female by means of this fetish, the boy has simultaneously recognized his danger and denied it. But, as Freud remarks, "everything has to be paid for in one way or another, and this success is achieved at the price of a rift in the ego which never heals but which *increases* as time goes on. The two contrary reactions to the conflict persist as the centre-point of a split in the ego"(Freud [1905–38] 1963, 221).

I understand this creation of the fetish – which at bottom represents the resurrection of the phallic mother – as a deeper insight into the continuing evolution of the Oedipus complex within patriarchal civilization. That which the boy could not admit was not only the castrated (read "culturally impotent") state of his mother, but also the concomitant castrated (read "culturally impotent") state of his own majority self. The instinctual demands that press for expression are those modes of being/understanding central to his majority self's sensuous body-ego awarenesses. The reality demanding that he relinquish this mother-accomplished majority self or face castration (cultural impotence) is that of the patriarchal culture, which has developed and reinforced over millennia the definition of femininity as inferior, primitive, and regressive.

The special insight I offer into this state of affairs is that the rift widening in the ego is directly reflective of the growing split between masculinity and femininity in patriarchal cultures today. This rift is the result of the Oedipal repression of the boy's majority self and the Oedipal denial to the girl of her minority self. As technological and scientific knowledge explodes and advances, the rift between the domains assigned to men and those assigned to women widens. The increasing power of communications and men's increasing powers over cultural communication also give impetus to the ever-widening psychic rift between men and women and between the majority and minority selves of each split ego.

However, it is not only the young masturbating boy who has created a fetish. The whole of patriarchal society has also created a fetish. This fetish permits to patriarchal society an alienated expression of the majority self's sensuous body-ego and also permits this society to deny the castrated state of women, in this way assuaging masculine guilt. The result is a masturbatory heterosexuality that is in actuality a masturbatory *homo*sexuality because its norms derive from one sex only, the male (*homo* here meaning "same"). This masculine fetish is none other than the body of the barely post-pubertal young woman. The fetish created is of the nubile girl entering womanhood, eternally young, eternally slender, eternally beautiful: She represents the unchanging goddess of youth and pleasure who denies the passage of time and in so doing condemns patriarchal men to obsessive and eternal repetition—and to sexual and emotional immaturity.

Freud states that the boy who by creating a fetish has resolved the conflict "between the demand of the instinct and the command of reality" has in fact taken "neither course, or rather he [has taken] both simultaneously, which comes to the same thing" (Freud [1905–38] 1963, 220). So, too, the man who fetishizes the sex-goddess girl-woman, has found a way in which to give expression to his longings without really satisfying them. (Her satisfactions are beside the point.)

Since the body-ego's sensory awarenesses dialectically evolve—or would evolve if unrepressed—in accomplicity with more cognitive awarenesses, dissatisfaction breeding repetition (repetition compulsion) becomes the heritage of this fetish. For by fetishizing the body of the girl-goddess, men also fetishize their own majority selves, condemning *themselves* as well to increasing repression and stagnation. Because this fetish complex denies to men the pleasures of their body-egos, and especially denies access to their proximity senses, society becomes an addict: Men are doomed to an ever-intensifying and compulsive consumption of sensory pleasures that yield them less and less satisfaction. As the survivors of the Oedipus trauma and its splitting of the self, men entering into cultural and economic potency carry a heavy load of guilt. By pointing to the seductive power of their fetishized girl-goddesses, men attempt to lessen their own survivors' guilt.

The consequences for the womanhood struggling to life with the girl's adolescent Oedipus crisis are no less catastrophic. All young, and many not so young, women in patriarchal cultures are more or less alienated from their own bodies—and this alienation is intensifying. Studies indicate that anorexia and bulimia, for example, are on the increase among young women (Moses, Banilivy & Lifshitz 1989, 83:396–97). Although the increasing interest in exercise and body-building appears to be a countervailing trend, exercise must be linked with enthusiasm for good nutrition and for maintaining good mental as well as physical health. Anorexics are known to exercise and starve themselves to death at the same time. Recognizing their own castration as women, at least on an unconscious level, adolescent girls are initiated into the cult of Woman as Goddess through cultural media images and through the attitudes of the adult men and women around them. No matter what her other attributes, the young girl soon learns that the ultimate criteria for her success are her degree of beauty and her youthfulness, the latter equated with a prepubertal slimness that denies and defies corporeality. The body itself comes to symbolize her despised majority self, which must be beaten and starved into submission. The girl's instrumental attitude toward her own body becomes even more exaggerated than that of her masculine counterparts.

Fear of fat becomes absolute, and the girl's life becomes obsessively diet-ridden (ibid., 393-97). I am speaking here of the average adolescent, *not* of those girls afflicted with terminal anorexia who are carrying the patriarchal culture's directives to their logical conclusion by literally starving themselves into the nonbeing to which their majority and minority selves have been consigned. The bulimic's cultural illness reveals her ambivalence and also informs us that bulimics are not so firmly ensnared in self-hatred: Stuck between majority and minority selves, their binging and purging reflects the obsessive cycle of repeatedly taking "neither course, or rather [taking] both simultaneously, which comes to the same thing" (Freud [1905–38] 1963, 220).

The female bulimic's ambivalence toward life as a young woman in patriarchal culture is the mirror image of the male fetishist's ambivalence toward his repressed majority self. The striving for purity and for perfection means striving for an existence outside of time, represents a denial of the rhythms, the temporal modalities, of the body and of the body-ego's sensuousness, all of which constitute the essence of the majority self. Undoubtedly, there also exists a strong relationship between the suppression of the girl's clitoral masturbation and her turning to anorexic and bulimic modes of "self-control." Depriving the girl of clitoral sexuality — central for women's sexual pleasure — is the first step in her initiation into the forms of masculine sexuality wherein her primary duty is to give pleasure, not to receive it. So, also, do the problems of virginity, the double standard, sexual intercourse, and pregnancy present themselves: In order to solve the epidemic of teenage pregnancies, especially in America, the adolescent girl must have returned to her the primary responsibility for her own pleasure; the clitoral eroticism of her majority self must be made available to her. Along with this validation of women's sensuality, the adolescent girl must also be given the economic means and nurturing necessary for the development of minority self competency.

Incredible as it may seem, sex therapists Lorna and Philip Sarrel report that "a recent survey of families in Cleveland found that 85 to 95 percent of the parents *never* discussed sex or intercourse with their three-to-eleven-year-old children. Forty percent hadn't even discussed menstruation with their daughters" (Sarrel & Sarrel 1984, 204). For the Sarrels these sad statistics mean that "for some people, sex is so far outside the realm of ordinary human experience that we dare not speak of it" (ibid.). The Sarrels' findings are echoed by June Machover Reinisch, director of the Kinsey Institute for Sex Research, who says, "The sexual revolution is mostly in the media. In our homes, we're still struggling. Sex is so scary that students in sex education classes devote most of their energy to sitting quietly, trying not to giggle or blush. They often don't even hear the information they need" (Hall 1986, 20:36). As essential as sex education is for developing children, it will not halt teenage pregnancy until it is understood that "sex" education must also encompass education regarding the *value* of the female sex. Our culture must liberate the mother-accomplished majority selves of both girls and boys.

Unfortunately, many women are as alienated from their own bodies as are the men whose ultimate insult to each other is "Mother-fucker!" (We can now begin to gain a deeper understanding of this insult and its equally ubiquitous sibling, "Go fuck yourself!") Sociologist Ann Oakley reports in *Becoming a Mother* (1980) and *Woman's Work* (1976) that many mothers believe that breast-feeding is "nauseating," or "animal," or "disgusting," and that it is just not "nice" and somehow "sexual" (Oakley 1980, 169; Oakley 1976, 195). Here we have more proof that women view their own bodies from the perspective of patriarchal culture, that is, as sex objects.

In recent decades many doctors have discouraged women from nursing their children. Certainly the patriarchal culture does not facilitate breast feeding: One not infrequently reads letters to the editors of newspapers and magazines in which outrage is vented at young mothers who have dared to nurse their infants in public. The gentle beauty of the nursing couple — celebrated in religious iconography — is indignantly trundled off to the restaurant's or park's toilets, where sanitary facilities are often lacking. Constantly reassured by the patriarchy that their "queendom of the natural" is valuable, women are unceremoniously packed off when attempting to exercise their natural gifts. In truth, the very existence of an organization such as La Leche League, which teaches women how to nurse and which encourages them to continue nursing, gives the lie to the patriarchal myth regarding the naturalness of women's mothering.

Far from naturally inhabiting their bodies, women are driven from their bodies and are trained, like their masculine counterparts, to see the young, slim adolescent female body as the ultimate symbol of sensuousness — a sensuousness that has been collapsed into male genital sexuality. The difference between the girl and boy is that the girl is simultaneously, and contradictorily, trained to identify herself with her masculine-defined body, whereas the boy is trained to regard his body as his instrument because his identity lies with his mind and vocational capabilities. However, because the patriarchal culture's ideal feminine body is an impossible one, a fetishized version of reality — perfect at all times, and therefore outside time, forever slender, young, and pretty — the girl's own body betrays her more continuously than the culture or her parents.

What both girl and boy share in patriarchal cultures as they grow into women and men is that "time sickness" of which psychologist Rollo May (1986) spoke and which represents an illness caused by an amputation of the temporal modalities of the majority self. In fact, I believe that all neurosis can be analyzed as a time sickness, an illness that occurs when we are not grounded by the proximity senses, represented most specifically by our majority selves.

With the onset of adolescence the girl's body begins changing, and changing rapidly. Her body's annoying new rhythms defy her control: Just as she becomes aware of the dominant culture's contradictory injunction that she exist in suspended animation within a fetishized corporeality, her skin hosts ugly eruptions, her abdomen bloats premenstrually, she bleeds irregularly as her menses establish themselves. And, finally, the ethereal eludes her as her weight increases no matter which diets she follows while her sexual needs become at least as urgent as any adolescent boy's. In brief, the adolescent girl feels that her body is an out-of-control mess; she feels that she cannot trust her own body. French writer Simone de Beauvoir summed up the girl's dilemma when she said, "Not to have confidence in one's body is to lose confidence in one's self" (Nelson 1985, 7:4). Indeed, the present-day production of femininity within patriarchal cultures coincides with the production of no-confidence votes by young women passing judgment upon their own bodies. Only a liberated future will know to what an extent the girl's partial loss of her majority self and of its body-ego awarenesses has worsened the normal ups-and-downs of physical-sexual maturation.

In brief, a paradigm change for girls from the dominance of the majority self to that of the minority self remains a rare occurrence, whereas it is the norm, if a precariously based norm, for boys. Most adolescent girls find themselves trapped in transition between their two selves and the bridges do not hold their weight; they have no solid ground under their feet. The narcissism or preoccupation with self with which girls and women are reproached can now be more fully understood: Women do often remain self-involved because they have not been able to accomplish the task of integrating and completing a culturally respected and therefore a culturally viable self. In fact, the dynamics of accomplicity are presently such that, as Freud remarked regarding the growing split in the ego, even men are finding it increasingly difficult to maintain social-self integrity. Instead of pointing the finger of blame at the growing number of narcissists, social psychologists would do well to understand the psychoanalytical dynamics behind the phenomenon and to realize that the narcissists are not individuals irresponsibly enjoying themselves at the expense of those around them. Most of them have lost the capacity for enjoyment and are nonindividuals painfully seeking self-healing — or, failing that, self-obliteration.

The truth remains that without the sensory awarenesses of the majority self's body-ego, women *and* men are cut off from their origins and neither can continue to develop the necessary integration of their unknown selves. Until this integration occurs neither woman nor man will have achieved the necessary "reunification of the sexes in the self," the healing dialogue between feminine and masculine parts of the self, of which Norman O. Brown has spoken.

Women's sexuality is threatening to men, not because it awakens visions of the threatening mother, nor because it challenges sexual potency, but because sexual demands by women awaken men's repressed mother-accomplished majority selves and the sensory/temporal body-ego awarenesses repressed along with them. Indeed, these latter elements represent the temptations of a "lost paradise" all men are supposed to find irresistible. In truth, without the freeing to development of these lost portions of the self, the cognitive self — patriarchal civilization's proud reason — is also doomed to sterility and to self-destruction.

But women's wounds are doubly deep because women are alienated from their own mother-accomplished majority selves and prevented from developing their father-accomplished minority selves. Sociologist Jessie Bernard describes women's situation as follows: "Women have been left sort of bereaved — psychologically high and dry. Women give emotional support to their husbands twice as much as husbands give it back. It leads to severe emotional deprivation, especially in housewives, whose mental health I regard as the Number One public health problem in this country" (Friday 1978, 222). Here an essential question must be answered: Since children's majority selves are produced through mother-child accomplicity, how healthy can male or female children be who are products of such severely deprived mothers?

Writer Phyllis Chesler defines the full scope of the problem facing women in patriarchal societies when she asserts: "Paradoxically, while women must not 'succeed,' when they *do* succeed at anything, they have still failed if they're not successful at *everything.* Women must be perfect (goddesses) or they're failures (whores)" (Chesler 1973, 277). Clearly, the double standard does not operate only in the bedroom; it operates also in terms of one's success as a human being. This sexual and social double standard represents the widening split in patriarchal culture between masculine and feminine, between repressed majority selves and underdeveloped minority ones. To hide this split from themselves, to affirm it while denying it, men have made a fetish of the young female body. In this way they hope to retain the pleasures of their mother-accomplished majority selves while denying to this self — and therefore to themselves as much as to women — its essential evolution.

The denigration of the feminine has become a vicious circle: The majority self was formed over centuries by mother-child accomplicity as mothers slowly took on more and more responsibility for child-rearing. As they were able to spend more time with their children, they slowly withdrew or were withdrawn from essential economic activities. This was especially true among middle- and upper-class women toward the end of the nineteenth century and until the middle decades of the twentieth century, the very period which gave birth to Freudian psychoanalysis and our current gender problems. The withdrawal of large segments of the female population from public production led to further denigration of women, which in turn led to the greater repression of the male's growing mother-accomplished majority self. Although this schema is cursory and oversimplified, I believe that it nevertheless reveals the essential dynamics that explain the growing split in the modern egos of both men and women. Healing of this split will require more than increasing numbers of women taking low-level "maintenance" jobs within public production spheres.

All of the open, overlapping spirals of history may appear flat and closed as one views them from contemporary perspectives, but there is a real sense in which all history must be only a reconstruction. Unconstituted facts are mythical beasts, and even a resurrected majority self would not represent the original majority self. We may live in many overlapping, semi-autonomous modes and times, but time's arrow points in but one direction, and even with resurrection there is the tragedy of loss. There always will exist a sense in which one "cannot go home again," but the health and survival of our civilization depends upon rediscovering the origins of the majority selves of men and upon the liberation of the minority selves of women.

THE PRODUCTIVE POWERS OF ACCOMPLICITY

My theory of accomplicity asserts that the processes of interaction produce the structures of selfhood. Therefore, the majority self, produced through mother-child accomplicity, is inextricably involved with the child's essential being. A mother-raised child — boy or girl — can never be free of "contamination" by the feminine. There is no cord to be cut, for the cord is the self; dissolving bonds threatens to unglue the entire self. In order to grasp this new angle of vision, one which abrogates the masculine subject/object split and unifies mind and body, let us now examine in detail the theory of accomplicity. I will indicate how the processes of accomplicity produce the majority self and the minority self of girl and boy, selves that are different because of the child's differing interactions with mother and father.

In a system such as Freud's where principles of transformation (displacement and condensation) and interpretation are articulated, there can be no perfect one-to-one (isomorphic or indexical) relationship between elements existing upon different levels of analysis. Logically, differences must be understood as existing on a lower level of abstraction because differences are always isolated against a larger backdrop of similarities. Apples and oranges are different fruits, but as fruits they belong to a larger class of similar objects. Within any classification system, the magnitudes of differences and similarities are a function of the logical level upon which one operates. These systems are culturebound systems that grow up out of the experiences of their originators. Most patriarchal systems of thought construct indexical relationships between logical levels that maintain the categorical integrity of objects lying on disparate levels.

Freud's metapsychological system differs from other patriarchal systems because it is not merely an indexical system: It recognizes nonidentity and categorical gaps through which may enter chance, choice, movement, change, and progress. Conversely, as discussed in Chapter 2, the perfect correspondences, the homologous relationships between levels such as conscious/unconscious, inner/outer, and culture/nature, which are ubiquitous in patriarchal thought, foreclose the possibilities for movement, for creation, change, and progress. They do more: Perfect parallels between different universes of thought and being collapse interactive dualities into a sterile one-dimensional monism. All categories become transhistorical and the unique moment of change is lost.

On the level of consciousness, to be self-aware is to be simultaneously identical and nonidentical to self. In its haste to defend against contamination by the feminine, masculine thought has not recognized that culturally unified differences, *not* identities, are the locus of knowledge/being. Sexual differences represent primordial differences elaborated by cultures. Especially over the last two centuries, as men obtained greater cultural power, women and the cultural modes assigned to them were defined by men as primitive and inferior and akin to nature. To attain to masculinity and the cultural values assigned to masculinity — power, immortality, and dominance — men found it increasingly necessary to sever connections with the devalued feminine. Men, in fact, had to deny any structures or substance of the self that might contaminate them with the feminine. In this way was intensified the masculine drive for clear-cut categories, for categorical purity, for firm definition, for the self-identical. The major goal of patriarchal thought became to discover facts. Within the dominant culture reification became original sin; the idea of deconstruction was seen as nihilism; ambiguity became anathema, fantasy mere play, art merely emotion. The logical paradoxes that riddled patriarchal thought were noticed, but their philosophical consequences were denied or ignored; academic disciplines grew ever more compartmentalized, ever more one-dimensional, ever more sterile.

Fortunately, on the periphery of masculine disciplines powerful new ideas are arising to counter these prevailing views of reality. In Chapter 2, I drew upon striking new understandings concerning the nature of knowing/being that emanate from quantum physics. I also have cited some of the new empirical data accumulating in the social sciences regarding the nature of family dynamics. I have quoted some of the few sources now available from women as mothers. All these new sources undermine prevalent patriarchal mythologies.

If, however, children do not begin life merged with mother, how then are we to envision their early beginnings, their origins, and their development? Perhaps we should consider that children begin life merged with the unconscious social membrane, those folkways and social habits that have been incorporated into human nervous systems and that are absorbed by the child's body-ego during the critical early period of life when the brain's limbic systems are dominant. After all, as mentioned earlier, social contract theories — those political theories of identity and exchange — have been invalidated as theories accounting for the origins of families, clans, and nation states because social contracts depend upon already existing, although tacit, cultural mores.

Earlier, I also suggested that the social individual might emerge from a preexistent cultural mass or matrix. The tradition I am drawing upon here extends from the Freudian unconscious, which Freud understood as social, to the French sociologist Emile Durkheim's "social facts" or "representations," to the more recent assertions by the great physicist Werner Heisenberg that the "spirit of an age" is solidly real and factual. The understanding I am trying to convey is a complex one, foreign to Americans who view with suspicion ideas about any social body that, they fear, would compromise the ferociously defended American belief in the sanctity of the individual.

But as the nineteenth-century French writer Alexis de Tocqueville and the twentieth-century sociologist Robert N. Bellah (1986) have brilliantly argued, American society cannot survive an individualism that denies the individual's roots in community. In this study I have traced the American denial of social rootedness to the American male's fear of contamination by feminine values, values that patriarchal societies have identified with "habits of the heart." For patriarchal men, ideas regarding the social body connote annihilation of Faustian impulse and threaten the individual with absorption into reproductive immanence.

I am arguing that these fears of absorption and contamination have tainted the character of patriarchal culture's theoretical systems. I am further arguing that the survival of human civilization depends no less upon a lifting of these defenses; that our continuing individuation, the spiritual and material evolution of each man and each woman, depends, as Albert Camus has stated, upon a recognition of our "likeness to all." Specifically, this means that men must recognize and embrace the feminine in themselves and women must develop their masculine selves. Clearly, a new vision of early psychosexual development is needed that will supersede those defensive systems of the dominant culture. However, as French philosopher Jacques Derrida has warned, to explain in words ideas that are fundamentally nondiscursive is a difficult and contradictory undertaking. With this caveat in mind, then, I will try to communicate my vision of the embeddedness of social individuals in the cultural matrix and their emergence from it through the interactive powers of accomplicity.

Newborns arrive partially merged with the unconscious social membrane, and this condition of merging varies qualitatively and in degree as the body-ego awarenesses develop and as the other structures of selfhood emerge in what is an essentially nonlinear unfolding. The body must be understood as the basis for both cognition and creativity. Furthermore, this bodily ground for thinking and feeling is "essentially interactive" (Lynch 1985, 269). The most deeply embedded portions of the cultural surround penetrate to the genetic inheritance of each of us (Freud's phylogenetic inheritance), and in this way they function like the absolutes — the "unconditioneds" of which philosophers speak. The detailed ways in which cultural mores become individual body can now be glimpsed and guessed at only dimly. However, new discoveries in genetics, biochemistry, and psychoneuroimmunology are beginning to make ideas regarding the inheritance of acquired characteristics less fantastic.

Within the discipline of modern anthropology, it is now widely understood that neither during fetal development nor at birth does the child recapitulate the whole of species development; ontogeny does not recapitulate phylogeny for cultural beings. Although from birth onward the infant "thinks," that is, its body-ego has awareness, the latest studies of infant development point to central nervous system organization that privileges the limbic and perceptual systems during a critical period that allows for rapid learning; this learning may differ dramatically from the learning that occurs after the age of two or three (Winson 1986, 173).

Much is still unknown regarding the nature of this critical period and the pruning of neural connections that occurs during this time. Enough is known, however, to make plausible the suggestion that in some ways infants "pick up" the culture's developmental curve where they find it, that much of what appeared in the past to be genetically determined is passed from cultural agents to the infant through forms of communication unconscious to both infant and agents. I have called these forms of communication the processes of accomplicity, and I have specifically identified as centrally important to these processes the neglected proximity senses of touch, taste, and smell, along with a myriad of kinesthetic senses now poorly understood. In addition, these proximity senses of the body-ego communicate the culture's, as well as the body's, various temporal modalities.

Our first language is that of touch and *kinesics* (Montagu 1986, 108). In his fascinating study *Touching, The Human Significance of the Skin* (1986), Montagu reminds us that "Freud's view of the skin as an erotogenic zone differentiated into sense organs and special erogenic zones such as the anal, oral, and genital really refers to erogenized tactile zones [so that] what he calls infantile sexuality appears to be . . . largely tactuality" (ibid., 217). Moreover, both the nervous system and the skin arise from the embryo's ectoderm, so that our inner and outer "minds" — the nervous system and the skin — are united through their early origins (ibid., 4–5). During the course of his important research into the causes of blood pressure elevation, Prof. James J. Lynch found that "the notion of the human body as a communicative organ, one that can speak with an eloquence surpassing that of spoken words, gradually fused with the realization that it takes two or more human beings to carry on a conversation. When two human beings speak to each other with words, their bodies are also simultaneously engaged in an astonishingly complex dialogue" (Lynch 1985, 205).

However, these processes of communication by means of the proximity senses must not be mistaken for mere exchanges of information. The human interrelationships of accomplicity build the infant's selves; accomplicity constitutes the structures of selfhood. These structures of selfhood must be viewed as informed by everything that is known at the moment the child enters the culture because these structures remain forever in touch with the unconscious social membrane that simultaneously separates us from and unites us with others. Therefore, children begin their lives as social-selves. Here I underscore Freud's refusal to differentiate, as did Jung, between the personal unconscious and the collective unconscious. The two are one and separate simultaneously. The individual's unconscious participates via accomplicity in the collective, cultural unconscious. Herein also resides the explanation of the correctness of Freud's view that psychoanalysis is a social psychology. Freud understood that an individual was never an undivided, isolatable entity but, rather, was constituted by social relations, particularly those in his early family life.

We must also view the unconscious social membrane as simultaneously separating the infant's parents from and uniting them with other social individuals. The unconscious social membrane should be understood as a metaphor for that cultural matrix which embodies and communicates the temporal, sensory, and spatial concepts of the culture. In an important way, this social membrane also vivifies the bodily potentials of the individual. Because of their cultural "depth," that is, their length of time as cultural heritage, these sensory-temporal-spatial categories appear, as "unconditioneds" — as a priori categories of thought. However, the infant's parents also represent another aspect of the cultural heritage, that which Freud calls the superego, specifically, moral precepts, values, and rules. These more recent historical aspects of the child's cultural heritage also inform the processes of accomplicity.

Moreover, the child is never a receptacle into which the unconscious pours, or into which parents pour training and knowledge. The child brings to life from the moment of birth multiple "potentia," as well as the capacity for unique growth and creative interaction with parents whose own capacities were developed earlier through their own childhood accomplicity. As in the new sciences of complexity, the "butterfly effect" operates in infant-parent accomplicity: Small differences in initial conditions translate into large consequences (Gleick 1988, 11–31). Yet we must keep in mind that the infant-parent interactions are always asymmetrical: The power of the culture is greater than that of the mother or the father, whereas the latter two wield power greater than the child's.

The child's countervailing power in relation to mother and father is its greater plasticity, its wider repertoire of potential response. The parents' countervailing power in relation to the culture is their greater potential reflexivity, their greater creative potentialities. As accomplicity informs the child, precipitates of substantive self are formed activating some potentials, foreclosing others. The precise mechanisms of accomplicity will not be understood without much time and effort on the part of many researchers in many disciplines. However, we human beings are both matter and energy. At the present time we know much more about our matter selves than about our energy selves. To understand how our matter and energy selves interact through mechanisms of accomplicity would help to solve the formidable problem of body-mind relationships.

Besides the blood pressure effects studied by Lynch, researchers at the University of Miami Medical School and Duke University Medical Center have discovered that when infants are massaged, they become more responsive and develop faster neurologically. These researchers speculate that touching may release certain biochemicals, or certain others may be released when touch is absent (*Scientific American* 1989, 261:34 & 36). Also reinforcing my theory of accomplicity, Lynch discusses the possibility that mother-infant communication occurs "through hidden bodily reactions of which neither [parent or child] is aware" (Lynch 1985, 220). Montagu's analysis suggests that these hidden bodily reactions shape infants by means of "the differences in the kinds and modalities of the individual's tactile experiences within the family, especially in relation to his or her mother," and that these differences, in turn, are mostly determined by cultural differences (Montagu 1986, 295). My theory of accomplicity further suggests that different selves are generated for each social-individual by the different "hidden bodily" interactions of mother-infant and father-infant.

Parent-infant accomplicity has both qualitative and quantitative aspects. In some instances, depending upon the sensory modality and the developmental period involved, a quantitatively small amount of interaction can create a large or qualitatively deep precipitate of self. In other instances, long and involved interactions remain relatively trivial in terms of the self precipitates created. Again, I emphasize that the infant contributes to the interaction and is not a passive receptacle. The infant selects, controls, and constitutes to some degree its own self-substance. The principle of cultural indeterminacy operates here upon several levels: It is present in the juncture between the social-individual and the unconscious social membrane; it is also present in the processes of accomplicity and in the moments when these processes give rise to the structures of selfhood. It is equally present in the interrelationships between social-individuals' various sensory/temporal modalities and in their mind/body accomplicity.

To visualize more concretely what has been rather abstract explanation, let us consider the ways in which the body is multidimensional and also the ways in which the body thinks, that is, the ways in which the body-ego is aware from birth onward. The multidimensionality of the infant's sensory modalities relates to the differential processes of accomplicity between mother and infant and between father and infant. These differences are essential to the development of the infant's majority and minority selves. Each of the senses, each of the organs, can be understood to possess its own rhythm, its own temporal modality. Our brain waves, our heartbeats, our respiration, all of our circadian rhythms, as well as our senses of taste, touch, pain, pressure, sight, and hearing, our deep body sense, and the various senses of balance and position— each bears an intimate, and differential, relationship to time: They each have in effect their own nonidentical times. Much recent research deals with the phenomenon of social rhythms and demonstrates that infants and parents interact rhythmically. The essence of time is rhythm. I suggest that majority self and minority self are built up out of the differences between mother time and father time, out of the different sensory and temporal modalities and rhythms characteristic of mother-infant and father-infant interactions.

May has criticized what he calls the "traditional way of describing human beings in terms of static substances" (May 1986, 144). To the contrary, he believes that time is the "heart of existence" (ibid., 136). Future research must help us understand the relationship of our spatial selves to our temporal/energy selves. Certainly, studies now under way that demonstrate the influence of babies' buried memories upon their later activities point to the power of the body to carry meaning through time (*Psychology Today* 1989, 23:12). The new paradigms of human relationships now appearing will not only enable us to visualize our energy-temporal selves, and our majority and minority selves, they will also enable us to visualize ourselves as that which we truly are, multidimensional.

Other clues regarding the multidimensionality of our selves have come from studies revealing that the sensitivities of different body tissues greatly vary. For example, whereas many repetitions are required to condition certain glandular responses to given stimuli, it has been proven that the heart muscle can "remember" one single trauma, and react, years afterward. Psychoanalyst Daniel E. Schneider writes in *The*

Psychoanalysis of Heart Attack that "Freud had pointed out that a *single event* (in contrast to the 50 or 100 times a dog may need to be reinforced in his bell-meat-salivating conditioning) was often enough in a child's sensitive mind to influence the structure of his character by precipitating an anxiety-producing impulse against which he needed to defend himself" (Schneider 1967, 27).

Schneider reports on laboratory tests conducted at a V.A. hospital in Maryland by W. Horsley Gantt and others. These studies demonstrated that "often secretory (i.e., *salivating*) and motor reflexes are formed only after 50 to 100 reinforcements of a conditional stimulus (food or pain), whereas *the cardiac reflex formation may be precipitated by a single reinforcement.* . . . After an attempt to extinguish certain conditional reflexes in laboratory dogs, *the cardiac component appeared practically unaffected for as long as 4 or 5 years* after the secretory and motor components had been effaced" (ibid.). In sum, the extinction of a conditioned response is much more rapid in some body systems than in others. The point is that the individual self—that is, one unified and separate from its social, cultural, and body environmental surround—is a myth of patriarchal thought as well entrenched as the six myths regarding mother-child interaction already analyzed.

The social-self is social to its core because it is a self permeable to the unconscious social membrane by means of the processes of accomplicity. The social-self "invents" itself, but it does so in accomplicity with its caregivers. Accomplicity is the process whereby the structures of selfhood are precipitated. Accomplicity's processes must be envisioned as occurring through a dialectics of difference, that is, accomplicity involves dialogue among nonidentical temporal and sensory modalities that have cognitive import.

Caregivers also grow through infant-parent accomplicity, but mother's and father's self precipitates, the self structures accruing to them from the infant-parent relationship, are lesser than those accruing to the infant. This is true not only because of the fundamental asymmetry of the parent-infant relationship, but also because of the openness and malleability of the infant's nervous system. The infant's growth and development as a cultural individual depends upon a lengthy period wherein asymmetrical relationships, relationships of conceptual/perceptual difference, are salient. The culture's evolution also depends upon the meeting and mingling of nonidentities, that is, of differences represented by the ever-renewing (neotonous) qualities of the infant and by the folkways (praxis) of the parents.

Cultural anthropologist Victor Turner has noted that humans *conserve* through structure and *grow* through antistructure (Turner 1975, 298).

Antistructure is provided by the differences between the sensory/perceptual possibilities of infant humans and adult humans. Further difference, and therefore further growth potential, is provided by gender differences. Still further difference is inherent in each self's nonidentical sensory modalities, modalities that profoundly affect cognitive growth.

Cognitive researcher Gordon Rattray Taylor (1979) declares that perceptions have cognitive import; nowhere is this poorly understood insight more important than in grasping the development of consciousness in the young child. Even toddlers are incredibly sensitive geiger counters: The truth value of their instinctive reactions and perceptions often surpasses the reasoning powers of adults, as the story of the naked emperor amusingly confirms.

I submit that perceptual reality is not an interparadigmatic pool of simple unanalyzable stimuli existing in the hiatus between conceptual paradigm syntheses: Percepts and concepts interact dialectically; they carry on a dialogue with each other, particularly within the limbic brain systems. Perceptual reality is also synthetic; it does not remain behind with women and children in a natural primitive paradise of sensuousness. Perceptual and conceptual realities develop via the accomplicity of human interaction.

William James's statement that "the intellectual life of man [consisting of] his substitution of a conceptual order for the perceptual order in which his experience originally comes" may epitomize patriarchal wisdom, but modern empirical science is demonstrating that this formulation is fundamentally incorrect (James 1953, 77). The body thinks, and percept and concept grow up together. They grow together and apart in complex dialectical interactions in which percept and concept become substantive precipitates and in which both can be indeterminately destructured. Once again, in ways we now only dimly perceive, *difference* is the locus of knowledge/being, but it is a difference regulated through the unconscious social membrane and created over time by the sensory/cognitive accomplicities of *gendered* human beings.

At present I cannot pretend to give a complete accounting of the processes of accomplicity, of the processes whereby the infant social-self participates in the social-selves of caregivers, of the processes whereby growth and self structures are precipitated for both. I can only make the most tentative of beginnings, confident, however, that these initiatives are nonetheless more accurate than the dominant culture's descriptions of breakable ties or bonds, of object-cathexes, and of identifications.

For example, Norman O. Brown has commented that Freud was "unable to maintain consistently the correlation of identification with love of the father and object-choice with love of the mother" (Brown

1977, 42). Therefore, Brown declares that only one category should be retained, that of a "being-one-with-the-world" (ibid.). I trust that by now the reader will recognize once again the inevitable "solution" to a false dichotomy posed over and over again by patriarchal thought in countless manifestations. First, by way of defense, a sharp opposition is erected where none exists; next, as Brown demonstrates, the strategy is reversed and the duality is declared null and void, and both poles of the duality are collapsed into a frictionless and static identity. Both of these maneuvers serve the same cause; namely, they serve to keep the fortress self, the patriarchal self, secure on all frontiers.

The problem that patriarchal thought has in dealing with origins, development, and permeable categories can be understood only in relation to the male's gynephobia, in relation to men's need to keep themselves apart from that which they themselves have defined as the "slimy not-me." By making paramount the need for air-tight categories, by insisting upon the pristine, self-made self, patriarchal thought has erected insurmountable barriers between its self and any understanding of that self's origins.

Taylor writes, "The failure of science to provide even a sketchy but convincing account of emotion suggests to me, very strongly, that some major factor in the story [of mind] is still unidentified" (Taylor 1979, 291). Certainly there are many anomalies of mind, body, and emotion that the dominant culture's split between mind and body, between subject and object (with the mind/subject taking a manipulative and instrumental attitude toward body/object) cannot begin to penetrate and explain. The curious phenomena of the multiple personality is only one example that has begun to attract the attention of more researchers. A few years ago the American Psychiatric Association added multiple personality syndrome to its official diagnostic listing. A provocative finding of researchers in this field is that most individuals with multiple personalities have been shown to have a childhood history of physical and sexual abuse. Positing the origins of our divided selves in parental conflicts and differences that infants perceive and absorb through accomplicity is quite consonant with what is now known about the genesis of the multiple personality.

For the theory of psychosexual development this study presents, however, it is essential to understand that the proximity senses and the unconscious, both neglected by the dominant culture, are centrally involved in the production of the infant's majority and minority selves. However, just as the blind and deaf Helen Keller reported thinking with her tongue and fingers, indeed with all parts of her body, so also does an infant's majority self think in sensory and temporal modalities quite different from those of its minority self.

In fact, we all do have a general awareness of the body-ego: Illustrating this awareness by means of the "uncanny," let us consider the universal state of bereavement, including where the lost loved one was "only" a pet. I suggest that the "uncanny" feeling of presence that persists long after the bodily presence of the loved one has gone, represents the accomplicity remaining from the relationship: In our habits and movements, our bodily sensations, and our unconscious-preconscious undertakings, the dead are still present because they remain a part of us. It is this remaining cosubstance of self that makes their departure so unreal, so unbelievable; that almost convinces us that they are still present – as indeed they truly are when we adopt the theory and vision provided by accomplicity.

In "Women and Depression," researcher Maggie Scarf wrote that "women invest themselves so very powerfully in their affectional relationships and derive such a sense of self from these vital emotional connections that their inner selves become intertwined with other selves" (Scarf 1980, 26). The theory of accomplicity declares that this is indeed what happens to everyone, and that this process produces the structures of selfhood in all of us, in men as well as in women. Patriarchal culture at the time of the Oedipus crisis attempts to repress these understandings along with the mother-accomplished majority self. Oakley expresses insight into accomplicity when she states, "As mother and child grow together, love deepens" (Oakley 1980, 246). By contrast, the dominant culture's myths identify growth as separation, especially as separation from mother.

The theory of accomplicity explains why growth must necessarily be a growing together that in patriarchal cultures as now organized, has different qualitative aspects with the mother and with the father. Without accomplicity, no growth can occur; with the conflicting products of mother and father accomplicity (majority self and minority self, respectively), our divided selves are generated.

Patriarchal cultures must come to recognize accomplicity – the power of interrelationship, of love/caring – as a productive force, not merely a *re*productive force. Accomplicity as productive has been obscured by the patriarchal myth of love as a regressive force that, like the sirens' chant, pulls us backward toward a lesser state of being, toward the nonbeing of primitive symbiosis.

To measure the distance patriarchal culture has yet to travel, I will next consider the darker side of contemporary accomplicity as manifested in the conflicts between our divided selves. I will discuss how adolescent girls and young women develop masculine sexual attitudes and become erotic objects to themselves. Herein lies the truth of Freud's claim that the libido is masculine: In a patriarchal civilization with masculine sexuality dominant, how could it be other? Women are alienated from their own sexuality at the very moment when they are alienated from their majority selves. Women's sexuality in patriarchal cultures remains underdeveloped while men's sexuality remains deformed. Women lose access to their own sensuous body-egos, and yet they cannot feel comfortable with their roles as sexual "prey" within the masculine ethos, nor with masculine pornography — no matter how hard they try to be "good sports" for the sake of the men whom they love.

In Chapter 6, I will explore the banality of the sadomasochistic personality in patriarchal cultures, and in the light of the majority-self and minority-self divisions, I will explain some of the dynamics underlying sadomasochistic behaviors. Only by clearly understanding these aspects of the personal/cultural unconscious can one fully appreciate the truth in Rich's assertion that "the repossession by women of our bodies will bring far more essential change to human society than the seizing of the means of production by workers" (Rich 1981, 292).

6

The Denial of Life and the Resurrection of the Woman

And you will scarcely have failed to notice that sadism has a more intimate relation with masculinity and masochism with femininity, as though there were a secret kinship present; though I must add that we have made no progress along that path.
Sigmund Freud

Freud was right: our real desires are unconscious. It also begins to be apparent that mankind, unconscious of its real desires and therefore unable to obtain satisfaction, is hostile to life and ready to destroy itself.
Norman O. Brown

SADOMASOCHISTIC IMPULSE AND THE DIVIDED SELF

In Chapters 4 and 5, I sketched the foundation for my transformation of the Freudian Oedipus complex. I pointed out that many of the contradictions and inconsistencies found in Sigmund Freud's Oedipus complex theory were abolished when Freud's dual relational modes of object-choice and identification were eliminated. Instead, I put forward the idea that the qualitatively and quantitatively different modes of interaction between mother and child as opposed to father and child produce the child's dual — and divided — self structures. These productive processes I call accomplicity. The fruits of the latter are the child's dominant majority self, produced by means of mother-child accomplicity, and the child's secondary or less dominant minority self, resulting from father-child accomplicity. Instead of images of separation, division, projection, and identification, I evoked the concept, which Freud also uses, of interactive incorporations that are productive of self structures.

Next, I went on to explain that the Oedipus crisis results from that paradigm change of self which culminates for the male when his minority self seizes a dominant position and more or less successfully represses his majority self. This paradoxical revolution of dominant/subordinate parts of the self could not take place for the boy, I suggested, without strong support and reinforcement from the mother and the father, as well as from patriarchal culture. I further suggested that the girl's Oedipus crisis occurs much later than the boy's crisis because it is to the advantage of the patriarchal culture for her to maintain a dominant mother-accomplished majority self. At puberty the girl more fully understands that she will not be permitted to develop her minority self, and she begins to understand how this prohibition renders her impotent within patriarchal culture. Her struggles to effect a paradigm change of self similar to that of her brothers represents her Oedipus crisis — her attempted paradigm change is most often doomed to failure. The girl's minority self is stillborn or remains stunted, as does the girl's majority self, since, upon entering adult society, it is subject to the definitions and limitations imposed upon it by the patriarchal culture. In turn, the boy's majority self remains split off and in partial repression.

This new outlook upon Freud's Oedipus complex provides deeper insight into the norms of patriarchal society as well as into many aberrations of human interrelationship. We can now begin to penetrate the reasons for the banality of sadomasochistic behavior and begin to understand how, to paraphrase Norman O. Brown, the two sexes may finally be reunified within the self. To this end, let us consider in turn the secrets of sadomasochistic behavior and the taboos against incest and masturbation (autoerotic behavior). At this time I must limit myself to presenting a rapid glimpse of these complex and overdetermined behaviors. Much more clinical and theoretical work is needed so that my model may be given greater definition and color.

For Havelock Ellis and Krafft-Ebing, great turn-of-the-century sexologists, the human sexual instinct was not problematic, it was a natural mode of behavior. Freud rejects this view and instead presents sexual instincts or drives that develop during the pre-Oedipal mother-involved period. These various drives arise from the erotization of the child's body zones, which, according to Freud, are each in turn central to a given stage of development. Here we have the now familiar oral, anal, and phallic stages of the libido—a term used by Freud to cover all the component forces of sexual instinct. For Freud these sexual drives had neither a natural aim nor a natural object, but must traverse successfully each of the stages in order to finally come together in so-called normal adult genitality.

By relating this "evil" period of pre-Oedipal development wherein all children are "polymorphously perverse" to the (supposed) lack of development of "perverts," Freud was able to explain homosexuality, necrophilia, and so on, based on a "fixation" or stalled development of the sexual instincts. "The detaching of sexuality from the genitals has the advantage of allowing us to bring the sexual activities of children and of perverts into the same scope as those of normal adults" (Freud [1925] 1963, 71). Freud further extended the idea of sexuality by insisting that all "affectionate impulses were originally of a completely sexual nature but have become *inhibited in their aim or sublimated*" (ibid., 72).

Note that while broadening the concept of sexuality to cover all of the body's early sensuous modalities, Freud simultaneously narrows the meaning of all human interrelationships to that of adult genital sexuality. In this way Freud effectively collapses the sensuous-erotic into the male genital. Actually, Freud is correct in so doing because patriarchal culture *does* identify sex, woman, and the body. Because Freud's system was partially embedded in the subject/object split, Freud was unable to understand how patriarchal culture separates all of us—men and women alike—from the sensuous pleasures represented by the majority self, formed, I suggest, when the brain's limbic centers and the proximity senses are dominant. Far from representing perversion, polymorphous or other, the majority self represents that lost paradise without which mankind "is hostile to life and ready to destroy itself."

According to Freud, the libido—the combined sexual drives—is active, persistent, ingenious, and continuous. Freud also relates the libido to the masculine. The little girl during her pre-Oedipal period of clitoral masturbation is, according to Freud, a "little man"—this despite Freud's insistence upon the fundamental bisexuality of both girl and boy. Curiously, Freud holds that at the time of her Oedipus crisis the girl must turn from her mother and repress her masculinity, causing "a considerable part of her general sexual life [to be] permanently injured," while he simultaneously declares that women are crippled sexually if they cling to clitoral excitability (Freud [1905–38] 1963, 208). Freud attributes some of the mystery women hold for men to women's repeatedly alternating between periods where either masculinity or femininity is dominant. This alternation represents for Freud the expression of bisexuality in women's lives (Freud [1916–33] 1966, 595). Of course, I am suggesting that the conflicts between majority and minority selves that women continue to experience better explain what Freud sees as women's alternating masculinity and femininity.

As previously mentioned, Freud first posited a symmetrical Oedipus complex for the girl, which his disciple Carl Jung named the Electra complex. Herein the girl feels rivalry with the mother (just as the boy does with the father) and, by resolving the complex finally identifies with the mother and takes the father, and eventually men, as her object (just as the boy's identification with father allows him to retain a female object, but to renounce his longing for mother). With the help of women colleagues, Freud soon realized that both girl and boy take the mother as their original incestuous sexual object. Freud then came to believe that the girl has a more difficult task than the boy in overcoming her Oedipus complex: She must change not only her object but also, according to Freud, her leading genital zone from that of the clitoris to that of the vagina.

The theory of accomplicity eliminates all the complications and convoluted thinking psychoanalysts go through trying to maintain an elusive consistency within this model. My model is much simpler: The girl and the boy both develop two interrelated but relatively autonomous selves based upon their interrelationships with mother and father (or their surrogates); both selves are mediated by the patriarchal culture and the unconscious social membrane. A deeper understanding of this new model of psychosexual development will emerge as we next examine deviations from the culture's norms that commonly appear in both genders.

If, for Freud, homosexuality and other so-called perversions are explained by unevolved or fixated behavior, adult neuroses are brought about by current frustrations that force regression to the periods when the sexual drives of childhood are being brought under the dominance of the genital zone. Freud finally came to believe that nearly all adult neuroses could be explained in terms of unresolved Oedipal conflicts. Freud viewed the sexual act itself as "an act of aggression with the purpose of the most intimate union" (Freud [1940] 1969, 6). Although Freud claimed that he did not know why "sadism has a more intimate relation with masculinity and masochism with femininity" (Freud [1916–33] 1966, 568), he appears to present a solution when he asserts that "the accomplishment of the aim of biology has been entrusted to the aggressiveness of men and has been made to some extent independent of women's consent" (ibid., 595). Freud goes so far as to claim that the man who first overcomes a woman's sexual resistance places her forever in bondage to him.

In this way Freud presents sadism as a normal and *necessary* part of masculine sexuality. Freud explained that sadism occurs when a subject's sexual satisfaction requires that humiliation, abuse, and pain be inflicted upon a sexual object, whereas in masochism it is the subject who desires pain, humiliation, and abuse. The essential point for Freud, however, was the existence of "a certain admixture of these two trends" in all normal sexual relations (Freud [1916–33] 1966, 568).

The idea of the banality of the sadomasochistic personality underscores the key role that phenomena generally considered abnormal have in enlarging our understanding of that which is considered normal. In fact, I believe with Freud that the abnormal is so ubiquitous and shades so gradually into the normal as to make untenable hard and fast distinctions. I also go further than Freud and argue that the norms of patriarchal heterosexuality are themselves distorted and unbalanced, and that masculine heterosexuality is fundamentally morbid. Therefore, these norms themselves are responsible for the generation of much unhappiness and neurotic behavior; these norms themselves are responsible for the commonplaceness, the banality, of violence against women and children. Rape, incest, wife battering, sexual and other abuses against children and women — such are the stuff of our everyday lives in patriarchal societies.

Because the norms of masculine sexuality centrally include the idea of women as prey, and sexual intercourse as a violent taking of the woman by the man, rapists are said to have "no profile"; they can be anyone: the boy next door, the young college student, the loving husband. It is instructive to listen to the words of a seventeen-year-old upper middle class white man who made an "instantaneous decision" to attempt to rape a nurse while alone with her in a doctor's office: "I had never been violent before this happened, and I haven't been violent since. The attack took everything out of me, in almost all ways. I had to interrupt my schooling, and I never went back. You might say it ruined my life. It was my doing, but I was also a victim. *I had no image of a man who could be gentle and kind and still sexual.* The emphasis was always on being superaggressive. If that's what you believe you should be, you're going to end up committing some act of violence" (Russell 1975, 249–50) (my emphasis). To claim that rape or sexual abuse is not about sexual desire is incorrect; in patriarchal societies, sexual desire is structured by power hierarchies that are fundamentally violent and sadomasochistic.

The standard psychoanalytic definition of sadism describes it as an unconscious or conscious "infliction of physical or mental unpleasure, pain, or humiliation, in order to obtain gratification or pleasure; the ability to experience a specific kind of pleasure connected with the simultaneous gratification of both libidinal and aggressive tendencies" (Eidelberg 1968, 385). A masochist is one who "is interested in aims which are not only unpleasant to us, but are also unpleasant to him. A masochistic pervert, who has to be beaten in order to achieve a genital stimulation, experiences the pain inflicted on him as unpleasant, but he accepts this unpleasure because, without it, he is unable to obtain a genital discharge" (ibid., 235). Freud notes that the most striking characteristic of sadomasochistic behavior consists in both aspects, that is, sadism and masochism, regularly being found in the same individual.

Freud also found the phenomenon of masochism to be a puzzle and a stumbling-block for his libido theory in which instinctual drives operate according to the pleasure principle. Why, Freud asked, should individuals seek pain instead of pleasure, especially when they do so compulsively? Freud's original libido theory gave way before the compulsive reenactment of traumas in both dreams and waking life by shell-shocked veterans of World War I. Freud believed that he had solved the problem of sadomasochistic behavior by going beyond the pleasure principle to a new fundamental instinctual duality, that of Eros and aggressiveness. In place of his polarity sexual instincts/ego instincts, operating under the auspices of the pleasure principle and the reality principle, respectively, Freud brings forth the idea of two great classes of instincts.

The first class contains Eros, or the life instincts, uniting and binding individuals together into groups; the second contains the instincts of aggressiveness and destruction, which attempt to go "beyond the pleasure principle" and restore earlier inorganic states of being. Freud thought that this latter formulation better explained sadism, which he now could describe as a fusion of Eros and the destructive instinct; masochism he now explained on the basis of this same fusion directed inwardly. Even Freud, however, remained dissatisfied with some aspects of his last formulation and admitted that apparently we must choose destruction of others if we are to avoid the impulse toward self-destruction. "A sad disclosure indeed for the moralist!" Freud exclaimed (Freud [1916–33] 1966, 569).

In order to move beyond Freud's dark pessimism, I point to the stunted, repressed majority selves of both men and women as the source of compulsive destructiveness and sexual addictions. The dominant self of patriarchal culture, that which began as a father-accomplished minority self, cannot develop further because it has been cut off from the rich sources of knowledge, emotion, and intuition, and from the sensory memories — particularly those of the proximity senses — represented by the body-ego modalities of the majority self. This rupture of self brought about by the Oedipus paradigm change of self wherein the boy's mother-accomplished majority self is murdered, that is, split off, castrated, repressed, represents for the remaining self a fundamental loss, not of mother, nor of symbiotic paradise, but of nourishing links to important portions of the self. Vital connections are cut away from conscious awareness, and these sources of knowing are then hidden away in the unconscious.

At least Freud's explanations of sadomasochistic behavior were based upon real external threats to the ego, either castration threats in the child's present or the same threats actualized in the phylogenetic heritage. After Freud, various followers diluted, trivialized, or made inherent and therefore natural — and thus finally inexplicable — these powerful emotions of sadism and masochism. For child psychoanalyst Melanie Klein, the children themselves very early developed powerful sadistic wishes toward the parents. According to Erich Fromm, some people are necrophiliacs — lovers of death — and others are biophiliacs — lovers of life. Fromm tended to root extreme necrophilia in genetic inheritance, a rather strange nonexplanation for a purported culturalist (Fromm 1974, 365–67). Erik Erikson traces sadomasochism to the "evil dividedness" that comes to a nursing child whose budding teeth cause the mother to withdraw her breast; the child is scarred by this "general impression that once upon a time one destroyed one's unity with a maternal matrix" (Erikson 1963, 79).

Surely, phenomena far deeper, far more traumatic and intractable than being taught not to bite the mother's nipple while nursing are at stake here. (What about all the bottle-fed babies? Do they lack sadomasochistic impulses?) Note also that Erikson's explanation relies upon male myth number one regarding the symbiotic unity of mother and infant, a myth deconstructed in Chapter 4.

Phenomena that Freud, as well as numerous writers (Franz Kafka comes readily to mind), philosophers (Soren Kierkegaard, for example), and contemporary feminists have noted regarding human self-destructiveness linked with voluptuousness deserve more penetrating answers than those briefly mentioned above. Freud did speak at length about "beating fantasies" that surfaced regularly during sessions of psychoanalysis. The fantasy "A child is being beaten" gives the neurotic pleasurable feelings, Freud said, and terminates in masturbation. Freud traces this fantasy in both female and male to the Oedipus complex and to *"incestuous attachment to the father"* (Freud [1905–38] 1963, 127). Freud's complete explanation for this fantasy — too lengthy to be reproduced here — seems especially convoluted, and in the end, as in many of his case histories and dream studies, something appears to be lacking. Freud's arguments do not totally convince. In fact, Freud's analyses regarding sadomasochistic behavior are often incomplete and unsatisfying, not only because he could not fully transcend the limitations of his intellectual model but also because he lacked insight into how the sexes become divided within the self. Like many male writers, thinkers, and psychologists, Freud believed that women are more masochistic and that a part of a woman's unconscious welcomes sexual assault (Freud [1901] 1965, 181).

Here we have a subject that is central to the so-called masochism of women, a phenomenon uneasily admitted and commented upon by many women, feminists among them, but yet to be satisfactorily explained. I am speaking, of course, of the frequently uncovered "rape fantasies" harbored by women. Writer Nancy Friday states flatly that "in over seven years of research on women's sexual fantasies, the most prevalent themes I found were rape, domination, and force" (Friday 1978, 313). Psychoanalyst Dorothy Dinnerstein claims that women "may also enjoy (at least in fantasy) [a man's] power to rape her or beat her up..." (Dinnerstein 1976, 243). Feminist leader and writer Gloria Steinem acknowledges that some women are turned on by pornography, strongly support it, and enjoy rape fantasies (Steinem 1983, 228). Psychiatrist Natalie Shainess describes what she believes to be a widely spread sexual masochism in women that produces rape fantasies. Writer Susan Brownmiller describes the conscious rape fantasy of women as "a man-made iceberg" which "can be destroyed — by feminism" (Brownmiller 1975, 322). None of the explanations given for the prevalence of these rape fantasies in women strike me as entirely convincing.

Friday attributes rape fantasies to women's accepting the notion that sex is bad, only something enjoyed by "loose" women; the rape fantasy lets the "good girl" in every woman off the hook: "We make the other person *do it* to us" (Friday 1978, 313). This is perhaps the most common explanation for women's rape fantasies, and certainly there is enough truth in this explanation to lend it an air of plausibility. Yet, in the final analysis, it fails to convince because it assumes women's total alienation from *any* sexual desire that does not precisely reproduce that dominant masculine view of sex as something a man does to a woman. Moreover, this explanation confirms women as masochistic, which is why Shainess also subscribes to this particular idea regarding women's rape fantasies. Finally, and most important, although this explanation does remove from the woman responsibility for her own desires, it does not explain the sadistic aspects Freud found as always co-present in masochists.

Feminist writer Robin Morgan has argued that the fantasizing woman maintains control over the rape fantasy, and that it is this control which is the important factor. However, her explanation begs the question why, of all the imaginable fantasies one could conjure up, does submitting passively to rape or to other sexual abuse occur with such monotonous regularity in the fantasies of women? Dinnerstein supplies a novel response: It is emotionally fitting, she explains, that the man control the woman's body, since women as mothers controlled—they bribed and even punished—the child body of women and men. This explanation rests, of course, on male myth number five, the myth of maternal omnipotence whose apocryphal nature I have already explored in Chapter 4.

Steinem, Brownmiller and Shainess all point accusing fingers at patriarchal culture's power to brainwash women into accepting the masculine definitions of sexuality wherein the male is aggressive and the female passive prey. Sex is confused with violence in popular culture, Steinem points out (Steinem 1983, 220). Shainess blames male-generated pornography, the media, and even sex therapists for leading women "away from their own notions of authentic sexual response" (Shainess 1984, 95). Brownmiller claims that men have handed to women their sexual fantasies "on a brass platter" (Brownmiller 1975, 323). Women either accept them, she asserts, or they find themselves unable to fantasize at all. This latter explanation divides women with a stark dichotomy: suffer total mind control or have no mind at all. If these explanations are accepted as encompassing the whole story of women's sexual life and options, it is difficult to imagine a dialectical, or any, way out.

Once again, it is Freudian analysis that provides clues to dialectical openings and solutions—not only to the problems of women's rape fantasies and masochism, but also to the problem of modeling an authentic sexuality for women within patriarchal societies. Here the key is Freud's insistence upon the bisexuality of both girl and boy and the consequent dual possibilities open to each during the resolution of their Oedipus crises. Freud explained, "The Oedipus-complex offered the child two possibilities of satisfaction, an active and a passive one. It could have put itself in its father's place and had intercourse with the mother as he did, so that the father was soon felt to be an obstacle," or, Freud continues, the child could put itself in its mother's place, supplanting her and receiving love from the father (Freud [1905–38] 1963, 178–79). If we set aside this typical masculine either/or format of Freud's, along with his subject-object relational modes, and if we substitute my concept of majority and minority selves, then real insight into sadomasochistic behavior becomes possible.

For example, in one of his most famous case studies, that of *Dora, An Analysis of a Case of Hysteria*, Freud traces Dora's hysterical symptoms to her frustrated sexual impulses. Freud states that, on the deepest levels, Dora was harboring homosexual impulses because in a dream she represented "the phantasy of defloration . . . from the man's point of view." Freud concludes that "cruel and sadistic tendencies find satisfaction in this dream" (Freud [1905–09] 1963, 133). The essential clue is provided when Freud asserts, "An hysterical symptom is the expression of both a masculine and a feminine unconscious sexual phantasy" (ibid., 151). Freud's assertion makes sense under the light shed by my theory of accomplicity: Dora's hysteria reflects the continuing Oedipus conflicts between her majority and minority selves.

Dora had not yet resolved her Oedipus complex in the usual manner for girls, that is, by means of a partial abandonment and repression of her majority self and resignation regarding the undeveloped state of her minority self. The perfidy of her father's adulterous affair, of his "offering" her to the husband of his paramour, plus Dora's mother's neurasthenia, all of these unhappy circumstances, coupled with Dora's own acute intelligence, caused her to keep alive her majority self and, with it, her own hopes for the development of her minority self. What Freud reported as "homosexual impulses," as "sadistic tendencies" resulting in the compromise formations of coughing attacks and loss of voice and appetite could better be described as attempts by Dora's warring selves to work through patriarchal sexuality's power imbalances; its sexual aggression, penis orientation, and separation of sex from love; its objectification, fetishism, and uncontrollability (Coveney et al. 1984, 14–16).

Since the struggle for power and control characteristic of patriarchal sexuality infect to varying degrees both the majority self and the minority self, Dora's inner sexual charades could not help but be sadomasochistic. Dora had not yet opted for the usual resolution forced upon women by their situation within patriarchal culture, namely, a partial repression of their majority selves in favor of the impotent majority self defined by the patriarchy, along with a renouncing of the development of their minority self; and so the strong homosexual, sadistic trends Freud found were those of Dora's minority self attempting to effect a paradigm change of self akin to that of the Oedipal boy. It is my contention that in a society where women's sexuality and the majority selves of girl and boy are repressed and/or distorted, *all* heterosexuality must necessarily take on sadomasochistic characteristics. The inherent meaning of sexuality in patriarchal cultures becomes "deform or be deformed"; however, because of the processes of accomplicity, both boy and girl are paradoxically "deforming and deformed." It is within this context that Freud's gloomy observation regarding the need for civilized man either to destroy himself or to destroy others becomes transparent.

The light that majority self/minority self conflicts casts upon sadomasochistic behavior also better permits us to discern phenomena commented upon by some women writers. Ruth Herschberger speaks of the "permanent stain on her honor" suffered by a raped woman and comments that "in some occult way, she has been *forced* into a state of psychological identification or relationship with the person who criminally assaulted her" (Herschberger in Roszak & Roszak 1969, 125). What has actually occurred is that the rape has loosened the woman's Oedipal repressions and reawakened earlier conflicts, centered on the minority self, the patriarchy's fifth column within the woman. Ironically, because of the predominantly mother-involved childhoods of boys, even when repressed the man's majority self constitutes a still more powerful fifth column of femininity within the male.

Feminist Shulamith Firestone has stated that "women are the only 'love' objects in our society, so much so that women regard *themselves* as erotic" (Firestone 1979, 148). My model of majority and minority selves provides insight from another angle: Within patriarchal cultures the only portion of a woman's minority self that does regularly develop is that portion imbued with a masculine sexual outlook. Paradoxically, women in patriarchal cultures come to experience sexuality through the eyes of their minority selves, while those of their majority selves remain closed.

Friday repeats a frequent theme of the mother-blaming contingent when she attempts to pin the rap for sadomasochism on "mother's silent and threatening disapproval [which] adds dark colors to the girl's emergent sexuality [and] this fear becomes eroticized in such strange forms as masochism, love of the brute, rape fantasies—the thrill of whatever is most forbidden" (Friday 1978, 93). Even Freud does not go this far. He explicitly mentions the coercive power of social mores that force women to be passive and that suppress women's aggressiveness. Freud mentions, too, the masochism often found in men and concludes, "All this is still far from being cleared up" (Freud [1916–33] 1966, 580).

Unquestionably, it is beyond the scope of this study to "clear up" the complex human phenomena called sadomasochism. Whether the works of the Marquis de Sade represent the warped productions of an aberrant praxis or whether as has been suggested recently, de Sade's works were a critique of patriarchal society's abuse of women, matters little. What counts is why sadomasochistic behavior, now as then, infects and fascinates us all. Freud came closest to decoding the puzzle when he emphasized the co-presence of sadism and masochism in each individual, when he related these factors to sexuality as it develops through early childhood, and when he normalized all the perversions by relating them to the individual's stalled development. However, my model of accomplicity extends Freud's insights by asserting that the manner in which the patriarchal culture's power structures cause mother-accomplished majority selves and father-accomplished minority selves to be produced assures the reproduction of sadomasochism and stalled development in everyone.

Again, the mother-child unit does not exist as an isolated island floating peacefully in the middle of a family lagoon; the realities of most family life place the child in turbulent seas grasping for support and often torn between the tempestuous emotions, conscious and unconscious, of father and mother. We live in violent patriarchal cultures in which the physical and psychic integrity of women is attacked daily: Wife beating is currently being called normal and routine for half the couples in America. Jean Baker Miller cites data estimating that "rape occurs to one out of four women in the United States, that one third of female children and adolescents under the age of eighteen experience significant sexual abuse, and that violence occurs in one third to one half of U.S. families" (Miller 1986, xxii; see also Langley & Levy's *Wife Beating, The Silent Crisis* 1978; Stacey & Shupe's *The Family Secret* 1985; Straus et al. 1980; Russell 1975 & 1986).

Freud emphasized that "quarrels between parents and unhappy marital relations between the same determine the severest predispositions for disturbed sexual development or neurotic diseases in the children" (Freud [1905] 1962, 85). Such quarrels and such unhappiness are the *norm* in patriarchal cultures, wherein the male is viewed as all powerful and exclusively produces the cultural values by which the female is devalued.

Given this power hierarchy, the relationship between the majority self and the minority self in each of us is inevitably one of sadomasochistic conflict and ambivalence. Interestingly, sex researcher Diana Russell found that the more traumatic and serious cases of incestuous abuse were just those cases in which "the victims responded ambivalently" (Russell 1986, 55). For both sexes in patriarchal cultures, the wells of love truly are poisoned at their source. Psychoanalyst Erik Erikson explains Gandhi's renunciation of marital sexual relations by way of Gandhi's "aversion against all male sadism — including such sexual sadism as he had probably felt from childhood on to be part of all exploitation of women by men" (Erikson 1969, 194). Both Freud and Erikson emphasize an area that has received surprisingly little attention in the psychiatric literature, namely, the effect of the sexual power imbalances between female and male, between mother and father, upon developing children.

In conclusion, the positing of deeply divided majority and minority selves of women and men provides deeper insight into the commonplace female rape fantasy: The fantasy can now be understood as a manifestation not only of women's masochism but also of the sadism of the woman's minority self.

Moreover, sexual violence by men can in fact be interpreted as masculine hysteria, a compromise formation developing, as Freud explains, *"only where the fulfillments of two opposing wishes, [each arising] from a different psychical system, are able to converge in a single expression"* (Freud [1900] 1965, 608). In the accomplicity model the two psychical systems are, first, the partially repressed mother-accomplished majority self, whose repression has created the man's psychic wound, his symbolic castration, and his loss of self structures, that is, the body-ego modalities; and, second, his more consciously retained minority self.

Men's sadistic behavior toward women is richly over-determined. It permits men at once to maintain their participation and kinship with society's aggressors – the few truly powerful males – and to retain their relative position of power vis-à-vis the female. By maintaining aggressive-sadistic ascendancy over the female, the male assuages his guilt at being culturally favored ("If she were worthy, she would not submit to such treatment"), while masochistically and unconsciously experiencing the drama by means of his repressed majority self.

The greatest hope for a transformation of patriarchal heterosexuality lies in this masculine fifth column, which must continuously be reburied. It not only permits men the experiencing of women's subordination but also represents the lost body-ego modalities whose resurrection is necessary for the continued cognitive development of men's minority selves. The continuous resurfacing of the repressed majority self's desires – and the concomitant need to maintain their repression – motivates compulsive and hysterically sadistic masculine sexuality.

Women's psychic wounds are multiple: Subjected to the definitions and praxis of the patriarchal culture, a woman, also, has been forced into a partial repression of her majority self's body-ego modalities. This culture considers her inferior and attempts to limit her existence to that fetishized masculine image of woman, forever young, beautiful, pure, and perfect. Her guilt, too, multiplies with the growing inauthenticity of her majority self and with the growing inferiority of her undeveloped minority self. She masochistically experiences as justified the aggressiveness and sadism of the male – justified, she comes to believe, because of her majority self's imposed inferiority – while through her own minority self she participates in the male's sadism. Women's actual and potential strengths are not recognized by the patriarchy. Women have often been accused of harboring a martyr complex, but it is their situation within patriarchal culture that frequently forces them *actively* to seek martyrdom, that is, to sacrifice the self and renounce cultural immortality, as the only alternative open to them.

Freud's model maintains the subject/object split while presenting dialectical clues through the medium of bisexuality (the passivity/masochism of the male and the activity/sadism of the female). Some feminist models undialectically oppose the brute sadism of unfettered male power to the powerless and victimized status of the female. If this latter model were literally true, no change would be conceivable. The accomplicity model overcomes the subject/object split because it does not ignore the simultaneous existence of masculine masochism and feminine sadism.

Because autoerotic behavior awakens their repressed majority selves men require women as fetishized objects, as prostitutes, as mistresses, as receptacles, purchased or preyed upon, for their sexual desires. Masculine desire is rendered unquenchable and therefore compulsive as long as the masculine minority self remains cut off from the majority self's body-ego and sensuality. Women remain, as Freud noted, trapped between two selves characterized as masculine and feminine. Neither of women's selves can develop within a cultural surround that defines one self as masculine and superior, yet closed as an option to women, and the other as feminine and inferior. The patriarchal culture's hierarchy of masculine and feminine brings about the conflicts of our divided selves and accounts for the fact that everyone suffers from some degree of sadomasochism. However, because everyone is bisexual, that is, because everyone has both mother-accomplished and father-accomplished majority and minority selves, everyone also has the capacity to understand and transcend these deep divisions within the self.

I have spoken about the power of accomplicity to build the self structures of developing girls and boys. Left to emphasize is the correlative building of substantive selves for the parents or parent surrogates: Erikson noted that parents are raised by their babies as much as they raise them; on a different time scale, Ashley Montagu (1981) explained human evolution as humanity's progressive incorporation of the neotonous qualities of children. However, on the time scale of the individual parent-child relationship, there remains a fundamental asymmetry because for children the very foundations of social-self are laid down during infancy's critical periods of nervous system development. Although the changes effected for the parents' self structures are profound, they do not constitute the same order of importance. Perhaps the positive results of engaged accomplicity for fathers lies in the partial release of fathers' repressed majority selves. This partial resurrection and development of fathers' majority selves, I speculate, grants fathers qualitative satisfactions that may obviate the compulsive needs of normal masculine sexuality.

Greater accomplicity reawakens the possibilities of the sensuous body-ego for fathers. Engaged fatherhood is, therefore, an effective vaccine against the disease of incest (Parker & Parker 1986, 56), helping transform and broaden masculine sexuality along healthier lines by means of the structures of selfhood built up for fathers during accomplicity with their children. Not incidentally, widespread preoccupation with nurturing their own children would bring men abundant cognitive rewards as well.

IMPOSSIBLE NORMALITY

By declaring the normality of a degree of sadomasochism, Freud is merely carrying on a well-established tradition within sexology, a tradition that justifies the violence or some degree of force/aggressiveness in masculine sexuality, attributing these to men's primitive instincts and the need for males to subdue and impregnate females. This opinion can only flourish, of course, in cultures that deny the sexual impulses of females. Surprisingly, only within the last two decades have women's sexual desires begun to attain a certain legitimacy. Even so, the high rate of adolescent pregnancy appears to stem in great part from the desire of young girls to deny responsibility for their own sexual needs. Rather, they want to be "swept away" by romantic feelings they believe would be compromised by the premeditative use of contraceptives. More important, young women report that young men often refuse to use contraceptives. Ignorance of the consequences of sexual activity, of course, along with the "it won't happen to me" syndrome remain large factors in adolescent pregnancy.

Lorna and Phillip Sarrel, sex therapists quoted earlier, cite a study carried out in the early 1980s by Tampax, which discovered that a third of girls getting their first menstrual period did not "know what was happening to them" (Sarrel & Sarrel 1984, 16). A typical newspaper article, one among many of late, reports the shocking statistics in regard to teenage pregnancy and sexual experimentation in an equally shocking ambience of sexual ignorance regarding contraception. The results in one middle-class suburban high school were that one in five girls, some only fourteen years old, had become pregnant the year before. The article, entitled "The Secret We Don't Want to Hear," claims that 90 percent of parents are not educating their children regarding sexuality (Sanderson 1985, V:3). This article was written in 1985, not 1955. The question is painfully clear: Just where is sexual liberation? Sexual liberation appears to consist only in boys' and men's freedom to impregnate "nice" girls as opposed to "loose" girls.

The Sarrels report the following incident:

Among college students, sexual relationships are usually perceived as being between sexual equals, not between a horny male and a reluctant, chaste female. About fifteen years ago, at the end of a lecture we gave for several hundred college students, a young woman raised her hand and asked, 'Can a female ever feel horny?' The students all looked at us with expectant curiosity. And we (we blush to tell) hesitated, started to say no, then reluctantly halfway reversed ourselves. Today it seems inconceivable that anyone would even ask such a question, and we hope our 'Yes, of course' response would be without hesitation. (Sarrel & Sarrel 1984, 92)

This acknowledgment of female sexuality constitutes a healthy, if belated, beginning; but it is far from widespread. There still exists today a strong tendency to model feminine sexuality after masculine sexuality. This denial of women's sexuality represents a backward step, away from the necessary transformation of sexuality in patriarchal cultures.

A women studies group in England has published a brief, but important, analysis of masculine sexuality entitled *The Sexuality Papers* (Coveney et al. 1984). Based upon their content analysis of men's magazines, literature, and the work of conventional sexologists, as well as their own experiences as women, they have developed a profile of the characteristics of normal male sexuality. These characteristics are *power*: the need to dominate women; *aggression*: those sadistic aspects of masculine sexuality ranging from mild humiliation to rape, torture, and murder of women and children; *penis orientation*: "having sex" defined as penis penetrating vagina; "*the separation of sex from loving emotion*": an attitude urged upon women as necessary for their liberation and espoused by some feminists; *objectification*: the inability of men to respond to women sexually unless they turn them into objects; *fetishism*: the need for some men to relate only to a part of a woman or to an article of female clothing. As regards this latter characteristic, I have asserted that the slim young woman's body as a whole is the principal masculine fetish and represents a part-object when extracted from the temporally changing myriad manifestations of womanhood. Last is *uncontrollability*: men believe that their desires are urgent and imperial: to deny them is unhealthy. The women studies group notes that the latter "leads to a quantitative approach to sexuality – gaining a sexual conquest is described as 'scoring'" (Coveney et al. 1984, 14–17).

This group of writers quotes with approval Ethel Spector Person, an American psychoanalyst, who argues that masculine pride in powerful sex drives should be seen as a compulsive sexuality that serves to control women (ibid., 17). The theory of accomplicity adds the insight that the fetishization of young women and the compulsiveness of masculine sexuality also serve to keep repressed the majority selves of the men themselves. This fetish is what allows men to remain addicted to sex (or rape, and so on); the addiction, in turn, serves to keep men from integrating their lost selves.

Unfortunately, there exists a tendency within contemporary sex therapy to be penis orientated and to validate unhealthy trends in sexuality as constructed by patriarchal culture. The Sarrels report how they tried to reassure a male client who felt uncomfortable with his own objectification of women; he felt that he should give up his childish fantasies in order to attain mature sexual love. Not at all, insisted the Sarrels, following the prevalent attitude that "whatever turns someone on sexually" is all right. They explain that giving up these fantasies "in fact isn't necessary or even desirable [because throughout] life, many men will continue to be 'leg men' or 'tit men' or 'ass men', without those desires interfering with adult sexuality" (Sarrel & Sarrel 1984, 52). What they are really saying, of course, is that these fantasies are a part of adult *male* sexuality. It is my contention that such fantasies are unhealthy and that they do interfere with the quality of sexual relationships for *both* sexes.

In accepting their clients' sadomasochistic or other fantasies, the Sarrels are merely acquiescing in a long tradition going back to Havelock Ellis and beyond. For example, the British feminist study group mentioned above quotes sexologist Paul Gebhard, who claimed that "varying degrees of fetishism, voyeurism, bondage, flagellation and sadomasochism [are] common in most males; only the most extreme forms could therefore be considered abnormal" (Coveney et al. 1984, 79). Another sex researcher, Prof. Neil Malamuth, vice-chairman of the University of California at Los Angeles's Communications Studies Department, has become internationally recognized as an expert in the field of sexual violence. Malamuth has found that a third or more of the male population might commit rape if they were certain they would not be caught. He has also found that violent pornography and media portrayals of sexual violence do increase the acceptance of violence toward women. Malamuth has concluded that major cultural changes must occur or women will continue to be subjected to attacks from men.

Other experts in many fields have testified that persons—the vast majority male—committing crimes such as incest, rape, and murder seem so normal; they are such "nice guys." Expert opinion unanimously reports that the child molester has "no profile" and is "impossible to identify." Among the researchers who think that rape is a learned behavior and that rapists have much in common with the majority of normal men are Profs. Diana Scully and Joseph Marolla of Virginia Commonwealth University (Shainess 1984, 154). Brownmiller has claimed in her exhaustively documented study of rape that "the typical American rapist might be the boy next door" (Brownmiller 1975, 174). Brownmiller points out the existence of what she calls "the myth of the heroic rapist. As man conquers the world, so too he conquers the female" (ibid., 289).

There exists a widespread masculine attitude in which women are prey to be hunted and taken. Brownmiller reminds us that "the very words 'slave girl' impart to many a vision of voluptuous sensuality redolent of perfumed gardens and soft music strummed on a lyre. Such is the legacy of male-controlled sexuality under which we struggle" (ibid., 170). Brownmiller views the continual threat of rape under which women in patriarchal societies live as an effective way in which men keep women under control. Although historian Edward Shorter has criticized Brownmiller's historical analyses, he agrees that "Brownmiller is brilliantly, prophetically, right in proclaiming the political nature of rape today. Violating and degrading women has become as much a political act as the stiff-arm salute or the torchlight parade" (Rohrbaugh 1979, 335–36). Sex researcher Shere Hite agrees, stating that "forcible physical rape stands as an overwhelming metaphor for what has been the rape — physical, emotional, and spiritual — of an entire gender by our culture" (Hite 1985, 742).

I must emphasize that much of the garden-variety violence against women and children takes place, not in secret or in isolation, but within the sanctity of the home in full view of other family members. The subject of family violence surfaced during the 1970s and has been gathering steam since then. Some family counselors believe that up to 70 percent of American families are dysfunctional. Since the divorce rate is approaching 50 percent and many families stay together despite sexual or other abuse, this figure does not appear outrageously high. In fact, after more than twenty years of family life study, Prof. Murray Straus, director of the Family Research Laboratory at the University of New Hampshire, believes that violence is as normal in Western families as love. Strauss cites the cultural norm that allows "the marriage license [to be considered] a hitting license. . . . The highest level of violence is in male-dominant households" (Jones 1983, I-C:12; Strauss 1980, 211).

It is both interesting and significant that Freud should assign central importance to mother-son incest when, in fact, "more than 90 percent of children sexually abused by adult relatives are female, and the vast majority of abusers are males, even when the child is male" (Janeway 1981, 10:78). Father-daughter or stepfather-daughter incestuous relationships are infinitely more prevalent than those between mother and son, yet Freud claimed that these types of incest were all but halted by men (the brothers) early in human history.

One of the most significant studies on the incidence of incest was carried out by Dr. Diana Russell (1986) of Oakland's Mills College. Dr. Russell's random survey of 930 women revealed that of every six adult women, one had been assaulted sexually by a member of her family before she reached age eighteen (Russell 1986). Other reports estimate that 250,000 U.S. children are molested sexually every year and that 75 percent of the encounters are between daughters and their fathers (Trotter 1985, 19:10; see also Herman 1981).

In addition, sociologists report that up to 60 percent of couples in America admit to violence within their marriages. The fastest-growing crime of violence in the U.S. is rape, with the number of reported forcible rapes up over 20 percent since 1978 according to the U.S. Department of Justice (marital rape is seldom recorded, let alone prosecuted) (Jamieson & Flanagan 1988, 482). Child sex abuse cases in the United States have increased more than twentyfold over the last ten years (Gelman 1989, 114:99), while reports of child sexual abuse jumped 71 percent from 1976 to 1979 (Russell 1986, 75). Russell reports that "both incestuous abuse before eighteen and extrafamilial child sexual abuse before fourteen have quadrupled between the early 1900s and 1973" (ibid., 81). Violence and pornography are growing more commonplace and more graphic in magazines, in films, and on T.V. Some studies, among them those by Malamuth, have linked media violence with men's increased readiness to commit violent or sadistic acts (Malamuth & Briere 1986, 75–92). As elements of sadism and violence have increased within rock videos, their popularity has soared.

Violence, especially sexual violence toward women, has always existed in patriarchal societies. Now it is simultaneously becoming more frequent and more blatant as women begin to attain the power to protest and to change the conditions generative of this violence. At the heart of sexual violence, as of tabooed sexual behaviors, lies an original crime: It is not the patricide upon which Freud founded his Oedipus complex and the origins of male self and society. The primordial crime is the symbolic murder of the mother-accomplished majority self of men; this majority self lies buried in uneasy repression within the psyches of men, and it is stunted, distorted, and bound within the psyches of women.

The patriarchal cultural ideals of love, both unconditional mother love and romantic-erotic love between adults, are corrupt reflections of the unbalanced power relations existing between men and women. These corrupted ideals burn into our unconscious the fetishized images of martyr mothers and seductive Lolitas, all ready to immolate themselves on the altar of heroic manhood. The production of such cultural stereotypes serves to assuage the consciences of individual men by attributing to women spurious power and a perverse will to self-victimization. Tragically for both men and women, these stereotypes — sacrificing mothers, enticingly perfect nymphets, virile heroes — serve only as wardens ensuring that repressed potential selves do not escape our inner dungeons.

Freud notes that a common wish men hold is that they might become "fathers of themselves." Until the present this wish has reflected men's denial of their origins in the mother-accomplished pre-Oedipal period. As the benefits of the acknowledgment and freeing of their majority social-selves are understood, I predict that "fathering themselves" for men will come to mean accepting the responsibility each of us has *to change* the social circumstances that presently perpetuate the divided selves of women and men, thus crippling the evolution of femininity and masculinity.

Freud argued that the advance of civilization brings about increasing guilt. I suggest that this guilt-ridden divisiveness of the self occurs because patriarchal civilization is masculine and that, therefore, the further this civilization advances, the greater is the repression of the majority (feminine) self. The participation via accomplicity in this advance by all of us — female as well as male — assures a heavy portion of increasing guilt to each of us. Freud's disciple, psychoanalyst Otto Rank, noted that "the development of the paternal domination into an increasingly powerful state system administered by man is thus a continuance of the primal repression, which has as its purpose the ever wider exclusion of woman" (quoted in Marcuse 1974, 68). Rank's observation requires but one essential modification: The repression in question is not just primal; it occurs most decisively with the repression, with the symbolic death, of the majority self during Oedipus crises.

The madness in Freud's cultural paradox, in Freud's assertion that advancing civilization causes ever-increasing guilt, culminates in his statement that the destructiveness released by this guilt can find but two outlets: It must be directed either outward toward others or inward toward the self. The accomplicity model decodes this paradox by referring to the warring majority and minority selves: Either one directs one's aggression outward in escalating intensity and compulsive sadism upon the world, or one directs it inwardly and masochistically upon the majority self (this is especially true, of course, for men). Our only hope for a solution to these dilemmas is to unleash the majority selves of men and to develop the minority selves of women. Such a revolution in our sex/gender system is possible because we are all dual: Men, too, harbor a feminine fifth column that suffers with the suffering of women.

THE MEANINGS OF SYMBOLIC DEATH

Besides the concepts of culture as memory and as metaphor, I mentioned in Chapter 3 that Freud's system holds immanent a concept of culture as madness. To explore this aspect of Freudian social psychology, I must further trace the evolution of Freud's instinct theory. Freud insisted upon maintaining the integrity of his instinctual dualisms although he was aware of the inconsistencies this caused him. Freud may have rooted love (sexual-instincts) in hunger (ego-instincts), but hunger itself was rooted in unconscious drives, in the libido, in the hungers of sexuality. However, when Freud discovered that the ego itself is subject to libidinous striving and thus can become an object to itself, and when he failed to find a solution he could derive from the unconscious pleasure principle to explain the obsessive repetitions in dreams and symptom formation by traumatized patients, Freud realized that he must transform his first dualistic opposition of ego-instincts to sexual-instincts.

Freud then claimed that a tendency more fundamental than the pleasure principle existed; he claimed that the psychical system had to master and bind external excitations. Traumatic stimuli must produce anxiety, Freud reasoned, in order for repression to occur. When a trauma occurs suddenly and unexpectedly, it may thereby overwhelm an immature psychic apparatus. In this case, successful repression cannot occur and the neurosis of compulsive repetition of the trauma becomes the means by which the patient attempts to master the trauma by retrospectively producing anxiety. According to Ernest Jones, Freud's official biographer, Freud equates

the tendency to repetition with that of restoring a *previous* state of affairs, an equation which is far from obvious. Be this as it may, Freud came to the conclusion that the fundamental aim of all instincts is to revert to an earlier state, a regression. And if instincts aimed at the past, why should they stop before reducing a living organism to a pre-vital state, that of inorganic matter? So the ultimate aim of life must be death. In this way arose Freud's celebrated concept of the *Death Instinct.* (Jones 1961, 405)

Freud's new dualism opposes the entropy, the regressive destructiveness of the death instinct (Thanatos) to Eros, which Freud describes as the progressive building up and binding of libidinal energies into larger and larger communities.

Earlier I remarked that Freud had effected a transvaluation of patriarchal values by rooting conscious reason in the passions of unconscious libidinal striving. Now, in his final dualism, Freud has carried this transvaluation one step further. The "seething caldron," the formless chaos of unconscious desire, now becomes responsible for binding humans into more inclusive communities. The other pole of Freud's duality, once occupied by the ego-instincts, is now invaded by the *"urge inherent in organic life to restore an earlier state of things"* (Freud [1920] 1961, 30). In his first equation, which unequivocally opposed individual needs for self-preservation (ego-instincts) to society's needs for reproduction (sexual-instincts), Freud reinforced the patriarchal idea of the regressive nature of sexual love. In his last equation, Eros emerges as the triumphant source of ever-enlarging community. Thanatos, or the instincts of death and aggressiveness, linked by Freud with the satisfactions of sadism and of the ego's "narcissistic enjoyment," now become "the greatest impediment to civilization" (Freud [1930] 1961, 69). From ringing endorsements of patriarchal individualism in his early work, Freud has arrived in late maturity to an appreciation of the origins of human solidarity in sexual (sensuous, bodily) relations.

Freud himself remarks that other analysts were resisting his new ideas regarding a death instinct. In fact, even in recent times, modern psychoanalysis has managed to disregard much of Freud's later production. In the United States the only notable attempts to comment upon and extend Freud's later ideas came during the 1950s and 1960s from philosophers and cultural theorists such as Herbert Marcuse and Norman O. Brown. These last formulations and dualisms of Freud's, especially Freud's implicit concept of culture as madness, hold much promise for womanist psychology.

Unfortunately, Freud inadvertently cut off avenues to development for his Eros and death instinct dualism. Anticipating the resistances to his new formulations, and realizing the theoretical objections they would occasion, Freud sought out a multitude of biological, physiological, and even physiochemical parallels and examples with which to ground these new instincts. In this way, Freud himself partially closed the door to the symbolic and metaphoric dimensions he had originally opened with the validation of his patients' psychical realities. Freud's biological reductionism serves only to underline the gap between biological knowledge as it then existed and the potential symbolic meanings of his Eros/Thanatos dualism.

In my estimation, it is essential for the development of feminist thought that Freud's cultural theories be reexamined and that the dimension of the symbolic be explored: A theory of the symbolic death of the majority self complements that symbolic death all women suffer in patriarchal cultures. Psychoanalyst Robert Seidenberg has written sensitively of women's dilemmas in "The Trauma of Eventlessness." Seidenberg acknowledges the symbolic death of the self to which I am referring when he states, "Deaths can be many, the biological is but one. People worry about their survival: professional, social, and political, as well as biological." Seidenberg emphasizes that "loss of self encompasses matters of quality of living, accomplishments or the lack of them, meeting or falling short of one's ego ideals, and . . . success in object relations. . . . The self [can slip] away and only the fortunate get a warning signal" (quoted in Miller 1978, 361). Following are several aspects of symbolic death that, unfortunately, I can touch upon only briefly in this chapter.

Interestingly enough, Norman O. Brown assimilates Freud's death instinct, which Brown identifies as the "core" of human neuroses to infants' inability to separate from their mothers (Brown 1977, 284). I discussed the ubiquity of such an assimilation when analyzing the dominant masculine myths in Chapter 4. Brown goes on to characterize the infant's separation from mother as that which "confers individual life on all living organisms" (ibid.). Here Brown's conflating of literal birth-separation (what else could his phrase "all living organisms" mean?) with the symbolic separation of the child from the mother at the times of the Oedipal crises becomes highly symptomatic. Brown goes on to explain most conventionally that the death instinct begins with separation from mother because birth inevitably leads to death. In the light of my explanation of the genesis and repression of the mother-accomplished majority self, an entirely different and striking new understanding is now within reach.

The first meaning of symbolic death refers to the symbolic death of the child's majority self, most particularly the boy's; that the child cannot reconcile itself to the loss of this essential portion of self is not a regrettable failing, as in Freud's *and* Brown's formulations. I suggest that the concept of cultural madness immanent in Freud's later work—a madness intensifying in actuality within late twentieth-century patriarchal cultures—can be understood, in part, through this symbolic murder of the mother-accomplished majority self. I argue, in fact, that our survival and our cultural evolution depend upon successful revolt against the majority self's symbolic death. Other aspects of symbolic death will also shed light upon infamous twentieth-century suicidal, irrational impulse.

A second meaning of symbolic death involves the Oedipal girl who finds herself upon the brink of young womanhood. Here it is the denial of development to the girl's minority self, her lack of access to the patriarchal culture's symbols of immortality that constitutes a symbolic death. The Oedipal girl's minority self "slips away" as warning signals are smothered and muffled. Here, too, a revolt — a "raging against the dying of the light" — is essential. Furthermore, because of the dialectical nature of accomplicity, which forms the structures of selfhood, a third paradoxical meaning of symbolic death descends upon that very patriarchal civilization which over recent generations has brought about the first and second symbolic deaths of the boy's majority and the girl's minority selves. To obscure from itself these dialectical understandings of symbolic death and therefore seal itself off from contamination by the weak and dying feminine, patriarchal thought has had to collapse and conflate, to debase and deny, the blossoming, opening, full-blooded reality of the symbolic dimension. Just as Norman O. Brown ignores and denies the symbolic, metaphorical dimensions of death, so does other patriarchal thought — with the partial exception of Freud's — reduce the open apposite of the dialectical and overdetermined symbol to a one-dimensional mirror world filled with the impotent "imaginary" (see, for example, the work of Jacques Lacan, Lemaire 1981).

The problems of fantasy versus reality, that is, of psychic or inner reality versus patriarchal or outer reality, and of the symbolic production of the structures of selfhood hold the keys to my continuing transformation of the Freudian system. As noted earlier, taking his patients' fantasies quite seriously, Freud validated the importance and reality value of psychical events. Freud did even more than this, however: He proclaimed that the causative sexual traumas missing from the neurotic's real external world, past and present, were once present in the real external world of the ancestors of his patients. In other words, Freud developed the theory of the phylogenetic inheritance of primal fantasies and he related these to both the early sexual impulses of children and to their shame and guilt regarding these impulses. I am arguing that much which Freud attributed to phylogenetic inheritance is "inherited" in the sense that cultural selective systems and parents' individual and moral concerns pass into the constitution of infants' majority and minority selves very early by means of the hidden and partially unconscious body communications of accomplicity.

Freud believed that the incestuous desiring of the mother and the resulting murder of the father, committed in reality by our ancestors, are committed only in fantasy by children. Then, memories of these acts are repressed. Freud asserted that children believe that their thoughts are omnipotent, that magical thinking makes it so, and that committing a deed in thought is the same as committing that deed in reality. For the unconscious mind – for the modes of primary process thinking as opposed to the conscious, so-called rational modes of secondary process thinking – as persons thinketh in their hearts, so are they. But Freud's most important formulation is the one seldom analyzed: Freud concludes that sexual seductions are neither always true in reality, nor always true only in fantasy (based, remember, on prehistoric truth). Rather, Freud concludes that "the childhood experiences constructed or remembered in analysis are sometimes indisputably false and sometimes equally certainly correct, and *in most cases compounded of truth and falsehood*" (Freud [1916–33] 1966, 367). What counts, Freud said, was that the strong feelings, the dreams, the images, and the symbols, which are produced by the primary process thinking of the unconscious, must be founded upon something real, and that "*in the world of the neuroses it is psychical reality which is the decisive kind*" (ibid., 368).

Once again, Freud has uncovered an intersection of time with the timeless because by asserting the reality of children's fantasies of molestation, Freud has asserted the continuance in the present of the past. He has validated the reality of the psychic; by compounding past/present, reality/fantasy in recollection, he has dialectically opened up the dimension of the symbolic, the dimension essential to the further transformation and development of psychoanalysis.

First, we must understand that to deny sexual drives to children is in a fundamental sense to deny them agency or subjecthood. This is especially true when we understand the fundamental importance of gender drives as the major motivational system for both sexes of all ages. Second, we must understand that these drives are shaped in their specificity by mother and father accomplicity, which generates children's majority and minority selves. This means that the youngest of infants has already absorbed bodily at the earliest ages the contradictions and conflicts of patriarchal heterosexuality. Infants' psychic reality is already partially constituted and corrupted by the power relations of father and mother as their majority and minority selves are formed – and this occurs *long before* their Oedipal crises. Here we have uncovered the hidden meaning and truth of Freud's "phylogenetic heritage" and of the "evil" impulses Freud claims exist in the smallest children.

The corrupted power relations of father and mother constitute a psychic or symbolic rape of children that is as real and harmful as any physical trauma. In fact, it is the cultural meaning of sexual relations in patriarchal societies that causes the greatest injury to both girl and boy children. In patriarchal societies female children are psychically raped and molested throughout childhood and beyond: The vulnerability of their mothers is the vulnerability of their mother-accomplished majority selves, it is their very own vulnerability. This is why even boys experience symbolic rape. Freud is right, for psychic reality is as real as any other because human beings are cultural beings, are symbolic beings, as much as they are natural beings. Furthermore, the natural, that is, the sexual, is as compounded and as constituted as is the factual. "Sticks 'n stones" – and words – not only break bones: Broken minds, too, often result, minds that mend more slowly than broken bones, if they mend at all. However, infants are also agents, and the indeterminacy of parent-child accomplicity explains why most do not succumb to extremes of mental illness.

In brief, the Oedipus complex must be understood as a symbolic structure signifying the wish of the child, whether female or male, not for sexual possession of the mother, but for repossession and development of its own repressed mother-accomplished majority self. This latter represents the body-ego and includes the rich signification of the proximity senses with their rootedness in the body's temporal modalities. The "killing of the father" signifies the wish of the child to overturn the patriarchal world whose monopolization of economic and cultural power has brought about the repression, the stunting, the castration, of femininity and therefore of each child's majority self. Freud, however, did understand the dialectics of reality and fantasy in constituting the multidimensional self as well as the multidimensional cultural surround.

Early in his development of psychoanalysis, Freud took the fateful step of endorsing the reality of his patients' fantasies: Psychical reality became for Freud as important as external reality. By validating the productions of his patients' dreams, memories, and symptoms, Freud validated the truth of symbolic dimensions; he implicitly recognized the metaphoric constitution of culture and of the social-individual. By so doing, Freud was also implicitly recognizing what philosopher Jay Ogilvy (1979) meant when he proclaimed that for twentieth-century humans, culture – our symbolic constitution – has become more important than nature – our biological constitution. Moreover, late twentieth-century philosophers are now beginning to realize that the relationship between nature and culture, between body and mind, between sex and spirit, and, I would add, between female and male, remains forever partially indeterminate.

I have extended the Freudian concept of a phylogenetic cultural inheritance by suggesting that this inheritance is the power relationship of mother and father, which becomes incorporated by the infant and child's majority and minority selves by means of accomplicity. I have further extended the meanings in Freud's endorsement of the psychical dimensions of his patients' seduction memories by sketching a theory of psychic rape: In patriarchal societies where women and children are denied access to the cultural symbols of immortality and serve at the pleasure of powerful males, their very beings are violated. Excluded from the dimension of the symbolic, they are in truth castrated beings who suffer symbolic death based upon the fatality of gender.

Freud understood that the very same touch, caress, or gesture can have many nuances: The child *feels* when its meaning is affection and when lascivious domination is intended. Freud believed the patient as child. Unfortunately, Freud was trying to work within the dominant patriarchal paradigm, so that it was not possible for him to completely understand the importance of his discovery. Although he apparently took one step backward with his emphasis upon seduction fantasies, Freud took two leaps forward with his discovery that we are symbolic beings whose very substance is violated with the patriarchal degradation of women. Freud insisted that the "imaginary [can appear] before us in reality" and that "a symbol [can take] over the full functions and significance of the thing it symbolizes" (Freud [1917–23] 1958, 152). As theorist Juliet Mitchell has argued, Freud uncovered patriarchal culture's construction of adult sexuality from elements of childhood eroticism (Mitchell 1975). But these erotic organ modes of childhood, which Freud projected into our phylogenetic past, are already contaminated in infants and small children by the power struggles of father and mother.

Freud's comment that "neurotics are dominated by the opposition between reality and phantasy" would seem an apt indictment of the neuroses of patriarchal culture, which is dominated by its worship of the either/or, by a phobic avoidance of any ambiguity, by a need to separate all reality into neat little packages with watertight boundaries (Freud [1905–09] 1963, 132). However, for some readers, questions may still remain: Are little girls (or little boys) only imagining their Oedipal difficulties? Are they inventing (along with their brothers) stories of sexual molestation by fathers to screen their own guilty autoerotic activities?

I do not deny, as Freud did not deny, the reality of sexual molestation. Recent investigations are uncovering an astonishing prevalence of family incest, the overwhelming majority of which are those of uncle-niece, father-daughter, or stepfather-daughter (Russell 1986; Herman 1981).

I do, however, support Freud's assertion regarding the absence of physical molestation in some cases — this is Freud's infamous one step back, but I then expand Freud's proper emphasis upon psychic reality ("phantasy") to include the dimension of "psychic rape": In cultures where women and children are denied respect, dignity, and access to the cultural symbols of immortality, where they are valued primarily for their ability to bring pleasure to the all-powerful male, *the very processes of socialization*, of the imbuing of patriarchal cultural codes, of the production of majority and minority selves through accomplicity, constitute *a symbolic rape* of the developing child, whether female or male. The significance of this symbolic rape is a symbolic death for the boy's feminine self and a living death for the girl's feminine self.

Power is sexualized in patriarchal cultures, and men are socialized to sexualize only those whom they can dominate. Similarly, and this is the crucial point for feminist thinkers, *women are also socialized from infancy onward to sexualize only those who can dominate them.* This situation would indeed be hopelessly impervious to change if it were not for what Freud saw as the constitutional bisexuality of males and females. Without the ambivalence built into their divided selves by the processes of mother and father accomplicity, sadomasochistic conflicts would not exist. The naturally sadistic boy would find his desires met by the naturally masochistic girl; she, in turn, would also find her desires met in the same intimate dance.

But Freud explicitly denied access to such a simplistic interpretation, and he was equally explicit in his tragic vision of relations between the sexes. What Freud called the negative Oedipus complex described each sex's psychic reality existing in the heart of its opposite. Sadism and masochism are always found together in each individual, Freud declared, just as he proclaimed the mingling of femininity and masculinity and of reality and fantasy in each individual.

The tyranny of the either/or as it manifests itself in modern psychology has glossed over these complexities of Freudian thought. Freudian psychoanalysis is important to feminist thought not only for its emphasis upon bisexuality and the hidden dimensions of the unconscious; not only because of its dialectical elements, which sketch out a theory of gendered becoming based upon power and difference; and not only for the social construction of sexuality via power and difference. Indeed, Freudian psychoanalysis is important to feminist thought also because the epistemology immanent within psychoanalysis describes the social-self as a *symbolic* being: Psychoanalysis comprehends the metaphoric constitution of cultural realities and validates the importance of psychical reality. Anatomy is destiny only as long as culture says so.

However, cultures speak in many tongues besides the scripts written and spoken by fathers; the mother tongue is the primordial language learned by girls and boys in infancy, and its silent ministrations form the majority self of both. The reality of patriarchal culture is never pure but is contaminated at its inception by the real fantasies that inhabit the differences between masculine power and feminine power. Incestuous urges color the reality of both sexes and harm both even when they remain covert and repressed (Russell 1986, 392).

Freud understood that reality is often other, is often equally compounded of fantasy and reality. To paraphrase William James, without the validation of the community the reality value of fantasy cannot be recognized. And before Freud, no fantasy, no psychic reality, could be given its proper weight. But Freud built the edifice of psychoanalysis upon the hysteria of women and the sexual desires of children, and until we complete the task that Freud began, we will not penetrate into the dungeons where the potential for better femininities and masculinities lies trapped.

To know what is real and what is imagined is indeed difficult when one begins to realize that the imaginal and the fantasized themselves are important constituents of the real, and that both change dramatically with age and experience, with sex and circumstance. In *Women and Violence* (1981), Miriam F. Hirsch presents a case history that illustrates just how difficult it is for women to know their own reality in a culture that fails to validate it. As a child of nine, a woman had been fondled by her uncle, but since her parents did not believe her when she told them, she reports having "a lot of difficulty with men in [her] teens as far as what was real and what wasn't" (Hirsch 1981, 350). It was not until years later when, she was a married woman and this same uncle again approached her that she realized for the first time that "all the fears I had as a teenager were real" (ibid.)

A further example of the difficulty of sorting out reality and fantasy when the viewpoints of children and adults collide is provided by the testimony of a reporter covering the well-publicized McMartin Pre-School child molestation case. After a three-month comprehensive investigation, Cynthia Gorney of the *Washington Post* reports that the intensely charged atmosphere surrounding this case caused "both children and the adults listening to them [to lose] the capacity to sort the imagined from the actual" (Shaw 1990, A:36). The point is that for children this young, the imagined constructs the actual as much as the reactions of the community of adults help to construct the actual. Further, there could be no "letting the children express what happened to them in their own words," as was suggested, since young children often do not possess the words with which to name their experience and a neutral and objective language of molestation does not exist. All understanding, even that of scientific theorizing, is expressed in language that at bottom is metaphoric and is never innocent of viewpoints and values.

Freud himself was explicitly aware of the metaphoric dimensions of thought. In an example previously mentioned, Freud complained that the concepts of his fledgling science must remain only metaphors until new knowledge was gathered, and that this was quite unlike the concepts found in physiology and chemistry. Then as if to modify his latter assertion, Freud added, "These [physiological, chemical concepts] too only constitute a metaphorical language, but one familiar to us for a much longer time and perhaps also simpler" (Rickman 1957, 165). The use of temporal categories in relation to metaphoric thought should be noted. If Freud had stated, "these metaphorical languages appear simpler and more straightforward because familiar to us *for a much longer time*" (my emphasis) he would have been closer to the truths now being elaborated by the poststructuralist movement led by French philosopher Jacques Derrida.

There are other ways in which Freud penetrated beyond literal, indexical reality, however. As Edward Hall notes, Freud distrusted spoken words, understanding that they can hide as well as reveal. Freud knew how to read body language and all forms of nonverbal communication; for Freud the symbolic structure of gestures reveals secret desires. The neurotic symptom, like the dream, is a metaphoric communication that not only reveals a specific illness or trauma but also provides insight into the whole illness-producing situation of the patient. To those present-day structuralists for whom the unconscious is structured like an indexical language, Freud opposes the metaphoric dimensions of human communication; he does not assimilate the symbolic language of the unconscious to the language models of patriarchal science.

Those who have assimilated the unconscious and its messages to so-called scientific language, Norman O. Brown correctly accuses of "byzantine scholasticism in which 'word-consciousness' is [substituted] for consciousness of the unconscious" (Brown 1977, 319-20). Here we must remember that logical paradox of which I spoke earlier: Paradox arises when we consciously focus upon unconscious processes and structures. Awareness of this paradox must be self-consciously incorporated into our theorizing. By granting to the body-ego consciousness and thought processes, however primitive, and by discerning the production of meaning in the structures of bodily movements and interactions, Freud gave the lie to the patriarchal truism that everything not expressible in words is mere feeling. Once again, the domain reserved to the female — that of body and affect — gains both dignity (because imbued with cognitive meaning) and access to development (because imbued with structures).

Freudian psychoanalysis gives substance to linguist Edward Sapir's insight that "national languages are all huge systems of vested interests which sullenly resist critical inquiry" (Sapir 1956, 60). The dominant psychologies of the patriarchy often fail to penetrate beneath the surface because they adopt narrow scientific language structures as their paradigm, in this way reducing the metaphorical aspects of language to homological, indexical ones. Movement from one level of reality, mind, and so on, to another is blocked except via homologies; that is, any item on a given level becomes the identical equivalent to an item on another level without remainder. Implicit, then, are rules of correspondence linking levels, and these correspondence rules operate like a priori, transhistorical categories of mind. Thus is established another neo-Kantianism, yet another masculine identity theory, similar to that of Suzanne Langer's "new key" philosophy (1963) wherein symbolization becomes the first spiritual need of men and self-consciousness becomes awareness of a self-identical entity.

Freud saw more truly when he asserted that self-consciousness arises, not out of identity, not out of sameness, but out of difference, out of *"any consciousness colored by intrapsychic conflict and anxiety"* (Fingarette 1965, 312). The loci of change, movement, development, and knowledge—of self and of other—are differences apposed within a cultural matrix.

Although various patriarchal psychologies and philosophies have incorporated an understanding of the symbolic or metaphoric constitution of the self, none of these except Freud's includes a means for the productive dialogue of reason and emotion, of conscious and unconscious, of concept and percept. All other patriarchal versions are closed, reductive, one-dimensional. Within masculine thought the openness of the symbol as metaphor becomes a "Flatland" prison, except in poetic language, where the metaphor's connotative powers become emotive islands floating in a sea of irrationality. "All poetry is a cry for help," a professor of literature once told me. In this patriarchal universe of discourse, concept is concept and percept is percept and never the twain shall meet. Anthropologist Eleanor Leacock correctly notes that masculine analysis uses "the metaphorical properties of language . . . [to] reduce analogies to homologies" (Leacock 1981, 300).

By ignoring the rootedness of the object in the richness of the nature/culture synthesis, by considering only the relations of signifier to signified, recent patriarchal thought once again has eliminated essential dimensions necessary for change and movement beyond the status quo. British social theorist Anthony Giddens alludes to these problems when he complains that the prevalent usages of *symbol* in modern sociology are *"merely equivalent to 'representation,'* and hence . . . symbols are presumed to have rigid boundaries" (Giddens 1979, 108). Once again, production – this time on the level of symbolic production – is foreclosed by a simple "re," the *re* of *re*presentation; and the "presumption" of rigid boundaries defends masculine categories from contamination by the categorically impure.

When patriarchal culture symbolically murders its own majority self, it forecloses possibilities for its own development. Without a dialectics of majority-minority self, of the body-ego's sensory modalities and the rational productions of the patriarchy, without a dialectics of fact and value, of objective reality and subjective reality (image, fantasy, and metaphor), patriarchal culture itself remains stunted. The compulsive repetitions necessary to keep the feminine majority self repressed can only intensify with the passage of time and with the expansion/domination of the minority self, which, remember, becomes the patriarchy's majority self. The greater the rigidity of symptom formation and the less mental mobility available for creative imagination, the more unbalanced become all social-individuals. This indeed is what is now occurring within patriarchal civilization. The only law of life is "evolve or die" – and the death of patriarchal civilizations may be more than just symbolic.

The dialectical processes of accomplicity, which produce the structures of selfhood of girls and boys, of women and men, ensure that fantasy is inextricably mingled with other dimensions of reality. The patriarchy's invidious hierarchies of power and prestige invade and corrupt the heart of reason and repress the reasons of the heart. Women thinkers must respond to the challenge of Freud and develop that "more subtle epistemology" which philosopher Abraham Kaplan finds unrecognized and underdeveloped in Freudian psychoanalysis (Nelson 1957, 212).

The repression of the female sex and the repression of the feminine selves of men are the oldest and deepest repressions humanity knows. The lifting of these repressions, thus permitting the reuniting of the sexes in the human person, will institute the most revolutionary changes in human culture and praxis yet witnessed.

HOW THE CATEGORIES OF REPRESSION CHANGE OVER TIME

Time is the key to a transformed Freudianism. An analysis of the dialectics of temporal categories is the key to a transformed psychoanalysis. We must grasp Proust's intuition of the importance of the conception of time as "incarnate," or, as Freud might have said, "of past years still held close within us." Our mind-body health – and our survival as a species – depends upon memories that can be unearthed only with the leverage afforded by cultural metaphors capable of explaining our origins and our present cultural madness. My accomplicity model of psychosexual development presents new insights into the temporal and bodily processes that constitute our divided selves and into the gender drives that inform these selves. This model emphasizes the unity of mind and body, of the individual and the culture, and of the feminine and masculine within each person. In the final analysis, cultures are *antientropy devices* that spatialize, or reify, time by means of the hardware of the cultural surround and through the unconscious social membrane that forms and informs the body-egos of each of us.

Each social-self has formed a mother-accomplished majority self and a father-accomplished minority self. These selves are similar and overlapping because both are mediated by the patriarchal cultural surround. They are also different from each other because of the different qualities and quantities of time spent by mother and father interacting with the developing child. The mother's interactions, her productive accomplicity, is more involved and continuous with early body-ego development and the modalities of the proximity senses. Mother-child accomplicity is more intensive during the infant's critical early months and years when body-ego awarenesses predominate. Typically, the father's accomplicity becomes somewhat more intensive later on, after the child reaches three, four, or five years of age, especially with young sons. This means that the majority self precipitates are closely allied with the multidimensional rhythms of the body, with the disparate organ modes, and with the proximity senses, whereas the minority self precipitates are more closely allied with patterns of feeling, thought, and speech that develop later.

However, when mother and father produce these specific social-selves of their infant, they are not themselves conscious of all they are producing. Certainly, conscious objectives of socialization are pursued by the parents. But important portions of the developing selves are also produced without their knowledge, not, as Proust thought, in the form of impressions, because "impressing" forecloses "selecting" and both "impression" and "selection" tend to imply conscious awareness on the part of either parent or child—or both. These important portions of the nascent self are *preselections* transmitted by means of the unconscious social membrane. Here I am simply intimating within the categories of an extended Freudianism how it is that, as social critic Ernest Becker has said, "the cultural sense of space, time, and perception of objects are literally built into the neural structure" (Becker 1973, 219). In brief, the theory of accomplicity clarifies that which Hall has called "the most difficult point to make and make clearly," namely, that "not only is culture imposed upon man but it *is* man in a greatly expanded sense" (Hall 1973, 188).

However, because accomplicity is a dialectical process and the infant an interacting subject, culture is not just "imposed upon man"; nor, as I have explained before, are "men" self-made. That which truly does take place between these masculine poles of imposition and self-production, between the tyranny of structure and the irresponsibility of unattached agency, are processes of interaction whereby the intangible, the spiritual, the mental, and the indeterminate — in short, our energy selves — become tangible, determinate, and *embodied* structures of *gendered* selfhood. Between these poles multiple times intersect with the timeless.

Historian and social critic Norman O. Brown has called attention to "the collapse of the rationalist notion of time [which] leaves the current theory of time irrationally culturally relativistic" (Brown 1977, 273). Brown goes on to laud Freud's discovery of the timelessness of the unconscious and to insist that healthy and unrepressed humans, "would not live in time" (ibid., 274). Here Brown's solution to human neurosis follows once again the familiar masculine pattern: We have found temporal categories to be culturally relative, Brown states, and therefore they are not immutable Kantian a prioris, common to all humans. Both modern and "archaic" rational times correlate with instinctual repressions; thus, our discovery of the relativity of cultural temporality signals the need for movement out of repression and into timelessness (ibid., 275). According to Brown, the principal human neurosis stems from the human incapacity to accept death, that cessation of individual time.

Again, I suggest that the binary time/timelessness gives us little insight into the problem of repression because if the unconscious is the site of repression and if it is characterized by timelessness (presuppositions this study has challenged), how then, precisely, will attaining a state of atemporality, that is, being able to live outside time, without fear of death, allow humans to live without repressions? Conversely, why would abolishing repressions permit humans to live outside time? In fact, Brown's analysis falters in the face of the reader's unwillingness to suspend disbelief: One simply cannot imagine either the unrepressed human or the atemporal human. Poet T. S. Eliot expresses greater insight when he declares, "Only through time is time conquered" (Bergsten 1960, 181) (paraphrased).

The solution to the problems of repression and temporal categories must be referred once again to the differing temporal categories of the majority and minority portions of the social-self and to their paradigm changes at the times of the Oedipus crises for girl and for boy. There are not just two times; not just different cultural times and timelessness.

There are, indeed, many simultaneous times within one culture. The timelessness that Freud discovered, the undeniable fact that the passage of time does not alter the repressed, as Freud put it, does not mean that the unconscious is timeless; it means, rather, that the structures of repression are locked into compromise formations that manifest themselves in unchanging symptomatic repetitions (e.g., fetishism, addictions, and compulsion neurosis).

Psychoanalyst Otto Fenichel, Freud's follower, understands this point well when he declares: "Not because primitive instincts are still effective within us do we have wars, misery and neuroses; rather, because we have not yet learned to avoid wars and misery by a more reasonable and less contradictory regulation of social relations, our instincts are still kept in an unfavorable form" (Jacoby 1983, 121). Humans cannot live without repression because they cannot live totally conscious, one-dimensional, self-identical lives. They cannot live without repression because they are *and* are not the unconscious social membrane that simultaneously connects them to the cultural body and separates them from it. Human beings are *and* are not the past history of their ancestors and the future history of their descendants.

In Freud's view the human superego, the seat of conscience and moral prescriptions, has many contacts with the phylogenetic heritage of the id. I have posited a dialectic of the id with the social heritage, represented by the superego. The latter is the culture's living unconscious represented by its living inhabitants, while the former represents a phylogenetic storehouse which I characterize as culture's contribution to instinct. I suggest that the deepest levels of unconsciousness are imprisoned in neural structures almost beyond the reach of reflexivity and are therefore dead to consciousness. While co-constituting itself in accomplicity with the outer world, the ego also co-constitutes its superego and deposits it within itself, that is, within the unconscious. Thus, I find in the Freudian system openings through which time can indeed be understood to interact with the timeless: the categories of repression themselves change over time. Norman O. Brown clearly understood that the structures of repression can change, that temporal categories — experiential and conceptual — themselves evolve over time.

However, I must add that there are limits to the depth of cultural repressions. At a certain distance elements repressed into the unconscious social membrane congeal into signifying natural patterns. These patterns, in turn, become through time the atemporal unconditioneds — the reifications, if you will — of our instinctual heritage. The human body-ego and human senses have developed over centuries in interaction with developing human cultures. The human nervous system becomes the phylogenetic heritage. In addition, I have also suggested that ontogeny does not recapitulate phylogeny, that infants "pick up" the curve of the cultural spiral where they find it. And as Dr. Ashley Montagu has so cogently argued in *Growing Young* (1981), the ever-increasing prolongation of youthful potential (neoteny) is the impulsion driving and guiding human evolution. But human evolution is presently locked in place because those youthful potentials are locked in the limbo of repressed majority selves. Freud's primal fantasies exist only because they are unrecognized and continuing contemporary problems; they are gender conflicts locked into the neural networks of infants by the mothers and fathers who battle over their cribs.

Because of Freud's insistence upon the importance of childhood memories in the etiology of the neuroses, he has often been accused of the "genetic fallacy," as when critic Philip Rieff declares, "While an oak does originate in an acorn, the mature tree cannot be held to be still 'essentially' acorn-ish" (Rieff 1961, 51). In typical masculine fashion, Rieff wishes to suggest that men evolve beyond their origins. I do not dispute this possibility, provided that origins are correctly understood, their challenges resolved, and these resolutions assimilated. By insisting on the phylogenetic inheritance of the primal fantasies (the Oedipus complex, the castration complex, incestuous acts and longings, and so on), Freud is acknowledging the contemporaneousness of impulses he identifies as both primitive and repressed. I have been suggesting that these impulses are not both primitive and imperishable but, rather, are impulses held in repression and therefore kept primitive by the power of patriarchal culture.

As patriarchal man defined the female by her sexuality, he also linked this sexuality to the sensory modalities of the body-ego. As the economic and cultural power of man grew, his stunting of the feminine became a stunting of the body-ego and, by intermediary of the majority self, a stunting of patriarchal man himself. When patriarchal man cut the female off from access to cultural symbols of immortality and transcendence, thus castrating her, he condemned himself as adult oak to eternal acornhood. This is my dialectical interpretation of the significance of the Freudian phylogenetic heritage.

The resurrection of body-ego awarenesses and modalities will entail the resurrection of other time senses, and in this way humans will indeed begin to live, not in timelessness, but in new and richer times. The repressed cultural unconscious is predominantly constituted at this historical juncture by the repressed structures, the repressed body-ego modalities, the repressed temporal categories, of the mother-accomplished majority selves of social-individuals. Herbert Marcuse has noted that "under the predominance of rationalism, the cognitive function of sensuousness has been constantly minimized" (Marcuse 1974, 180). I suggest that this negligence can continue only so long, and then reason itself begins to decay, reason itself begins to produce those repressions upon which aggression and, finally, madness feed.

In *The Natural History of the Mind* Gordon Rattray Taylor presents evidence that feelings have cognitive import; he describes dreams as consisting, not primarily "of images or actions," but of feelings combined with knowledge. (Taylor 1979, 151–52). Taylor also explains how perception "makes only relative judgments – and then treats them as absolute" (Taylor 1979, 207). Taylor asserts that this characteristic of perceptual functioning has important philosophical implications. The most important implication provides us with insight into the manner in which cultural paradigms may change over time. For if cultural categories become embedded as instincts, then there exists a type of cultural unconditioned, or absolute that is at once both relative and absolute, and, most important, this cultural absolute can change and evolve over time with the evolution of the culture's individuals. Therefore, the weakness of arguments involving a "renaturalization" of the world becomes patent: Love, sensuousness, peace and happiness cannot arise out of a resurrection of the body, because body, like nature, does not exist to be uncovered or liberated, any more than does women's sexuality. Liberation consists only in the releasing of repressed portions of the self into renewed processes of human interaction that *may* lead to fuller development.

Symptoms and dreams, then, could be recognized as attempts by the repressed portions of the self to "reclothe" concepts with the affectively toned symbols and metaphors that express the knowledge the conscious self needs in order to change and evolve. It is an attempt by the self to attain that dialectical wholeness which is dependent upon metaphoric partialization, upon a recognition of the symbolic constitution of all levels of reality, and upon the reuniting of majority and minority social-selves.

In so far as the gender conflicts of female and male, of majority and minority social-selves, are of long duration and have been exacerbated by cultural developments over the last 100 years, these conflicts exist within both the unrepressed and the repressed cultural unconscious. Their existence on the deepest levels of the unconscious accounts for the great difficulty in raising and resolving these conflicts. In a profound sense we *are* the conflicts, just as Freud's disciple Sandor Ferenczi stated that an individual *is* his character flaws. Most important, the depth to which gender conflicts penetrate the cultural unconscious – testimony to their longevity – ensures the revolutionary nature of any progress made toward their unleashing.

Freud believed that psychoanalytic theory will lift repressions and slowly integrate ego and id within the self. He relates this slow process to "a work of culture — not unlike the draining of the Zuider Zee" (Freud [1916–33] 1966, 544). Yet because of the dialectical relationships existing among levels of social-self consciousness and the levels of the unconscious, repressed and unrepressed, new precipitates are continuously produced, and new conflicts and contradictions are created, just as some are pressing to be lifted. Therefore, Freud's cultural Zuider Zee is continuously being refilled by the rush of events and by the precipitates from interacting temporal modalities. It is, in fact, the nonidentity of these temporal rhythms that creates the substrates of self.

Important in this context is the insight provided by modern physics and philosophy that the ways in which we know codetermine knowledge itself. A corollary understanding asserts that the very process of cognitive focusing codetermines the qualitative categories themselves, including those of time. The moment that we begin to analyze what we are feeling, we have changed our feelings. Therefore, we must understand that the discontinuous quality of the ego's, and the body-ego's, cognitive awareness creates a punctuation of phenomenal flow, of the id's timeless continuity.

In other words, psychic energies are bound in different ways by the qualitatively different focusing of awareness of the body-ego's different sensory modalities. These latter, in turn, create the structures of selfhood; again, awareness varies along several dimensions, and the body-ego has many qualitatively different awarenesses corresponding to its various sensory modalities. As these bound structures become the self structures over different body times, they are reified in habit and in material structures. But Freud also describes the opposite movement: Recollections directed psychoanalytically can destructure habits, which is another way of describing the lifting of repressed material from the unconscious.

Hall has written about the problem of "cultural indeterminacy" in *The Silent Language* (1973), where he summarizes his argument by stating, "When working with cultural data, *one can only be precise on one analytic level at a time and then only for a moment*" (Hall 1973, 114). So, too, there exists a need for such a principle of indeterminacy in order to account theoretically for change and development. All masculine theories of identity are static and cannot account for change. Theories of change and development require a logic of paradox, a moment wherein a thing both is and is not itself. The indeterminate moment is that moment of change. Furthermore, for the same reasons, change requires more than one valid level of analysis, more than one reality. Hall has noted the hostility of Americans toward accepting the different cultural realities existing within American society. Americans are preoccupied, he believes, with content rather than with form or structure (Hall 1969, 183). In fact, as long as American culture remains locked in mythic Faustian individualism, it will continue to lack the theoretical vision required to resurrect family, community, and country.

During the course of this study, I have repeatedly asserted that this patriarchal neglect of cultural theory is closely related to the repression of women's differences and, most specifically, to the repression of the mother-accomplished majority self whose contamination men fear. For this reason, the concept of culture, like that of the psychoanalytic unconscious, is resisted. Both resistances were explicitly noted by Hall and equated to each other. Patriarchal men deny their origins in the mother-accomplished majority self by insisting that they are self-made; for these self-made men that which occurs pre-Oedipally is mere emotion, fantasy, and the imaginary. But, as I have also suggested, when the multidimensional self is flattened out to one-dimension by such repression and denial, the possibilities for change and progress are forfeited. Along with the majority self are repressed the body-ego's sensory modalities, particularly those of the proximity senses. These are the very aspects of awareness that make learning through the body more powerful than secondary process learning.

The female body as a symbol of this early period is also repressed and replaced by patriarchal culture with a one-dimensional fetish – the forever young, stylized sex-goddess body of woman. Hall understands that humans "can be viewed as having visual, kinesthetic, tactile, and thermal aspects of [their selves] which may be either inhibited or encouraged to develop by [their] environment" (Hall 1969, 63). Hall also describes how Western cultures suppress memories through the suppression of odors (deodorants, air-conditioning, perfumes, and enclosed spaces). Smell, touch, and taste, like the taste of Proust's notorious madeleine, evoke the deepest memories because these senses are closely linked with the repressed majority self, formed during the early critical pre-Oedipal period when the infant's limbic system was becoming bound (ibid., 62–63).

Sapir has called attention to patriarchal neglect of the enculturation of children. He criticizes the metaphor of the "givenness" of culture and asserts that "the supposed 'givenness' of culture . . . is the most serious obstacle to our real understanding of the nature of culture and cultural change and of their relationship to individual personality. Culture is not, as a matter of sober fact, a 'given' at all . . . but something to be gradually and gropingly discovered. We then see at once that elements of culture that come well within the horizon of awareness of one individual are entirely absent in another individual's landscape" (Sapir 1956, 205). Part of these differences Sapir notes can be accounted for by the different cultural universes of the female and of the male. Moreover, on a higher level of abstraction, as various aspects of culture are integrated into the consciousness of cultural individuals, new contradictions arrive on the scene, which generate new deposits in the cultural unconscious.

Again, Freud's Zuider Zee may be drained by increased psychoanalytical knowledge, but temporal flows assure that it also is constantly being refilled. Some aspects of one generation's repressed unconscious may become future generations' unrepressed unconscious, and contemporary reinforcement of old conflicts may cause a reversal of relationship between these aspects of unconsciousness. It is not, as Erikson declares, that the generation is the "chosen unit of observation"; any understanding of time, change, and development requires more than one unit of observation, more than one level of analysis for intelligibility.

Complementary models must be developed to treat the individual as "unit of observation" and the generation or generations as "unit of observation"; but, most important of all, models must also be developed to treat the relationship between these models. Again note that, as Hall explains, *"one can only be precise on one analytic level at a time and then only for a moment"* (Hall 1973, 114). Within all these models a cultural principle of indeterminacy is operative. The passage of long periods of time flattens the interlocking and asymmetrical spirals of human development into closed, one-dimensional circles that from our limited perspective and with our usual lack of imagination we then mistake for monolithic truth – or call them "vicious" circles.

I have discussed above a possible reinterpretation of Freud's famous, if scientifically suspect, theory of the phylogenetic inheritance of acquired traits. I have suggested that Freud's importance to a transformed psychoanalysis also adheres in these immanent concepts of culture, resisted by patriarchal thought as ferociously as is the concept of the unconscious. For it is not that the unconscious is feminine but, rather, that the unconscious harbors those hidden and repressed aspects of the social-self, especially those of the majority self, that bear an intimate relationship to the formation and deformation of patriarchal femininity. If time is incarnate, as Proust declared, and past years still held close within us, these years are the time, and times, of the mother-accomplished majority self – the years during which this self has been developmentally frozen by repression.

The Freudian residues produced by overdetermination represent the tragedy of loss all genuine development requires. Earlier I suggested that the idea of metaphoric knowledge points beyond the individual self to the culture in which the self is grounded. Metaphors are not homologies; metaphors are cultural means by which wholeness is carved from infinite possibility. Metaphors regulate possibility and open up potential, just as they tend to cut away possibility. To understand the nature of cultural metaphor is to understand the nature of culture as tragedy.

The elements of uncertainty and ambiguity brought about by Freud's insistence on causal overdetermination entail the necessity Freud saw for interpretation. Interpretation, in turn, ensures that psychoanalytic theorizing and healing remain rooted in the specificities of each social-self's situation. Furthermore, Freud's emphasis on overdetermination of symptom, symbol, and motive points to a principle of cultural indeterminacy that respects the reality of interactive dualisms and of the dual existential realities of the sexes.

It must remain beyond the scope of this present study to examine all aspects of symbolic and metaphoric Freudian psychoanalysis. As already mentioned within various contexts, Freud's system contains its own elements of one-dimensionality and Freud reproduces his own brands of identity theory. But, as also noted, Freud gives us more than another identity theory: Freud gives us the indeterminate, the multiple, the ambiguous, and the means by which something is simultaneously both itself and other. Freud gives us a logic of paradox, along with his principles of transformation and complementarity. For Freud, the metaphoric dimensions of the dream and symptom both reflect and constitute important aspects of the social-self. For Freud the social-self is a bisexual structure of difference united by the matrices of the unconscious — what I am calling the unconscious social membrane — as well as by primal fantasies. For Freud, psychic reality, the dimension of the symbolic, is as real as other dimensions. For Freud, reality and fantasy meet and mingle, destructuring each other and constituting new symbolic realities.

Freud's system destroys isomorphic relationships and homologies by recognizing the symbolic dimensions of the social-self, by validating the metaphoric constitution of cultural realities, and by granting to fantasies a weight equal to other realities. In these ways Freud denies the identity theories upon which patriarchal philosophies and psychologies are founded. Freud's metapsychology constitutes a nonidentity theory of transformation across levels. Freud's thought produces the bridges whereby genuine development proceeds via differences dialectically apposed. Freudian explanation evolves from the interpretations of disciplined subjectivity, which dignify with recognition the realities of women.

Culture is more than an aide-memoire: Culture spatializes times within our very nervous systems. A developed concept of culture is indispensable to social theory. And a transformed psychoanalysis that emphasizes the temporal intersections of the majority and minority selves with the levels of the unconscious is indispensable to a concept of culture. In order that a viable concept of culture be incorporated into social theory, Faustian man must be willing to recognize that he is not as free as he believes, so that through this recognition he may gain more freedom than he now actually enjoys.

Finally, this new vision regarding cultural realities and their relationship to the divided selves of men and women serves to validate psychoanalyst Jean Baker Miller's insight that women embody the unsolved problems of the dominant culture (Miller 1986, 56).

7

Sisterhoods and Brotherhood

---

*The love between the sexes is undoubtedly
one of the first things in life, and the com-
bination of mental and bodily satisfaction
attained in the enjoyment of love is literally
one of life's culminations.*

Sigmund Freud

*It seems that Man Alone is a figure of
profound, tragic and noble philosophical
significance, while woman alone is a welfare problem.*

Mary O'Brien

TOWARD A WOMANIST PSYCHOTHERAPY

To center modern *angst* in gender conflicts is not to reduce the grand
nineteenth- and twentieth-century traditions of philosophical and
psychological speculation to the narrowness of sexuality. Rather, it is
finally to give serious consideration to the larger half of humanity who
have been ignored and often despised; it is, quite simply, to take women
and their differences from men seriously. Cultural theorist Anne Parsons
found that "what is therapeutic in one social context may very well be
sick-making in another" (Parsons 1969, 284). For example, Parsons
discovered that American models of psychoanalytic therapy resulted in
unintended "sick-making" with working-class patients in Italy.

Similarly, I am suggesting that applying the present types of patriarchal psychotherapies to women may also be sick-making. I am suggesting that a feminist or womanist psychotherapy will differ markedly from prevailing therapies, and that the principles of this psychotherapy may, in the final analysis, be more therapeutic for men than those now prevailing. Above all, I am suggesting that Sigmund Freud's vision of a psychoanalysis of patriarchal cultural neurosis and malaise is necessary in order to further advance our understanding of the depth psychology of social-individuals, whether female or male. Most psychotherapists today do view the therapist-patient relationship as a complex system of interactions wherein a "therapeutic alliance" must be established. I submit that the most important part of this therapeutic alliance resides in the articulation of a new world-view that recognizes the fundamental importance of gender to unleashing the potentials of our divided and healing selves.

Although a complete and detailed exposition of a new psychotherapy lies outside the scope of this study, important principles for such a future therapy do arise out of the model of psychosexual development presented here. I believe that this womanist psychotherapy is highly consonant with the work of many distinguished feminist psychotherapists, including Jean Baker Miller, Judith Herman, and Miriam Greenspan (1985).

The most important principle of a womanist psychotherapy declares that the *differences* of women from men — as mothers, as daughters, as human beings — must be culturally respected and validated. This tenet presupposes analyses of patriarchal culture, such as this study represents, that will explain patriarchal gynephobia and sexual fetishism, as well as clarify the origins of our social-selves, of cultural solidarity, and of culture/self conflicts. On the level of theory and philosophy, feminist thinkers must develop models of being/knowing that make differences central and respectable, thereby transforming masculine models of identity. Above all, feminist theory must clarify the relationship between feminine and masculine differences and similarities.

Philosopher Paul Ricoeur believes we must learn that "to see *the like* is to see the same in spite of, and through, the different. This tension between sameness and difference characterizes the logical structure of likeness. Imagination, accordingly, is this *ability* to produce new kinds by assimilation and to produce them not *above* the differences, as in the concept, but in spite of and through the differences" (Ricoeur 1978, 5:148). Ricoeur's theory explaining the imaginative construction of metaphor can also help us to understand the structure and importance of cultural metaphors and of the cultural construction of sexuality/gender:

For only by learning to understand and cherish the differences that are imaginatively productive through their very quality of difference can we hope for human growth and resolution of gender conflict. Unless we can learn to live in the multiplicity of times — "body" times — represented by the majority self, we will continue to experience that "time sickness" Freud understood as the repression of primal memories. Unless we can learn to embrace and tolerate difference, we will continue to exist divided from our selves and from others, unable, as Larry Dossey states, to "escape to new levels of internal [and external] richness" (Dossey 1982, 133).

Womanist psychotherapy affirms Freud's emphasis upon the interpretation of patient's dreams, fantasies, symptoms, and unconscious symptomatic actions and gestures. However, the womanist psychotherapist will teach patients how to interpret their own dreams, fantasies, and so forth, by putting them in touch with their body-egos through exercises which reawaken and reintegrate the proximity senses. In this way, the therapist will also put patients in touch with their majority selves, and she will awaken them to the aspirations of their minority selves; she will facilitate healing dialogues between these two selves.

Although in our agitated culture both sexes need all of the above, men most particularly need to be put in touch with their body-egos and with their repressed majority selves; women most particularly need to be taught how the patriarchal culture has distorted their body-image. Women also need to be put in touch with their stunted minority selves and to be encouraged to recognize the "traumas of eventlessness" and triviality in their lives. They need to develop beyond these unnamed problems — long ago named by Betty Friedan — and master objective cultural disciplines and cultivate the disciplined subjectivity that is women's strength. Equally important for women is recognition of the ways in which patriarchal culture has trivialized the exceedingly important productive work that women do with children by means of accomplicity.

Above all, womanist therapists must encourage women to challenge those aspects of patriarchal culture that handicap women and to join groups and organizations that are acting to transform society. Womanist psychotherapy is an active psychotherapy.

Parsons has pointed out that too much neutrality on the part of a therapist can increase a patient's conflicts rather than temper them (Parsons 1969, 326–29). Parsons states, "Active psychotherapy means . . . that it is the responsibility of the therapist to know about his [*sic*] patient's social norms and to consider them as crucially relevant to the treatment process" (ibid., 323). Certainly, this sensitivity to social norms must also apply to the cultural norms of women in patriarchal societies. In these cases, the psychotherapist's capital responsibility is to understand the multiple double binds with which patriarchal society hobbles women. Moreover, Parsons presents an excellent example of what I have called the sterility of one-dimensional thought when she points out that barriers to insight can come, not only from _not_ speaking the same language, but also from sharing _too closely_ the same (professional) language (ibid., 330).

Finally, when describing the client-therapist relationship, I once again emphasize the importance of Erik Erikson's insistence that "the psychotherapist must include in his field of observation _a specific self-awareness_ in the very act of perceiving his patient's actions and reactions. I shall claim that there is a core of _disciplined subjectivity_ in clinical work — and this both on the side of the therapist and of the patient — which it is neither desirable nor possible to replace altogether with seemingly more objective methods" (Erikson 1964, 53). Erikson goes on to ask, "How [do] the two subjectivities join in the kind of disciplined understanding and shared insight which we think are operative in a cure . . . ?" (ibid.). Erikson's reply to this question underscores the historical nature of the psychoanalytic encounter, that is, that this encounter develops empathy over time. Essentially correct, Erikson's reply must be further enlarged, I believe, by the concept of a cultural matrix and by the dialectics of accomplicity: The client-therapist relationship should be viewed as a relationship that repairs those faulty aspects of parent-child accomplicity by simultaneously destructuring the old and precipitating new structures of selfhood.

This way of viewing the client-therapist relationship holds the key to the problem of transference resolution. Womanist psychotherapy focuses on the mentorship of the therapist in the resolution of that which Freudian psychoanalysts call the "transference neurosis." Freud understood that human neurosis involves problems related to the social construction of sexuality, which can be traced to origins in the patient's childhood. I have reinterpreted these neurosis-generating problems as originating in majority self and minority self conflicts, which derive from mother and father cultural power differentials. Freud came to realize that during the psychoanalytic cure "a new edition" of the original parent-child relationship, and therefore a new edition of the childhood neurosis, is created. By treating and curing this transference neurosis, the therapist also treats and cures the original illness. Therapy was supposed to end with the "dissolution of the transference." But, as Norman O. Brown notes, both Freud and our common sense tell us that transferences cannot be completely dissolved (Brown 1977, 146).

From the standpoint of my new model of psychosexual development, this problem of the dissolution of the transference is a false problem that reflects the original masculine reluctance to acknowledge the permanence of feminine contamination of the child's majority self by the processes of mother-child accomplicity. Because *all* human accomplicity creates self-structures on levels both conscious and unconscious, the true problem then becomes one, not of dissolution, but of qualitatively changing the structures of self.

Ideally, the transference neurosis is resolved — and not dissolved — by the lifting of the repressions holding both body-ego and majority self in bondage and by the encouragement of engagements that develop the minority self. The processes of therapist-client accomplicity should create new structures of selfhood by involving clients in creative initiatives that contribute to changing their cultural surround. By encouraging the patient's gaze "outward" as well as "inward," and by revealing to clients the relationship between inner and outer, the therapist creates in the client minimal new "dependencies" on the therapist herself.

In fact, competent therapists are able to develop in clients the social-self knowledge, interpersonal coping skills, and flexibility that permit richer and broader engagement in life. It is neither possible nor necessary to eliminate the emotional involvement of therapist and client; it is possible and necessary, however, for that emotional involvement to work toward enlarging the present and future possibilities of the client. Furthermore, clients bring satisfactions and enlargements of life to the therapist as well, aside from monetary considerations: By sharing therapeutic accomplicity with clients, the psychotherapist builds knowledge and skill from which she or he, the profession, and future clients will all benefit.

The suggestions for a womanist psychotherapy outlined above are, of course, brief and preliminary attempts to draw out some clinical implications from the theoretical transformations of Freudian psychoanalysis contained in this study.

Many critics have noted that psychoanalysis, along with other psychologies in the modern world, has become a substitute for religious belief systems. These critics use such comparisons in order to denigrate and dismiss the importance of insight-based psychotherapies. This disparaging attitude toward psychoanalysis on the part of some social critics is corollary to the patriarchal attitude toward subjectivity mentioned earlier: Take one step outside the fortress of objectivity, says patriarchal thought, and one sinks into the quagmires of subjectivity and absolute relativity of belief. I trust that the validation of disciplined subjectivity will help to dispel this pernicious attitude. Indeed, the masculine eschewing of the subjective in favor of the objective motivated Freud to deny that psychoanalysis had any "Weltanschauung" (world-view) other than that of science itself. To make psychoanalysis acceptable to the scientific traditions of his day, many of which continue in force today, Freud emphasized the objectivity of psychoanalytic findings, in this way obscuring recognition and development of the new "subtle" epistemology that Freudian psychoanalysis foreshadows and that, I predict, will finally come to fruition with the birth of feminist psychoanalysis and womanist psychotherapies.

UNLEASHING OUR UNKNOWN SELVES

As we approach the twenty-first century, I submit that we are not entering the postindustrial age, nor the postmodern age, nor even the information age. Quite simply, we are in transition toward the *age of relationship*, an age in which humanity's headline story will be of revolutions in relationships. In particular, a revolution is now occurring in gender relationships because new insights into gender drives are permitting us to understand how our selves are constituted by our relationships. When we fully understand that we are, in part, our relationships, then we will be able to understand why children cling to the most abusive of parents, as psychoanalyst Alice Miller (1985) has shown. A "partnership order" (Eisler 1988) is liberated as we acknowledge the essential and inextricable involvement of the other in the constitution of the self; as we acknowledge that human beings can neither exist nor develop outside of human relationships, however violent and impoverished; as we acknowledge the inevitable contamination of each masculine self by the feminine, and vice versa.

Communication between human beings is more than an exchange; it represents the constitution of the structures of selfhood. These structures of selfhood are constituted through a dialectics of difference within a cultural matrix. Theorist Sandra Harding rightly proclaims that "existing bodies of belief do not just ignore women and gender; they distort our understanding of all of social life by ignoring the ways women and gender shape social life and by advancing false claims about both women and gender" (Harding 1987, 189). The new questions the age of relationship must answer are these: How have cultural gender divisions prevented us from understanding the relationship between body and mind, between feminine and masculine, and between the culture and the individual? And, how has the patriarchal culture's denigration of all things feminine perpetuated men's wars against the environment, against women and children, against his fellow men, and against his own majority self? For if feminist and womanist thinkers do not relate the denigration and estrangement of women and the feminine to the crises of patriarchal man, amply documented in the philosophical and scientific literature, then they will be overlooking a principal means of enlisting men in their movement toward freedom, equality, and psychosocial evolution.

As Thomas S. Kuhn might point out, anomalies are multiplying. Modern science cannot explain how multiple personality arises, how the mind controls the body during hypnosis, hysteria, biofeedback, and immune system enhancement; nor can science now explain the phenomenon of the *idiot savant* or the miracle of the child prodigy. And, despite his monumental contributions to human knowledge, Freud admitted toward the end of his career that even he did not understand the origins of neurosis, nor what its "ultimate, its own peculiar *raison d'être*" was. Freud said, "After tens of years of psychoanalytic labours, we are as much in the dark about this problem as we were at the start" (Freud [1926] 1959, 75).

My response to Freud's puzzlement is that in our unique historical moment, the genesis of most neurotic behavior will be found, not, as Freud thought, in sexual drives — drives based on instinctual urges — but in gender drives — those drives shaped by the cultural construction of femininity and masculinity. These drives are violently distorted by patriarchal culture's denigration of all things feminine. An examination of how femininity and masculinity are formed in accomplicity with parents or parental figures during infants' earliest months of life will reveal that the wells of sexuality and gender are poisoned at their source by the physical, emotional, and symbolic violence visited upon mothers by the patriarchal order. The accomplicity model of psychosexual development outlined here explains how human selves are divided by the violent suppression of the masculine selves of women and the feminine selves of men.

Today we are witness to a widening split within patriarchal cultures between definitions of masculinity and femininity and between the worlds of men and of women. The rising tides of violence against women and children, the growth of pornography, the increasing prevalence of sadomasochistic behavior, even the prevalence of addictive alienation from the body and the massive degradation of nature, all these testify to great divides. Until now the fundamental asymmetry of human interrelationship, of accomplicity in the adult-infant relationship, has been obscured by the politics of symmetry and by the myth of the founding of social intercourse in social contracts. Our unique moment in time demands new insight into the origins of our divided selves; our only hope is that dialogues concerning gender drives will heal the selves that have been broken apart along the fault lines of femininity and masculinity.

My accomplicity model of psychosexual development indicates the openings for change in both men and women. It suggests that the majority self constitutes a feminine fifth column in men just as the minority self constitutes a masculine fifth column in women. By means of these unrecognized fifth columns each sex unconsciously incorporates and lives the realities of the other. By unleashing the potentials of the majority self in men and the minority self in women both sexes will become more complete sensuously and cognitively. The battle between the sexes will finally end.

Prevalent in patriarchal thought is the idea of original social contracts among men in which women were exchanged in order to prevent incest and to solidify ties between tribes, clans, and nations; this idea presupposes a natural hostility, egocentricity, and aggressiveness among men. However, the facts of modern anthropology do not support this picture of early man, "red in tooth and club." The distinguished paleoanthropologist Richard Leakey has written a book, *The Making of Mankind* (1981), in which he refutes the idea of a natural aggressive instinct in humankind. Leakey explains that "when you actually look at the [very distant] past, the evidence for aggression and violence does not exist. The only evidence of what people did in that primitive period is what they left behind, and no weapons of death and destruction—no clubs—have been found" (*U.S. News & World Report* 1982, 92:62). In fact, Leakey asserts that "if there is any one thing that makes humans human, it is cooperation, not aggression"(ibid.).

World-famous anthropologist Ashley Montagu has written *The Nature of Human Aggression* in order to put to rest "the idea that human beings are inescapably evil" (Montagu 1976, 52). Montagu concludes that "aggressive behavior is frequently the response to the frustration of the need for love" and that "no child who was ever adequately loved ever became a delinquent or a murderer" (ibid., 324).

My study raises the question as to how women as mothers and as unnurtured—inadequately loved—nurturers can be expected to produce nonaggressive children. The answer is, quite simply, they cannot.

My reinterpretation of Freud's Oedipus complex provides clues for a deciphering of masculine aggressiveness and patriarchal authoritarianism. Many critics have already noted that masculine individualism, founded in an identification with the aggressive, castrating father, is a spurious individualism that represses genuine uniqueness.

Social theorist Richard Lichtman, for example, comments, "The secret of the resolution of the Oedipus complex is that *individualism is born in terror*" (Lichtman 1982, 157) (my emphasis). I suggest, however, that an even more closely guarded secret is that of the repression of the feminine majority self during the boy's Oedipus crisis. It is this repression that ensures that the Oedipus complex can never be completely resolved, given our present sex/gender system.

The massive studies of the authoritarian personality carried out by T. W. Adorno and others during the 1950s suggest that individuals most susceptible to authoritarian prejudices are likely "to keep important personality needs out of consciousness, [to keep them] *ego-alien*" (Adorno 1950, 55) and that "the extremely unprejudiced individual tends to manifest a greater readiness to become aware of unacceptable tendencies and impulses in himself" (ibid., 474). I differentiate between these two poles (authoritarian/nonauthoritarian) by reference to the *degree* of majority self repression. It is interesting to note that the ethnocentric or authoritarian individual fears above all contamination and being over-whelmed (ibid., 98). These are the very fears of men confronted with femininity and with their own repressed majority selves. I conclude that majority- and minority-self conflicts and divisions arising out of father and mother power hierarchies within the family represent the fundamental schisms of patriarchal cultural life. This insight validates and illuminates an important rallying cry of the 1960s and 1970s: Indeed, the personal *is* political.

Patrick Mullahy reveals Otto Rank's unusual insight into the problems of sublimation and desexualization when he summarizes Rank's views regarding men and women:

In order to pursue his supernatural aims, man has masculinized the world, including woman, and has forced a masculine ideology on her, who still preserves the "irrational" elements in human nature. Man has never accepted the fact of being mortal, that is, "never accepted himself." Hence his basic psychology is "denial of his mortal origin and a subsequent need to change himself in order to find his real self, which he rationalizes as independent of woman." (Rank quoted in Mullahy 1948, 198)

Of course, this "masculinization of the world" Freud describes as the Oedipal boy's father identification and his destruction-repression of object-cathexes to mother. These result in what Freud calls a desexualization and sublimation, and what I describe as the destruction-repression of the boy's majority self. Thus, desexualization entails the very real repression of the body-ego's sensory and temporal modalities and the symbolic repression of those feminine aspects of the boy's self developed in accomplicity with the mother. Desexualization equals defeminization because the patriarchal culture's symbolic construction of femininity makes women = body = sex. The tragedy of patriarchal civilizations, seen so clearly by Freud, is that the disembodiment, or castration, required by older men (and dead men, i.e., ancestors) of young men entering the symbolic world of masculine immortality leads to increasing guilt and sterility.

The multidimensional body-ego is essential to cultural evolution, yet it remains locked with the majority self in unconscious limbo; there it calls for release through dreams and symptoms, through the reembodiments of words in sensory images and symbols. Yet it goes unheeded; its productions are judged primitive and mere fantasy and despised as unthinking corporeality. Norman O. Brown has stated that "the aim of psychoanalysis — still unfulfilled, and still only half-conscious — is to return our souls to our bodies, to return ourselves to ourselves, and thus to overcome the human state of self-alienation" (Brown 1977, 158). I submit that this self-alienation is the alienation of majority self from minority self, which, in turn, is derived from the alienation of the cultural feminine from the cultural masculine.

"Strangely enough," muses Elizabeth Gould Davis in *The First Sex*, "no one ever considers what this absolute power given to men over women throughout the past few centuries might have done to the characters of the men themselves" (Davis 1979, 313). The answer I am suggesting is that this power has created conflicts and contradictions within the social-selves of both men and women and that the masculine nature of patriarchal heterosexuality limits and deforms this heterosexuality. Recent generations of patriarchal men have used their power to define women as inferior, yet nurturing, and to limit women more and more to the nurturing of infants and children. Ironically, because of the dialectical nature of accomplicity, these limitations have become limitations upon men and upon patriarchal civilization itself. The child's majority self, stunted and repressed, prevents the adult from further evolution; an inner fifth column, this majority self, reproduces the power hierarchy of female and male in conflicts with the minority self.

The continuing subordination and repression of women on all levels of patriarchal culture ensures the continuous and intensifying repression of men's majority selves and the stunting of women's minority selves. The denial of the majority self by men becomes a denial of life: vital energy must continuously be made available for maintenance of the repression and the resulting neurotic substitute-formations account for much that is bizarre and irrational in patriarchal heterosexuality. Psychoanalyst

Alice Miller writes that even Hitler's maniacal violence can be traced to childhood mistreatment. Killers must obsessively murder the helpless portions of their selves over and over again, she explains (Miller 1985, 240-43). However, the reader must understand that this symbolic murder of the majority self through real murders is rooted in the power hierarchy of father and mother within the patriarchal family.

However, in the final analysis, the majority selves of men cannot completely die; their symbolic deaths must be achieved over and over again. In order to trap in structures of symptom-formation the increasing guilt deriving from majority self/minority self conflict, patriarchal men in recent centuries have developed new myths and rituals. In *The Flight from Woman*, Karl Stern notes the modern occidental, post-Renaissance myths of Faust and Don Juan. These archetypical modern men, committed to rootless adventuring, obsessively seducing, perpetually unsatisfied, condemned (as Sartre says) to freedom, represent men freed from the constraints of their body-egos and perpetually voyaging away from their origins in the majority self. Stern comments that "it is as though in the person of the seducer cold intellect, pure reflexion were out to trap and slay pure nature, unreflected substance, personified in the girl" (Stern 1966, 217). But it is a symbolic murder that must be committed and recommitted endlessly. Stern's remarkable insights validate those being developed here because Stern firmly roots modern anguish — that of Soren Kierkegaard is but one telling example — in "the schism between the paternal and the maternal" in the origins of each of us (Stern ibid., 223).

Just as patriarchal structures of heterosexuality reveal majority-minority self conflicts, so also do patriarchal institutions such as the double standard (still alive even in the 1990s) serve to assuage guilt: First must be denied the guilt over the split in self, and then denied the guilt brought into being by compulsive sexual acts themselves. In a review of Susan Griffin's *Pornography and Silence*, Marcia Yudkin points out that "contemporary pornographic works continue the obsession with turning virgins into whores. Bodily desires that would be degrading to a spiritual being are projected onto a female whose animal nature is revealed and punished. To the pornographic mind, sexual acts are acts of humiliation to the soul" (Yudkin 1982, 10:41). The crux of the problem resides not only in the patriarchal construction of bodily desires as degrading but also in the prior denigration of the feminine and in its equation to body. "Mankind" denies bodily desires while affirming them through sexual sadism and symbolic or actual rape.

Philosopher Herbert Marcuse interprets Freud's concept of the accumulation of guilt with the advance of civilization in terms of mankind's remembrance of its victims. This accumulation of remembered guilt darkens "the prospect of a civilization without repression," Marcuse thinks (Marcuse 1974, 237). Yet I submit it is *not* conscious remembrance that accumulates guilt and maintains repression. Freud understood that, to the contrary, guilt remains and accumulates precisely because we forget, because accumulated guilt is "close held" within the very structures of our nervous systems and within the unconscious social membrane that is also the ground of our unconscious. Brown takes Marcuse's problem of remembrance one step further and declares in a weak climax to his seminal book *Life against Death*, that "modern secular Faustian man is strong enough to live with irredeemable damnation [i.e., irredeemable guilt]" (Brown 1977, 280).

However, I must agree with Ernest Becker (1973), who criticizes Brown's solution to the problems of man's "denial of death" and the resulting repressions that deny life. Brown's call for a resurrection of the unreflected body, after nearly 300 pages spent demonstrating masculine sublimation's negativity, is no solution to the body-spirit split. It is instead yet another confirmation of patriarchal thought's inability to reason its way out of spurious dualisms. Brown protests the degradation of the body implied in sublimation's desexualization, but his solution is not a higher synthesis of mind and body. His solution remains an exorcism of mind from body. Guilt and repression are bearable within Brown's resurrected body because they, too, are dissolved along with Brown's dissolution of time, history, and culture. The unreflected body Brown resurrects is as mythical a being as pure pleasure or as nature apart from culture.

Brown is right, though, to take seriously Freud's concept of culture as madness, which occurs because advancing civilization simultaneously advances man's "dis-ease"—man's burden of guilt. But in the final analysis Brown's efforts fail because he has not broken out of the reified structures of masculine meaning: Brown remains within the poles of yet another identity theory, of yet another spurious dualism.

For those of us who took the "Sexual Revolution" seriously—and I wager that was most of us at one time or another—so much indeed was expected: the end to the war between the sexes, yes certainly; and perhaps even, in some quarters, the end of war ("Make love, not war"); at least a more peaceful coexistence between ourselves and nature, between our minds or spirits and our bodies—*at the least* an increase in simple physical enjoyment for all concerned. As it turns out, simple physical enjoyment is not so simple after all.

One of Freud's most fervent followers, Wilhelm Reich, predicted that all manner of happiness, health, and peace of nonauthoritarian mind would follow upon universal orgastic potency. (Although Reich's formula, too, was not quite that simple.) Reich had questioned Freud's denial that neurotics could have healthy sex lives; Reich found that the "healthy" sex lives of many very disturbed people were not so healthy after all (Reich 1972, xvi). French philosopher Michel Foucault has observed that "the fact that so many things were able to change in the sexual behavior of Western societies without any of the promises or political conditions predicted by Reich being realized is sufficient proof that this whole sexual 'revolution,' this whole 'antirepressive' struggle, represented nothing more, but nothing less — and its importance is un-deniable — than a tactical shift and reversal in the great deployment of sexuality" (Foucault 1980, 131). My thesis, of course, overlaps Foucault's: Sexuality has indeed been "deployed" rather than "liberated," and this is so because neither women's sexuality nor women themselves have yet been liberated within patriarchal cultures.

The physical — as in "simple physical pleasures" — is neither simple nor pure; rather, it is constituted by cultural symbols and is as inextricably mixed with the mental/spiritual as are sexuality and gender realities. Sexuality has been "deployed" because Western heterosexuality is mas-culine and patriarchal and, as such, buttresses sexuality as consumption. Further, it maintains sexuality in harness to the same endless cycles of compulsive repetition as the Faustian sublimations it reinforces. Women who embraced the sexual revolution too often found themselves free only to service men outside the tenuous security of marriage; free to adopt the sensuality that pleases men who, in turn, were threatened and departed if "their" women dared to make any erotic demands of their own. Finally, women were free to pay their own way while earning much less than men in terms of both money and prestige — while still being held responsible for domestic duties. As sex researcher Diana Russell notes, "Sexual liberation without sex-role liberation can actually result in greater oppression of women" (Russell 1975, 209). In fact, far from liberated themselves, patriarchal men are still in thrall to that perverse logic of purity, virginity, and possession, that is, to the sexual double standard.

All of this explains why Norman O. Brown's resurrection of the body fails as a solution to repression and to the denial of death. Brown fails to acknowledge the reality of symbolic death and of symbolic immortality. Brown fails to understand the symbol as metaphor and sexuality and the body as symbolizing woman for patriarchal men. He fails also to recog-nize that woman, body, and sex all equal symbolic death in the masculine lexicon. In short, Brown fails to acknowledge the dimension of the symbolic. As Freud, Nietzsche, and Foucault all understood, far from representing "narrow" concerns, sexuality resonates on every cultural and social-self level from the highest to the lowest. Wilhelm Reich's analysis was more correct than even he realized, provided one recognizes that sexual repression equals repression, not of sexuality, but of women, and that this repression serves to preserve, not an existing structure of class, but an existing structure of caste that is broader and deeper than other hierarchies of unfreedom. The radical critique of capitalist societies (keep in mind that modern communist societies, too, are patriarchal) fails because it fails to understand the pleasures in production (the symbols of mastery and immortality) and the production in reproduction (the constitution of the majority selves of men and women).

Norman O. Brown, like Freud, linked the fear of the mother's castration with the fear of death. What they both failed to do was to understand the link between the mother's castration and the inevitability of children's symbolic castrations (through their majority and minority selves) and, in turn, symbolic castration's link with symbolic (cultural) death. To understand these links is to understand both Becker's characterization of the Oedipal project as a "flight from passivity, from obliteration" (Becker 1973, 36) and Brown's assertion that sublimation's hidden aim "is the progressive discovery of the lost body of childhood" (Brown 1977, 170).

Furthermore, unless these insights regarding the male Oedipal project's essential flight from womanhood in the repression of the majority self are assimilated, the lost body of childhood, the "infant sexuality" into which patriarchal culture collapses its body-ego, can never be recovered. As Becker put it, "The child wants to conquer death by becoming the *father of himself*" (Becker 1973, 36) because his origins in the majority self must remain repressed if he is to enter into the life of patriarchal immortality symbols. The same is also true for the girl, only her femininity—her essential self—depends upon the majority self (the fetishized one of the patriarchy and the partially repressed mother-accomplished one) in a way in which the boy's does not; and unlike the boy, her access to immortality is already foreclosed with the patriarchal stunting of her minority self.

But this double bind into which the patriarchy forces the girl-woman—if you abandon your majority self, you are no longer feminine; but, if you accept it or our counterfeit, then you are culturally dead—infects the boy-man also by means of the dialectics of mother-son accomplicity. The product of the advance of patriarchal civilization is an escalation of the war between the social-selves—and an intensification of guilt for both sexes.

In *Civilization and Its Discontents*, Freud remarked that "the theory of bisexuality is still surrounded by many obscurities and we cannot but feel it as a serious impediment in psychoanalysis that it has not yet found any link with the theory of the instincts" (Freud [1930] 1961, 53). These obscurities, too, I have tackled by way of the intersections of temporal categories: The greater continuity of care provided by the mother is responsible via accomplicity for the production of the majority self; this latter self intersects with the minority self produced by the more discontinuous father-child accomplicity. The rhythms of the majority self and minority self intersect, in turn, with those continuous rhythms of cultural life laid down in the unconscious social membrane. The transactions of the latter in particular are absorbed in infancy by the body-ego and are therefore closely related to the mother-accomplished majority self. Bisexuality and human instincts are related because the deepest principle of cultural organization is the polarity of male/female, and human cultures reify, that is, spatialize, their gender-specific structures into the very nervous systems of human beings.

Culture is to humans what instinct is to animals. I argue that what Freud called instinct — his "basal" concept on the border between nature and culture — is in fact those unconscious cultural attitudes and habits that become hard-wired into our nervous systems before the age of two. These forgotten attitudes, behaviors, and conflicts lie, not in the prehistory of our race as Freud would have it, but bound within our nervous systems below the level of conscious awareness. These instincts represent our cultural matrix, our culture's selective systems, its myths, paradigms, and symbols — and, above all, its gender conflicts. As such these unconscious cultural systems forming and informing each of us act to bind us to one another in uneasy ambivalence.

However, unlike the rigidity of animal instincts, our cultural instincts can be bent and changed by our very human ability to become conscious of that which has formed us and to change — "heteroplastically," as Freud has said — the cultural matrix that also deforms us.

Freud's vision is both profound and tragic — tragic because Freud recognized the great depths of human conflicts wherein both love and hate, masochism and sadism, Eros and Thanatos, culture and nature, mingle inextricably and inextricably give energy to human aspirations. Above all, Freud's tragic vision circles like a sun illuminating a newly discovered world in which all men and women are secretly bisexual, hopelessly compounded of elements both feminine and masculine.

Freud's shocking discovery was not that children have sexual feelings; as Freud himself dryly noted, every "nursemaid" knows this. Freud's shocking discovery was not that boys desire their mothers and wish to do away with their fathers; little boys' and girls' courting and nuptial schemes have not escaped the amused attention of generations of parents. No, Freud's truly shocking discovery — whose full explanatory power still awaits release — is that of the cultural construction of sexuality as well as gender, his discovery of the intertwining of femininity and masculinity within each man and woman. As long as civilization remains masculine and patriarchal, as long as the patriarchs in power denigrate the feminine in women and repress the feminine in themselves, Freud's tragic vision, which depicts guilt and aggressiveness increasing along with advancing civilization, will remain true.

Freud's revolutionary insight is that there is no natural sexual response: Sexuality is constructed through cultural symbolic systems so that under the conditions of patriarchal society it is indeed as impossible to know the true dimensions of women's sexual response as it is impossible to know the dormant creative and intellectual potentials of women. However, the crucial dialectical point of this study is that men also are crippled in their sexuality as well as in their capabilities for intellectual achievement.

Psychoanalyst Arnold Modell, in a chapter entitled "The Sense of Identity: The Acceptance of Separateness," comments, "Usually we are unaware of our own identities as we are unaware of our own bodies unless we are ill" (Modell 1968, 43). However, to be "unaware of one's body" *is* to be ill, and it is an illness originating in the majority self's repression. This illness, stemming from the male's repression of his majority self during the Oedipus paradigm change of self, manifests itself in the masculine hysteria of compulsive penis-orientated hypersexuality, which attempts to satisfy all sensuous urge by collapsing the erotic into the male genital. This illness manifests itself in the never-ending Faustian search for virgin-goddesses to violate and in the masculine fetishizing of barely post-pubertal young women, so slim as to be practically devoid of body. It manifests itself in all the masculine myths, but most particularly in the myth of love as a regressive force drawing us backward toward a lost mother-infant symbiosis. The ending "lived happily ever after" cuts off male romantic histories at their beginnings. Or like James Bond's women, the young women themselves are cut off by violent deaths that allow the saddened hero to seek solace, over and over again, in their clones. The "lived happily ever after" of masculine fairy tales ends the story of humanity at its beginning, at the point when the hero has won the heroine and adolescent longing must face the possibilities of adult maturity.

Finally, this illness resulting from masculine repression of majority selves creates all the invidious dichotomies of the either/or, including the depreciation of percepts, emotion, fantasy, and the subjective. It also causes sex therapists like Phillip and Lorna Sarrel to dismiss as innocuous mental games the most morbid, sadistic, or masochistic sexual fantasies — and to dismiss as well the anxiety, guilt and aggressiveness these sexual fantasies engender (Sarrel & Sarrel 1984, 129). Indeed, how could they take seriously such bizarre productions, since doing so would force a reexamination of the categories of modern psychoanalysis and would force a return to Freud's insistence upon the importance of psychic realities.

We can now return with deeper insight to William James's statement, *"The intellectual life of man consists almost wholly in his substitution of a conceptual order for the perceptual order in which his experience originally comes"* (James 1953, 77). We can now understand that if the body thinks, as Freud suggested, if the sensuous categories of the body-ego have cognitive import, then there is no "original perceptual order" and man's quantification of the sensible world clearly becomes a diagram of a diagram; it becomes mere metaphysics. In order to reground substantive reason, then, the one-dimensional "decorporealization" of patriarchal thought must be halted.

Norman O. Brown calls for a resurrection of the body as the solution to human neurosis and repression, which he believes is founded in an inability to accept death. Brown's contribution is to trace neurosis to the male child's relationship to the pre-Oedipal mother; Brown's mistake is to characterize this relationship as an "inherently" (i.e., naturally) ambivalent one. Brown compounds this error by locating human neurosis in a fixation to infantile fantasies, to infantile sexuality, and to its repression by the "fantasy of becoming father of oneself" (Brown 1977, 289). By so doing, Brown takes a step back from Freud: He reduces the importance of psychic reality to mere fantasy and suggests that the undoing of repression can be brought about by the recognition that guilt stems from infantile fantasy and that, in the final analysis, death anxiety stems from separation anxiety (ibid., 290). Sublimation, or the project of becoming father to oneself, "is a search in the outside world for the lost body of childhood" (ibid., 289). Brown does not see that the desexualization that sublimation entails is not a repression of infantile sexuality but a repression of the mother-accomplished majority self and, with it, a repression of the body-ego. Brown does not see that these repressions of majority self and body-ego, which occur for the boy at the time of the Oedipus paradigm change of self, come about not because bodily death is denied, but because the cultural symbolic death associated with feminine existence in patriarchal cultures is feared; with the repression of the majority self, this cultural symbolic death is fled.

Other thinkers, among them feminist thinkers such as Dorothy Dinnerstein and Nancy Chodorow, have repeated Brown's central errors. They have focused upon "human ambivalence towards the body of woman" (Dinnerstein 1976, 148), based upon an ambivalence toward the flesh. They claim that "the special link between woman and death will dissolve" (ibid., 149) if men will become equal to women as parents . The arguments I have developed in this study explain why women's seizing of economic, political, and cultural symbolic power is by far the more important factor in snapping the link between women and death: This is because the deaths most feared by men and by women are "living" deaths, that is, the deaths of cultural oblivion.

Furthermore, it is highly unlikely that men will share equally in parenting unless women have the economic and cultural power necessary to encourage such sharing. The resurrection of the body cannot be a *resurrection*: It can only be a freeing of women to cultural potency. In this way, the majority selves of men, too, will be released and the body-egos of both sexes can continue to evolve. Only if these liberations occur, can the cognitive elements of patriarchal culture and science further evolve; and, if these liberations do occur, *masculine* culture will be transformed . . . into *human* culture.

Patriarchal culture is entering the closing years of a century of extraordinary change, ferment, turmoil, conflict, hope, and disillusionment. The twentieth century has been a century of revolutions set in motion, not only by those late nineteenth- to early twentieth-century thinkers such as Marx, Einstein and Freud, not only by political leaders of vision, malignant and benign, but also by the efforts on an unprecedented scale of "ordinary" women and men to better themselves. This indeed has been the century of the "democratization of personhood" (Clecak 1983, 6). Yet I predict that the revolution that will create the greatest changes, qualitatively and quantitatively, is that long, quiet revolution still in progress, namely, the revolution of the female gender, of women. Because sexuality constitutes the most fundamental principle of cultural organization, evolution in the area of sexuality and gender will in turn, change every other area of human thought and endeavor.

Women as a gender stand on the brink of developing their capabilities for mastery, of discovering the passion of fulfillment in work and cultural potency. Men as a gender also stand to benefit greatly from this gender revolution. Men will become aware of the joyous production possible in reproduction as they participate more fully in the dialectics of accomplicity. Men will become individuals more sensitively and sensuously alive as their own body-egos and majority selves are liberated. Men and women will then be able to participate more intelligently in the formation of societies at once more creative and more just.

Raised to its full potential height, Freudian theory is indispensable for a deeper understanding of women and of the relationships between women and men in patriarchal cultures, and of the relationships between the femininity and masculinity of each man and woman. Itself transformed by the disciplined subjectivity of women theorists, Freudian psychoanalysis promises to advance social transformations now only incipient; these transformations will grant greater freedom to both sexes because, in late twentieth-century patriarchal cultures, the truths of masculine reality and the truths of feminine reality are beginning to confront each other. Freudian psychoanalysis represents the only masculine system in which the dualities of masculine and feminine, of the unconscious and conscious minds, and of primary process and secondary process thinking are centrally maintained. Freud himself did not take the final step of viewing neurotic symptoms and cultural conflicts as resulting from the overlapping, yet conflicting gender productions (majority and minority selves) of mother and father, but he did assemble all the elements so that, although momentous in its implications, this step remains a small one. Moreover, Freud dialectically related his stubbornly maintained dualities by means of principles that explain how the gaps of conflict and difference are bridged and how this bridging is productive of new realities.

Dinnerstein, Chodorow, and other feminist thinkers have urged the expansion of parenting by men as a solution to the masculine monopoly of mastery and violence. Dinnerstein understands that "expressive, aesthetic, humanistic values must shape the new world; that eroticism must permeate history, not be encapsulated in genital sex; that first-hand, emotionally vivid experience, not theory-dominated policy which violates such experience, must shape social action" (Dinnerstein 1976, 264). This study agrees that masculine parenting is desirable; but, this study asserts that far more important — because masculine parenting will follow from it — is the attainment of economic and symbolic cultural power and potency, by women generally and by women as mothers specifically. Women, however, will have to fight for these powers, alongside feminist men who recognize that they will also gain from women's cultural potency and that their children will gain from maternal cultural potency. At present most men will not share the thankless and culturally denigrated tasks assigned to women, such as child-rearing and housework, unless women obtain the economic and symbolic cultural power that encourages men to do so.

If we in patriarchal cultures are to produce more creative individuals capable of solving our cultural crises, then we must understand the hidden power of maternal accomplicity and learn how maternal cultural potency will unleash the powers of repressed majority selves and of stunted minority selves – not just among the privileged few, but among the many. Not to encourage women's impulses for growth in economic and symbolic cultural power risks exacerbating the present imbalance between the power of patriarchal culture to destroy and the power of unified selves to stop this race toward cultural self-destruction.

Finally, Freud argued not only for the existence and decipherability of the heart's reasons but also for the possibility of a disciplined subjectivity. Freud said: "I fail to see why the wisdom which is the precipitate of men's common experience of life should be refused inclusion among the acquisitions of science. The essential character of scientific work derives not from the special nature of its objects of study but from its stricter method of establishing the facts and its search for far-reaching correlations" (Freud [1901] 1965, 159). Women theorists must argue, along with Freud, for an infusion of wisdom into science and for the inclusion of women's "common experience" of life into that wisdom. When Freud critiqued patriarchal thought, as in this statement, he also validated the reality of the subjective life. I hope that this study adds to an understanding of the meaning of subjectivity – of the heart's reasons – and to an understanding of the limitations of patriarchal reason.

Women as mothers must refuse to continue as scapegoats for patriarchal neuroses. Women as mothers in patriarchal cultures are placed in yet another vicious double bind: They are supposed to be responsible for a myriad of ills, yet this responsibility implies freedom and choice. How, then, do women as beings confined by patriarchal thought to the intuitive naturalness of mothering find the freedom to err? How can natural beings be unnatural? The latest women's movement as yet has been unable to curb the blaming-the-mother propensities of behavioral researchers. This does not surprise me because matriphobia is rooted in gynephobia and both are, in turn, rooted in the Faustian complexes of the modern self-made man.

Albert Camus said that in order to nurture his difference as an artist, he was forced to admit his resemblance to all. The task of Faustian man who believes himself alone in a hostile universe is to recognize his origins and rootedness in a cultural matrix that includes the complementary differences of women. The task of women awakening to social consciousness is to nurture their own differences from men, at the same time admitting and cherishing their resemblances to each other. The hidden powers of women, their greater powers of accomplicity, will then serve to produce stronger children through maternal potency. These children – our children – may indeed change the paradigm of cultural patriarchy to one of cultural partnership.

Bibliography

NOTE: The references to Sigmund Freud's works indicate their date of first publication, followed by the date of the publication used in preparing this study.

BOOKS

Abbott, Sidney, & Barbara Love (1978). *Sappho Was a Right-On Woman*. New York: Day Books.

Adorno, T. W., et al. (1950). *The Authoritarian Personality*. New York: Harper & Row.

Al-Issa, Ihsan (1980). *The Psychopathology of Women*. Englewood Cliffs, NJ: Prentice-Hall.

Andersen, Margaret L. (1983). *Thinking about Women: Sociological and Feminist Perspectives*. New York: Macmillan.

Ariès, Philippe (1962). *Centuries of Childhood*. Translated from the French by Robert Baldick. New York: Vintage.

Bassein, Beth Ann (1984). *Women and Death*. Westport, CT: Greenwood Press.

Bauman, Zygmunt (1973). *Culture as Praxis*. Boston: Routledge & Kegan Paul.

Beck, Alan, & Aaron Katcher (1983). *Between Pets and People*. New York: G.P. Putnam's Sons.

Becker, Carol (1987). *The Invisible Drama: Women and the Anxiety of Change*. New York: Macmillan.

Becker, Ernest (1973). *The Denial of Death*. New York: Free Press.

Bellah, Robert N., et al. (1986). *Habits of the Heart*. New York: Harper & Row.

Bergsten, Staffan (1960). *Time and Eternity: A Study in the Structure and Symbolism of T.S. Eliot's Four Quartets*. Toronto: William Heinemann.

Bleier, Ruth (Ed.) (1986). *Feminist Approaches to Science*. New York: Pergamon.

Bronski, Michael (1984). *Culture Clash: The Making of Gay Sensibility*. Boston: South End Press.

Brown, Lester R., et al. (1989). *State of the World*. New York: W.W. Norton.

Brown, Norman O. (1977). *Life against Death*. Middletown, CT: Wesleyan University Press.

Brownmiller, Susan (1975). *Against Our Will: Men, Women and Rape*. New York: Simon & Schuster.

Caine, Lynn (1985). *What Did I Do Wrong? Mothers, Children, Guilt*. New York: Arbor House.

Capra, Fritjof (1977). *The Tao of Physics*. New York: Bantam.

———— (1983). *The Turning Point: Science, Society, and the Rising Culture*. New York: Bantam.

Chernin, Kim (1982). *The Obsession: Reflections on the Tyranny of Slenderness*. New York: Harper Colophon.

Chesler, Phyllis (1973). *Women & Madness*. New York: Avon.

Chodorow, Nancy (1978). *The Reproduction of Mothering*. Berkeley: University of California Press.

Clecak, Peter (1983). *America's Quest for the Ideal Self*. New York: Oxford University Press.

Cousins, Norman (1989). *Head First: The Biology of Hope*. New York: E.P. Dutton.

Coveney, L., et al. (1984). *The Sexuality Papers*. London: Hutchinson.

Davis, Elizabeth Gould (1979). *The First Sex*. New York: Penguin.

Deleuze, Gilles, & Felix Guattari (1982). *Anti-Oedipus*. Translated from the French by Robert Hurley, Mark Seem, and Helen R. Lane. New York: Viking.

Derrida, Jacques (1981). *Positions*. Translated and Annotated by Alan Bass. Chicago: University of Chicago Press.

Dinnerstein, Dorothy (1976). *The Mermaid and the Minotaur*. New York: Harper & Row.

Dixon, Keith (1973). *Sociological Theory*. Boston: Routledge & Kegan Paul.

Doi, Takeo, M.D. (1988). *The Anatomy of Self: The Individual Versus Society*. Translated by Mark A. Harbison. New York: Kodansha International.

Dossey, Larry, M.D. (1982). *Space, Time & Medicine*. Boulder, CO: Shambhala.

Dover, K.J. (1978). *Greek Homosexuality*. London: Duckworth.

Dowling, Colette (1982). *The Cinderella Complex*. New York: Pocket.

Eidelberg, Ludwig, M.D. (Ed.) (1968). *Encyclopedia of Psychoanalysis*. New York: Free Press.

Eiler, Mary Ann, & Thomas J. Pasko (1988). *Specialty Profiles: American Psychiatric Association*. Washington, DC: American Medical Association.

Eisenstein, Hester, & Alice Jardine (Eds.) (1987). *The Future of Difference*. New Brunswick: Rutgers University Press.

Eisler, Riane (1988). *The Chalice & the Blade*. San Francisco: Harper & Row.

Erikson, Erik H. (1963). *Childhood and Society*. New York: W.W. Norton.

———— (1969). *Gandhi's Truth*. New York: W.W. Norton.

———— (1964). *Insight and Responsibility*. New York: W.W. Norton.

———— (1962). *Young Man Luther*. New York: W.W. Norton.

Feyerabend, Paul (1978). *Science in a Free Society*. London: NLB.

Fincher, Jack (1980). *Lefties: The Origins & Consequences of Being Left-Handed*. New York: Perigee.

Fingarette, Herbert (1965). *The Self in Transformation*. New York: Harper Torchbooks.

Firestone, Shulamith (1979). *The Dialectic of Sex*. New York: Bantam.

Fisher, Seymour, & Roger P. Greenberg (1977). *The Scientific Credibility of Freud's Theories and Therapy*. New York: Basic Books.

Foucault, Michel (1980). *The History of Sexuality* (Vol. 1). Translated from the French by Robert Hurley. New York: Vintage.

Freeman, Lucy, & Herbert S. Strean (1987). *Freud and Women.* New York: Continuum.

Freud, Sigmund (1925/63). *An Autobiographical Study.* Translation by James Strachey. New York: W.W. Norton.

—— (1920/61). *Beyond the Pleasure Principle.* Translated & Edited by James Strachey. New York: W.W. Norton.

—— (1930/61). *Civilization and Its Discontents.* Edited & Translated by James Strachey. New York: W.W. Norton.

—— (1906–24/59). *Collected Papers* (Vol.2). Authorized Translation under the Supervision of Joan Riviere. New York: Basic Books.

—— (1911–23/59). *Collected Papers* (Vol.4). Authorized Translation under the Supervision of Joan Riviere. New York: Basic Books.

—— (1888–38/59). *Collected Papers* (Vol.5). Edited by James Strachey. New York: Basic Books.

—— (1916–33/66). *The Complete Introductory Lectures on Psychoanalysis.* Translated & Edited by James Strachey. New York: W.W. Norton.

—— (1917–23/58). *On Creativity and the Unconscious.* Papers on the Psychology of Art, Literature, Love, Religion. Selected, Introduced & Annotated by Benjamin Nelson. New York: Harper Colophon.

—— (1905–09/63). *Dora: An Analysis of a Case of Hysteria.* With an Introduction by Philip Rieff. New York: Collier.

—— (1923/62). *The Ego and the Id.* Translated & Edited by James Strachey. New York: W.W. Norton.

—— (1910/77). *Five Lectures on Psycho-Analysis.* Translated & Edited by James Strachey. New York: W.W. Norton.

—— (1927/61). *The Future of an Illusion.* Translated & Edited by James Strachey. New York: W.W. Norton.

—— (1926/59). *Inhibitions, Symptoms and Anxiety.* Translated by Alix Strachey. Revised & Edited by James Strachey. New York: W.W. Norton.

—— (1900/65). *The Interpretation of Dreams.* Translated & Edited by James Strachey. New York: Avon.

—— (1910/64). *Leonardo da Vinci and a Memory of His Childhood.* Translated by Alan Tyson. New York: W.W. Norton.

—— (1939). *Moses and Monotheism.* New York: Vintage.

—— (1940/69). *An Outline of Psycho-Analysis.* Translated & Edited by James Strachey. New York: W.W. Norton.

—— (1901/65). *The Psychopathology of Everyday Life.* Translated by Alan Tyson. Edited with an Introduction by James Strachey. New York: W.W. Norton.

—— (1927/69). *The Question of Lay Analysis.* Translated & Edited by James Strachey. New York: W.W. Norton.

—— (1905–38/63). *Sexuality and the Psychology of Love.* With an Introduction by the Editor, Philip Rieff. New York: Collier.

—— (1905/62). *Three Contributions to the Theory of Sex.* Translated by A.A. Brill. New York: E.P. Dutton.

—— (1913/50). *Totem and Taboo.* Authorized Translation by James Strachey. New York: W.W. Norton.

Friday, Nancy (1978). *My Mother, My Self.* New York: Dell.

Friedan, Betty (1986). *The Second Stage.* New York: Summit.

Fromm, Erich (1974). *The Anatomy of Human Destructiveness.* New York: Holt, Rinehart & Winston.

—— (1969). *Escape from Freedom.* New York: Avon.

———— (1980). *The Forgotten Language*. New York: Grove Press.
———— (1981). *Greatness and Limitations of Freud's Thought*. New York: Mentor.
———— (1967). *Psychoanalysis and Religion*. New York: Bantam.
———— (1955). *The Sane Society*. New York: Fawcett Premier.
———— (1963). *Sigmund Freud's Mission*. New York: Grove Press.
Gay, Peter (1988). *Freud: A Life for Our Time*. New York: W.W. Norton.
Giddens, Anthony (1977a). *Capitalism and Modern Social Theory: An Analysis of the Writings of Marx, Durkheim & Max Weber*. London: Cambridge University Press.
———— (1979). *Central Problems in Social Theory*. Berkeley: University of California Press.
———— (1977b). *Studies in Social and Political Theory*. New York: Basic Books.
Gilligan, Carol (1982). *In a Different Voice*. Cambridge, MA: Harvard University Press.
Gleick, James (1988). *Chaos: Making a New Science*. New York: Viking.
Glover, Edward (1957). *Freud or Jung?* New York: Meridian.
Greenspan, Miriam (1985). *A New Approach to Women & Therapy*. New York: McGraw-Hill.
Hall, Edward T. (1969). *The Hidden Dimension*. Garden City, NY: Anchor.
———— (1973). *The Silent Language*. Garden City, NY: Anchor Press/Doubleday.
Hamilton, Marshall L. (1977). *Father's Influence on Children*. Chicago: Nelson-Hall.
Harding, Sandra (Ed.) (1987). *Feminism & Methodology*. Bloomington: Indiana University Press.
Harding, Sandra, & Jean F. O'Barr (Eds.) (1987). *Sex and Scientific Inquiry*. Chicago: University of Chicago Press.
Hargreaves, David J., & Ann M. Colley (Eds.) (1987). *The Psychology of Sex Roles*. New York: Hemisphere.
Heisenberg, Werner (1962). *Physics and Philosophy*. Introduction by F.S.C. Northrop. New York: Harper Torchbooks.
Herman, Judith Lewis, with Lisa Hirschman (1981). *Father-Daughter Incest*. Cambridge, MA: Harvard University Press.
Hirsch, Miriam F. (1981). *Women and Violence*. New York: Van Nostrand Reinhold.
Hite, Shere (1977). *The Hite Report: A Nationwide Study of Female Sexuality*. New York: Dell.
———— (1985). *The Hite Report on Male Sexuality*. New York: Ballantine.
Horkheimer, Max (1974). *Eclipse of Reason*. New York: Seabury.
Horney, Karen, M.D. (1973). *Feminine Psychology*. New York: W.W. Norton.
Howard, Doris (Ed.) (1987). *A Guide to Dynamics of Feminist Therapy*. New York: Harrington Park Press.
Husserl, Edmund (1965). *Phenomenology and the Crisis of Philosophy*. Translation & Introduction by Quentin Lauer. New York: Harper Torchbooks.
Jacoby, Russell (1983). *The Repression of Psychoanalysis: Otto Fenichel and the Political Freudians*. New York: Basic Books.
James, William (1953). *The Philosophy of William James*. Selected & Introduced by Horace M. Kallen. New York: Modern Library.
Jamieson, Katherine M., & Timothy J. Flanagan (Eds.) (1988). *Sourcebook of Criminal Justice Statistics*. Washington, DC: U.S. Government Printing Office.
Janeway, Elizabeth (1971). *Man's World, Woman's Place: A Study in Social Mythology*. New York: Delta.
Johnston, Thomas (1965). *Freud and Political Thought*. New York: Citadel.
Jones, Ernest (1961). *The Life and Work of Sigmund Freud*. Edited & Abridged by Lionel Trilling & Steven Marcus. New York: Basic Books.

Keller, Evelyn Fox (1985). *Reflections on Gender and Science*. New Haven: Yale University Press.

Keohane, Nannerl O., Michelle Z. Rosaldo, & Barbara C. Gelpi (Eds.) (1982). *Feminist Theory: A Critique of Ideology*. Chicago: University of Chicago Press.

Kuhn, Thomas S. (1970). *The Structure of Scientific Revolutions*. Chicago: University of Chicago Press.

Langer, Susanne K. (1963). *Philosophy in a New Key*. Cambridge, MA: Harvard University Press.

Langley, Roger, & Richard C. Levy (1978). *Wife Beating: The Silent Crisis*. New York: Pocket.

Leacock, Eleanor Burke (1981). *Myths of Male Dominance*. New York: Monthly Review Press.

Leakey, Richard E. (1981). *The Making of Mankind*. New York: E.P. Dutton.

Lee, S.G.M., & Martin Herbert (Eds.) (1970). *Freud and Psychology*. Baltimore, MD: Penguin Books.

Lemaire, Anika (1981). *Jacques Lacan*. Translated by David Macey. Boston: Routledge & Kegan Paul.

Lerner, Harriet Goldhor (1986). *The Dance of Anger*. New York: Harper & Row.

Lichtman, Richard (1982). *The Production of Desire*. New York: Free Press.

Lynch, James J. (1985). *The Language of the Heart: The Body's Response to Human Dialogue*. New York: Basic Books.

Mannoni, O. (1974). *Freud*. Translated from the French by Renaud Bruce. New York: Vintage.

Marcuse, Herbert (1974). *Eros and Civilization*. Boston: Beacon Press.

Martin, Kay M., & Barbara Voorhies (1975). *Female of the Species*. New York: Columbia University Press.

Masson, Jeffrey Moussaieff (1985). *The Assault on Truth: Freud's Suppression of the Seduction Theory*. New York: Penguin.

May, Rollo (1986). *The Discovery of Being*. New York: W.W. Norton.

Medrich, Elliott A., Judith A. Roizen, Victor Rubin, & Stuart Buckley (1982). *The Serious Business of Growing Up: A Study of Children's Lives Outside School*. Berkeley: University of California Press.

Merleau-Ponty, Maurice (1965). *Phenomenology of Perception*. Translated from the French by Colin Smith. New York: Humanities Press.

Miller, Alice (1985). *For Your Own Good*. Translated by Hildegarde & Hunter Hannum. New York: Farrar, Straus, & Giroux.

Miller, Jean Baker, M.D. (Ed.) (1978). *Psychoanalysis and Women*. New York: Penguin Books.

Miller, Jean Baker, M.D. (1986). *Toward a New Psychology of Women*. Boston: Beacon Press.

Mitchell, Juliet (1975). *Psychoanalysis and Feminism*. New York: Vintage.

——— (1973). *Woman's Estate*. New York: Vintage.

Modell, Arnold H., M.D. (1968). *Object Love and Reality*. New York: International Universities Press.

Montagu, Ashley (1981). *Growing Young*. New York: McGraw-Hill.

——— (1976). *The Nature of Human Aggression*. New York: Oxford University Press.

——— (1986). *Touching: The Human Significance of the Skin*. San Francisco: Harper & Row.

Morgan, Robin (Ed.) (1984). *Sisterhood Is Global*. Garden City, NY: Anchor Press/Doubleday.

Mullahy, Patrick (1948). *Oedipus: Myth and Complex.* New York: Hermitage.

Nelson, Benjamin (Ed.) (1957). *Freud and the Twentieth Century.* New York: Meridian.

Oakley, Ann (1980). *Becoming a Mother.* New York: Schocken.

——— (1972). *Sex, Gender & Society.* New York: Harper Colophon.

——— (1976). *Woman's Work: The Housewife, Past and Present.* New York: Vintage.

O'Brien, Mary (1983). *The Politics of Reproduction.* Boston: Routledge & Kegan Paul.

Ogilvy, James (1979). *Many Dimensional Man.* New York: Harper Colophon.

Pagels, Heinz (1988). *The Dreams of Reason.* New York: Simon & Schuster.

Parsons, Anne (1969). *Belief, Magic, and Anomie.* New York: Free Press.

Piaget, Jean, & Barbel Inhelder (1969). *The Psychology of the Child.* Translated from the French by Helen Weaver. New York: Basic Books.

Pogrebin, Letty Cottin (1984). *Family Politics: Love and Power on an Intimate Frontier.* New York: McGraw-Hill.

Poster, Mark (1978). *Critical Theory of the Family.* New York: Seabury.

Rank, Otto (1958). *Beyond Psychology.* New York: Dover.

Reich, Wilhelm (1972). *Sex-Pol Essays: 1929–1934.* Edited by Lee Baxandall. Introduction by Bertell Ollman. Translated by Anna Bostock, Tom Dubose, & Lee Baxandall. New York: Vintage.

Reiter, Rayna R. (Ed.) (1975). *Toward an Anthropology of Women.* New York: Monthly Review Press.

Rich, Adrienne (1981). *Of Woman Born.* New York: Bantam.

——— (1979). *On Lies, Secrets, and Silence.* New York: W.W. Norton.

Rickman, John, M.D. (Ed.) (1957). *A General Selection from the Works of Sigmund Freud.* Garden City, NY: Anchor.

Rieff, Philip (1961). *Freud: The Mind of the Moralist.* Garden City, NY: Anchor.

Roazen, Paul (1968). *Freud: Political and Social Thought.* New York: Alfred A. Knopf.

Rohrbaugh, Joanna Bunker (1979). *Women: Psychology's Puzzle.* New York: Basic Books.

Roszak, Betty, & Theodore Roszak (Eds.) (1969). *Masculine/Feminine.* New York: Harper Colophon.

Rowbotham, Sheila (1976). *Hidden from History.* New York: Vintage.

Russell, Diana E.H. (1975). *The Politics of Rape: The Victim's Perspective.* New York: Stein & Day.

——— (1986). *The Secret Trauma: Incest in the Lives of Girls and Women.* New York: Basic Books.

Ryan, Mary P. (1983). *Womanhood in America.* New York: Franklin Watts.

Sanday, Peggy Reeves (1981). *Female Power and Male Dominance.* New York: Cambridge University Press.

Sapir, Edward (1956). *Culture, Language and Personality.* Selected Essays Edited by David G. Mandelbaum. Berkeley: University of California Press.

Sarrel, Lorna J., & Philip M. Sarrel (1984). *Sexual Turning Points.* New York: Macmillan.

Schaef, Anne Wilson (1985). *Women's Reality: An Emerging Female System in a White Male Society.* San Francisco: Harper & Row.

Schneider, Daniel E., M.D. (1967). *Psychoanalysis of Heart Attack.* New York: Dial Press.

Seidenberg, Robert, M.D. (1970). *Marriage in Life and Literature.* New York: Philosophical Library.

Sennett, Richard (1978). *The Fall of Public Man.* New York: Vintage.

Shainess, Natalie, M.D. (1984). *Sweet Suffering: Woman as Victim.* New York: Bobbs-Merrill.

Shepherd, Simon, and Mick Wallis (1989). *Coming on Strong: Gay Politics and Culture.* London: Unwin Hyman.

Sherfey, Mary Jane, M.D. (1978). On the Nature of Female Sexuality. In Jean Baker Miller, M.D., *Psychoanalysis and Women*, 136–53. New York: Penguin.
Shorter, Edward (1977). *The Making of the Modern Family.* New York: Basic Books.
Stacey, William A., & Anson Shupe (1985). *The Family Secret: Domestic Violence in America.* New York: Beacon Press.
Steinem, Gloria (1983). *Outrageous Acts and Everyday Rebellions.* New York: Holt, Rinehart & Winston.
Stern, Karl (1966). *The Flight from Woman.* London: George Allen & Unwin.
Straus, Murray A., Richard J. Gelles, & Suzanne K. Steinmetz, (1980). *Behind Closed Doors.* New York: Anchor.
Straus, Murray A., & Gerald T. Hotaling (Eds.) (1980). *The Social Causes of Husband-Wife Violence.* Minnesota: University of Minnesota Press.
Strouse, Jean (Ed.) (1985). *Women & Analysis.* Boston: G. K. Hall.
Tannahill, Reay (1980). *Sex in History.* New York: Stein & Day.
Tavris, Carol, & Carole Wade (1984). *The Longest War: Sex Differences in Perspective.* New York: Harcourt Brace Jovanovich.
Taylor, Gordon Rattray (1979). *The Natural History of the Mind.* New York: E.P. Dutton.
Terkel, Studs (1989). *The Great Divide.* New York: Avon.
Trebilcot, Joyce (Ed.) (1984). *Mothering: Essays in Feminist Theory.* Totowa, NJ: Rowman & Allanheld.
Turner, Victor (1975). *Dramas, Fields, and Metaphors.* Ithaca, NY: Cornell University Press.
Walsh, Roger N., & Frances Vaughan (1980). *Beyond Ego: Transpersonal Dimensions in Psychology.* Los Angeles: J.P. Tarcher.
Washton, Arnold M., & Donna Boundy (1989). *Willpower's Not Enough: Understanding and Recovering from Addictions of Every Kind.* New York: Harper & Row.
Watkins, Mary (1986). *Invisible Guests: The Development of Imaginal Dialogues.* Hillsdale, NJ: The Analytic Press.
Winson, Jonathan (1986). *Brain & Psyche: The Biology of the Unconscious.* New York: Vintage.

ARTICLES

Ainsworth, Mary D. Salter (1989). Attachments beyond Infancy. *American Psychologist*, 44,709–716.
Berardo, Felix M. (Ed.) (1980). Decade Review: Family Research 1970–1979 [Special Issue]. *Journal of Marriage and the Family, 42*, Minneapolis: National Council on Family Relations.
Bielby, William T., & Denise D. Bielby (1989, April). *The 1989 Hollywood Writers' Report: Unequal Access, Unequal Pay.* Santa Barbara: University of California.
Bordo, Susan (1987). The Cartesian Masculinization of Thought. In Sandra Harding & Jean F. O'Barr (Eds.), *Sex and Scientific Inquiry*, Chicago: The University of Chicago Press, 247–264.
Boris, Eileen, & Michael Honey (1988, February). Gender, Race, and the Policies of the Labor Department. *Monthly Labor Review, III*, U.S. Dept. of Labor, Bureau of Labor Statistics, 26–36.
Cairns, John, Julie Overbaugh, & Stephan Miller (1988, 8 September). The Origin of Mutants. *Nature, 335*, 142–145.
Campbell, Meg (1984, September). On Having a Second Child. *Ms, 13*, 140.

Cohen, Mabel Blake, M.D. (1978). Personal Identity and Sexual Identity. In Jean Baker Miller, M.D. (Ed.), *Psychoanalysis and Women*. New York: Penguin, 156–182.

Edwards, Thomas K. (1988). Providing Reasons for Wanting to Live. *Phi Delta Kappan, 70*, 296–298.

Eisler, Riane (1981). The Global Impact of Sexual Equality. *The Humanist, 41*, 9–15.

Eron, Leonard D. (1987). The Development of Aggressive Behavior from the Perspective of a Developing Behaviorism. *American Psychologist, 42*, 435–442.

Feingold, Alan (1988). Cognitive Gender Differences Are Disappearing. *American Psychologist, 43*, 95–103.

Field, Tiffany, et al. (1988). Infants of Depressed Mothers Show "Depressed" Behavior Even with Nondepressed Adults. *Child Development, 59*, Chicago: University of Chicago Press, 1569–1579.

Fineman, Mark (1988, 4 December). Bhutto's Rise – Paradox of Women in Pakistan. Los Angeles *Times I*, 8–9.

Galloway, Paul (1980, 23 October). What Boys and Girls Are Made Of. Los Angeles *Times V*, 24.

Gelman, David (1989, 13 November). The Sex-Abuse Puzzle. *Newsweek 114*, 99–100.

Gilligan, Carol (1982, June). Why Should a Woman Be More like a Man? *Psychology Today, 16*, 68–77.

Hall, Elizabeth (1986, June). Profile, June Reinisch: New Directions for the Kinsey Institute. *Psychology Today, 20*, 33–39.

Harding, Susan (1975). Women and Words in a Spanish Village. In Rayna R. Reiter (Ed.), *Toward an Anthropology of Women*. New York: Monthly Review Press, 283–308.

Hare-Mustin, Rachel T., & Jeanne Marecek (1988). The Meaning of Difference, Gender Theory, Postmodernism, and Psychology. *American Psychologist, 43*, 455–464.

Hartsock, Nancy C.M. (1987). The Feminist Standpoint. In Sandra Harding (Ed.), *Feminism & Methodology*. Bloomington: Indiana University Press, 157–180.

Herschberger, Ruth (1969). Is Rape a Myth? In Betty Roszak & Theodore Roszak (Eds.), *Masculine/Feminine*. New York: Harper & Row, 122–130.

Holt, Robert R. (1967). The Development of the Primary Process: A Structural View. In Robert R. Holt (Ed.), *Motives and Thought: Psychoanalytic Essays in Honor of David Rapaport. Psychological Issues*, Vol. 5, No. 2–3, Monograph 18/19. New York: International Universities Press, 344–383.

Jacklin, Carol Nagy (1989). Female and Male: Issues Of Gender. *American Psychologist, 44*, 127–133.

Janeway, Elizabeth (1981, November). Incest: A Rational Look at the Oldest Taboo. *Ms., 10*, 61–64 & 78.

Johmann, Carol (1985, May). Sex and Morality. *Omni, 7*, 20 & 80.

Jones, Verna Noel (1983, 9 December). Violence in U.S. Families Called "Normal." Los Angeles *Times, I-C*, 12.

Kahane, Claire (1985). The Gothic Mirror. In Shirley Nelson Garner, Claire Kahane, & Madelon Sprengnether (Eds.), *The (M)other Tongue, Essays in Feminist Psychoanalytic Interpretation*. Ithaca, NY: Cornell University Press, 334–351.

Kahn, Coppelia (1982). Excavating "Those Dim Minoan Regions": Maternal Subtexts in Patriarchal Literature. *Diacritics, 12*, 32–41.

Kaplan, Abraham (1957). Freud and Modern Philosophy. In B. Nelson (Ed.), *Freud and the Twentieth Century*. New York: Meridian, 209–229.

Keen, Sam (1988, December). The Stories We Live By. *Psychology Today, 22*, 43–47.

Keller, Evelyn Fox (1982). Feminism and Science. In Nannerl O. Keohane, Michelle Z. Rosaldo, & Barbara C. Gelpi (Eds.), *Feminist Theory, A Critique of Ideology*. Chicago: The University of Chicago Press, 113–126.

Leo, John (1984, 9 April). The Revolution Is Over. *Time, 123*, 74–84.

Levine, Robert, & Ellen Wolff (1985, March). Social Time: The Heart-beat of Culture. *Psychology Today, 19*, 29–35.

Malamuth, Neil M., & John Briere (1986). Sexual Violence in the Media: Indirect Effects on Aggression against Women. *Journal Of Social Issues, 42*, 75–92.

McCann, Hugh (1984, 6 December). Baby Talk: The Babble Has a Message. Los Angeles *Times, IB*, 7.

Miller, Julie Ann, & Joel Greenberg (1985, 15 June). Born Smart: Imitation of Life. *Science News 127*, 376.

Moses, Nancy, et al. (1989). Fear of Obesity among Adolescent Girls. *Pediatrics, 83*, 393–398.

Nelson, Martha (1985, 8 July). From the Editor. *Women's Sports and Fitness, 7*, 4.

New Perspectives Quarterly (1989). The Shadow Our Future Throws, *6*, 2–47.

New Perspectives Quarterly (1990). Prodigal Parents: Family vs. The 80-Hour Work Week, *7*, 2–49.

O'Brien, Justin, Translator (1958). Camus at Stockholm: The Acceptance of the Nobel Prize. *The Atlantic, 201*, 31–34.

Ostler, Scott (1984, 15 October). Was That Really a National League Team out There? Los Angeles *Times, III*, 3.

Parker, Hilda, & Seymour Parker (1986). Father-Daughter Sexual Abuse: An Emerging Perspective. *American Journal of Orthopsychiatry, 56*, 531–549.

Psychology Today (1989, April). Buried Memories. *23*, 12.

Quinn, Susan (1982). The Competence of Babies. *The Atlantic Monthly, 249*, 54–62.

Ricoeur, Paul (1978). The Metaphorical Process as Cognition, Imagination, and Feeling. *Critical Inquiry, 5*, 143–159.

Robinson, Paul (1984, February). Psychiatry's Secret Radical. *Psychology Today, 18*, 64–65.

Rubin, Gayle (1975). The Traffic in Women: Notes on the "Political Economy" of Sex. In Rayna R. Reiter (Ed.), *Toward an Anthropology of Women*. New York: Monthly Review Press, 157–210.

Ruddick, Sara (1984). Maternal Thinking. In Joyce Trebilcot (Ed.), *Mothering: Essays in Feminist Theory*. Totowa, NJ: Rowman & Allanheld, 213–230.

———— (1984). Preservative Love and Military Destruction. Some Reflections on Mothering and Peace. In Joyce Trebilcot (Ed.), *Mothering: Essays in Feminist Theory*. Totowa, NJ: Rowman & Allanheld, 231–262.

Sadker, Myra, & David Sadker (1985, March). Sexism in the Schoolroom of the '80s. *Psychology Today, 19*, 54–57.

Sanderson, Jim (1985, 14 August). The Secret We Don't Want to Hear. Los Angeles *Times, V*, 3.

Scarf, Maggie (1980, 5 & 12 July). Women and Depression. *The New Republic*, 25–29.

Schachter, Jim (1988, 17 April). Managing Diversity: Grappling with Change in the Work Force. Los Angeles *Times, IV*, 1.

Science News (1989, 4 March). Environmental Costs of Keeping Baby Dry, *135*, 141.

Scientific American (1989, September). Different Strokes . . . Premature Infants Gain from Being Handled, *261*, 34 & 36.

Seidenberg, Robert, M.D. (1978). The Trauma of Eventlessness. In Jean Baker Miller, M.D. (Ed.), *Psychoanalysis and Women*. New York: Penguin, 350–362.

Shaw, David (1990, 21 January). Media Skepticism Grew as McMartin Case Lingered. Los Angeles *Times*, *A*, 1 & 34–36.

Siegel, Lee (1984, 7 May). "A Sickness in Our Society": That (and More) Is What Watching Sports on TV Is Called at Psychoanalysts' Meeting. Los Angeles *Times*, *III*, 3.

Silverstein, Barry (1988). Will the Real Freud Stand Up, Please? *American Psychologist*, *43*, 662–663.

Stoller, Robert J. (1985). The "Bedrock" of Masculinity and Femininity: Bisexuality. In Jean Baker Miller, M.D. (Ed.), *Psychoanalysis and Women*. New York: Penguin Books, 273–284.

——— (1985). Facts and Fancies: An Examination of Freud's Concept of Bisexuality. In Jean Strouse (Ed.), *Women and Analysis*. Boston: G. K. Hall, 343–364.

Tavris, Carol, with Dr. Alice I. Baumgartner (1983, February). How Would Your Life Be Different If You'd Been Born a Boy? *Redbook*, *160*, 92–95.

Thurman, Judith (1982, September). Breaking the Mother-Daughter Code. An Interview with Nancy Chodorow. *Ms.*, *11*, 34–38 & 138–139.

Touraine, Alain (1989). Neo-Modern Ecology. *New Perspectives Quarterly*, *6*, 33–36.

Trotter, R.J. (1985, March). Fathers and Daughters: The Broken Bond. *Psychology Today*, *19*, 10.

U.S. News & World Report (1982, 15 February). Discarding the Concept of Man as "Killer Ape." A Conversation with Richard Leakey. *92*, 62.

Wallis, Claudia (1989, 4 December). Onward, Women! *Time*, *134*, 80–89.

Watney, Simon (1989). Psychoanalysis, Sexuality and AIDS. In Simon Shepherd & Mick Wallis, *Coming on Strong, Gay Politics and Culture*. London: Unwin Hyman, 22–38.

Weiss, Rick (1987, 25 July). How Dare We? Scientists Seek the Sources of Risk-taking Behavior. *Science News*, *132*, 57–59.

Yudkin, Marcia (1982, January). Silencing Eros. Review of *Pornography and Silence: Culture's Revenge against Nature* by Susan Griffin. *Ms.*, *10*, 41.

Name Index

Subject Index

ABOUT THE AUTHOR

FRANCE MORROW first became interested in gender studies as a graduate student researching art and perception. This interest deepened when she had the opportunity to study early child development while teaching preschool and kindergarten for the U.S. army in France and continued throughout her academic career. Ms. Morrow has taught graduate level courses in the fields of psychology, sociology, ethnic (women's) studies, and the fine arts, and is an active supporter of environmental and women's movements.